How Can They Hear Without a Preacher?

The Intersectionality of Gender, Sexuality, and Faith

Dr. Renay M. Scott

Copyright © 2023 by Dr. Renay M. Scott
All Rights Reserved

No part of this book may be reproduced or transmitted in any form or by any means, electronic or mechanical, including photocopying, recording, or by any information storage and retrieval system without the written permission of the author, except where permitted by law.

*To those who stood by me throughout the process,
especially my parents.*

Acknowledgments

I would like to acknowledge those who encouraged me to tell my story. You know who you are and while we have come a long way we still have a long way to go toward acceptance.

Table of Contents

Prologue i
Part I: A Journey of Discovery ....
   Chapter One: You Shall Know the Truth 4
   Chapter Two: Growing Up Different 20
   Chapter Three: Storm and Stress 44
   Chapter Four: The High School Years 64
   Chapter Five: Meet My New Friend 76
   Chapter Six: A Restless Night 82
   Chapter Seven: The Test 93
   Chapter Eight: I Like Dreaming 98
   Chapter Nine: The Journey Begins 104
   Chapter Ten: I Believe in Miracles 112
   Chapter Eleven: For Everything, There Is a Season 118
   Chapter Twelve: Until Death Do Us Part 125
   Chapter Thirteen: My New Best Friend 134
   Chapter Fourteen: How Do I Build a Friendship? 142

Chapter Fifteen: Falling 147

Part II: A Journey Toward Understanding ....

Chapter Sixteen: I Like Dreaming.. 160

Chapter Seventeen: The Beginning or the End? 167

Chapter Eighteen: Summer Love.. 175

Chapter Nineteen: Marching to Graduation 181

Chapter Twenty: Baptism 193

Chapter Twenty-One: How to Find Peace 200

Chapter Twenty-Two: To Do or Not to Do, That Is the Question 211

Chapter Twenty-Three: I Do 227

Chapter Twenty-Four: The Married Life 235

Part III: A Journey of Faith and Freedom..

Chapter Twenty-Five: Now What? 262

Chapter Twenty-Six: Coexistence 291

Chapter Twenty-Seven: The Professor 306

Chapter Twenty-Eight: One Moment in Time 317

Chapter Twenty-Nine: The Beginning or the End? 336

Epilog 350

About the Author...

Prologue

"For I know the thoughts that I think toward you, saith the Lord, thoughts of peace, and not of evil, to give you an expected end"

-Jeremiah 29:11 KJV.

When did I know I was gay? People who meet me ask me this question whenever they decide I'm gay or when the relationship develops enough for me to introduce them to my same-sex partner. However, the more important question is, "When did I accept that I was gay?" The journey toward accepting myself and my sexuality was complicated, spanning many years, including over 14 years spent married to a man who today I would characterize to be more like a brother than a husband.

My journey of discovery occurred when information about homosexuality, bisexuality, and sexual identity was less available and understood than today as I write. I trod the path when homosexuality was taboo and controversial. It was even considered illegal in several states. Discovering my sexuality and all its associated feelings was one step; accepting and embracing my sexuality was another journey altogether.

What complicated my journey of acceptance was my deep faith in Jesus Christ and the religion I chose to associate with because of my faith in Jesus Christ. In 1977, I vividly remember hearing a message about how "all have sinned" and that the "penalty for sin was death." The speaker explained that God had made a way to escape death and hell by sending his son, Jesus Christ, to die on the cross as atonement for our sins and that this was available to all who believed. I went home and prayed to God, telling him I accepted his atonement through the death of his son, Jesus Christ. I had little understanding at that moment of theology around what seemed like a simple message of hope. I acted like a little child and, by faith, entered the presence of Jesus Christ through prayer. Were my actions based on faith because I feared death and hell and believed I was a sinner and needed to act better? Or were my actions based on faith because I longed for a relationship of acceptance? Even today, I'm unsure what motivated me to take that leap of faith. However, I embrace that move because I enjoy my relationship with God through Jesus Christ. I value what my faith brings to my life. I also appreciate the freedom I've gained by throwing off legalistic religion based on man's interpretation of scripture for an honest relationship through prayer and Bible reading, which has helped me better understand God the person.

This child-like act of faith occurred in my early teenage years. Adolescence then, as now, is a time of turmoil, exploration, and growth. As I navigated high school and the social challenges it brought, I found a grounding from attending church, learning about my new faith, and making friends with people who shared it. My time in high school was spent playing sports, working on the yearbook, attending church, and working a part-time job. I had little time to date or even consider dating. It wasn't until my senior year in high school that I faced my first lesbian encounter, which left me confused and searching for answers.

This is an autobiography about searching for understanding and acceptance. I am sharing my journey toward understanding my sexuality, navigating the complexity of a society in turmoil over homosexuality, and a religion hostile to it. My journey was one of reconciling my faith in Jesus Christ with the message by some churches that homosexuality is wrong in hopes that those who read this come to accept Jesus as your Savior or those who have already accepted Jesus as your Savior come to understand that God loves you just as you are. My journey is one of love, heartache, discovery, and personal acceptance in the face of many friends, family, and colleagues who told me I was wrong when I shared with them my belief that I was gay or bisexual and who then walked away despite learning only one additional fact about me that they hadn't known or admitted to themselves the day before. I have learned the truth through my journey, and the truth has set me free.

Part I: A Journey of Discovery

*"How, then, can they call on the one they have not believed in?
And how can they believe in the one whom they have not heard?
And how can they hear without someone preaching to them?"*

-Romans 10:14 NIV.

Chapter One:
You Shall Know the Truth

"And ye shall know the truth, and the truth shall make you free"

-John 8:32 KJV.

Spring weather in Michigan is a mixed bag of wonderful warm days and cold, snowy days. It can be 70 degrees and sunny one day, rainy the next, and a blizzard by the end of that day. The spring of 1998 began pleasantly with growing warmth and sunshine. Spring is my signal that summer is arriving soon, and my teaching job will transition from full-time to part-time, allowing me increased time to enjoy things that bring me peace and joy. As the semester closed, I eagerly anticipated spending weekends at Lake Charlevoix, where my parents lived during their retirement. Being around water always brought me peace and relaxation. I loved playing on the lake, spending countless mornings waterskiing, afternoons soaking up the sun, and evenings enjoying amazing sunsets. Besides a love for the water, I love baseball. The West Michigan Whitecaps, a minor league baseball team, opened their season in April. I would spend many weekday nights at the ballpark watching future stars, with fans sitting around my seat, and enjoying the sights, sounds, and smells accompanying minor league baseball. I spent many mornings rollerblading along the shore of Lake Michigan between Holland and Grand Haven. These workouts kept me in shape, allowed me time to reflect, and gave me a lot of time to listen to audiobooks. These things brought me joy during my personal and emotional search to understand my complicated feelings, faith, and dreams.

I embraced a new life during the spring of 1998. I was enjoying spring activities and filled with great anticipation for a relaxing summer in 1998. I was excited about a new job and celebrated a measure of freedom by exiting a 14-year-plus marriage that constantly reminded me of the pain I felt due to rejection by a husband who took little interest in me and devoted most of his time to work. The new freedom also came from reconciling my questions about who I was with my faith in Jesus Christ. This new excitement was a stark contrast to the constant dread that hung over me at the beginning of 1997 when I decided I needed to change my life, even if it meant losing a job I loved, disappointing many whom I loved, and leaving a city that had been my home since I was four. What a difference a year can make.

January 1997 dawned as so many had previously since my marriage in 1983. As New Year's Day approached, my friends and colleagues at work would discuss their plans for New Year's Eve and their anticipation of the future. The future felt no different than the past, with more pain, emptiness, and excuses as to why Dan never attended school events with me or spent time at the lake or ballgames with me. While I participated in activities that brought me joy and hope, I attended them alone. My marriage didn't start this way, but gradually, my husband began working more and more while encouraging me to continue to visit my parents, attend ball games, and hang with friends after weekly softball games. I'm sure the distance between him and me grew greater over time without me even noticing because my life was so busy, including being with many friends and family whom I loved and enjoyed being around. We were very compatible in many ways, but we had been drifting apart the past five years, as I hadn't noticed while building a career I was proud of.

One Sunday in January of 1997, I was cross-stitching in front of the TV. Dan was at work as usual because he prepared income tax returns for his clients. I was alone with my thoughts when heavy, oppressive loneliness overtook me. The void I felt seemed dark and deep. I had just returned from a road trip with the women's basketball team from a local college where I was an assistant coach. I enjoyed the team's company, parents, and coaches on road trips, including leaving for a Saturday game on Friday afternoon and returning early on Sunday mornings. Returning home this weekend felt very different. Generally, I would spend Sunday afternoons preparing for my teaching responsibilities, longing for some downtime to read, run, or nap.

This Sunday afternoon was different because I had prepared for class while riding home after a parent had offered to drive while on the weekend road trip. This Sunday, I sat on the couch watching light snow falling as I looked out the window. The oppression and darkness I felt became so heavy that I just wanted to run and run and run to escape the pain. I knew that my depression was getting worse as these moments were becoming darker and lasting longer. I decided that on Monday, I would call and make an appointment with a counselor. Initially, I was skeptical of counseling. I had heard at church that as a born-again Christian who trusted in God and had the Holy Spirit indwelling in me, I would experience freedom from the darkness and the depression. The theology claimed that such darkness and depression were from Satan and that one needed faith and time with God to overcome Satan. In sermons, I heard how God would give me strength; that was all I needed to face every situation. I would often pray for strength and delivery from depression. I would implore God to strengthen my faith, thinking I lacked confidence, so I felt depressed. Yet, life was becoming increasingly overwhelming, and I was slipping further into the black hole of depression. Prayer was no longer enough.

Monday came, and I called for a counseling appointment. The counselor had an opening the following day. I took that as a sign. I wasn't sure if God was helping me or if Satan was enabling my lack of faith. I had little time to consider my thoughts because a lengthy practice session for the basketball team followed a full day of teaching with little downtime to reflect. I arrived home late to an empty house. That was expected because my husband was busy with tax preparation appointments by his clients, who knew they were getting a refund. I quickly prepared dinner after taking the dogs for a walk. I sat on the couch, turning on the news, only to realize some time later that I had drifted off to sleep.

Tuesday morning dawned quickly, and before I realized it, I was driving to the counselor's office. His office was close to home, allowing me to use my time efficiently. While I had no classes to teach, I had advising appointments and meetings in the afternoon before basketball practice.

My thoughts were racing as I sat in the counselor's waiting room, waiting for him to see me.

What would I tell him? Why was I even here? How can I summarize my life and feelings in an hour? Was this the first of many sessions I didn't have time for?

As my thoughts raced, the secretary announced, "Ken will see you now." I walked into his office and sat down. I don't remember much about the office or Ken, but I remember how I felt. I couldn't believe I was sitting before a stranger and about to tell him my most intimate thoughts and feelings. I had several close friends and family members with whom I hadn't even shared what I was about to share.

"Hello, what brings you in today?"

That was my first decision point. What was I to tell this stranger about why I was here? I decided to plunge in and put it all on the line. I explained that I was feeling empty and depressed without any genuine reason. We talked for an hour, and I made another appointment for the following week. During the second week, we discussed why I may feel so depressed.

"I just don't understand why, when I have exactly what I worked for my whole life: a college teaching position, a great home, a loving, supporting church, many friends…everything I need, but I feel so depressed."

Ken challenged me to consider what I didn't have. That seemed like such a selfish thought to me. After all, I was a Christian, and my religion taught me to "in everything, give thanks: for this is the will of God in Christ Jesus concerning you" (I Thessalonians 5:18 KJV).

I decided to peel back another layer of my soul. I just threw out another fact for discussion. "I just don't feel close to my husband."

Ugh, why was I going here? I didn't want to pick the scab to disclose the pain, yet I instinctively knew this was the root of the depression.

Ken explored why I didn't feel close to Dan. He prodded and probed, and I squirmed in my seat as I answered his questions honestly, feeling the anguish overtaking my heart and soul. I finally explained that Dan had shown little interest in sex or intimacy since our wedding day, leaving me frustrated, empty, and angry. I didn't think counselors would reveal their feelings, but Ken looked shocked. He paused for a minute, taking in what I had just said. I wasn't sure if he believed me or, perhaps, thought I was exaggerating. Finally, he appeared to accept what I said.

Then, he proceeded carefully, asking, "Why haven't you two been more engaged in intimacy all these years?" I didn't know how to answer that question. It wasn't like I hadn't tried to create romantic moments or ask Dan to be more attentive. As I shared my answer with Ken, I felt ashamed that I was only now dealing with this since we had been married for so many years. The question alone brought back many feelings of pain, confusion, anger, frustration, and shame. After a significant pause, I answered that I wasn't sure why I hadn't done more. I explained that Dan never seemed interested, and he withdrew whenever I asked for more. I added we were always tired between his work and mine. I continued by telling the counselor that I had tried to talk to Dan several times about this issue, but he didn't respond and even found ways to avoid the conversation each time. I also explained that he avoided situations where sex would be natural or normal for couples. He avoided holding hands, hugging, snuggling, and sitting close. He would even wait as long as possible after I went to bed to come to bed, hoping I had fallen asleep. I told Ken I was blaming myself for the lack of intimacy in our marriage. Ken was a little surprised by that comment. He asked me if I had ever considered that the lack of intimacy might be about Dan rather than me.

"No, I hadn't considered that," I responded frankly.

Then Ken dropped a bomb. "Could Dan be gay?" he asked me carefully.

Stunned, I sat quietly for a few moments. Just like I had left Ken speechless by my revelation about the lack of romance and intimacy in our marriage, so did his suggestion that Dan could be gay. After a few moments, I collected my thoughts and responded, "I guess he could be, but I can't imagine that he is gay."

I continued, "I don't have any indication or evidence that he is gay." I fell silent again, my mind racing.

Ken broke the silence, "I'm not suggesting that he has been unfaithful. I am merely suggesting that his lack of interest in sex is unusual and that being gay may be a way of explaining it."

Inside, I was screaming! I realized I had avoided pressing Dan on the subject for 14 years because I didn't want to explain that I was questioning my sexuality and wasn't sure how I felt about Dan since my anger toward him grew yearly. As I contemplated how to answer his question, Ken reminded me that we were at the fifty-minute point of the session and needed to end the week. I was happy we were through because I had enough discomfort for one session.

Ken asked if I wanted to make an appointment for the following week. I responded to Ken by saying that I didn't need an appointment for the following week because I needed time to talk to Dan about this before I came back again. I made an appointment for the next month and left the office.

I strolled to my car, opened the door, slid into the seat, and sat there. *Oh my!* I thought. *Dan, gay?* My thoughts raced. I didn't initially think it was about Dan being gay, but I had thought it might be about me being gay or, at the least, no longer attracted to Dan. I was wondering if it was about both of us being gay. I knew, regardless of whether Ken's suggestion that Dan might be gay was true, that I had to face and understand my sexuality. Shame rushed over me.

The months that followed that appointment would become a watershed in my life. With Ken's suggestion that Dan might be gay, I realized that I needed to address my sexuality. The depression I was feeling was partially because I needed to come to terms with who I was and whether being married to Dan contributed. I had become aware that I was craving intimacy and a close relationship, but perhaps what I desired wasn't with Dan. After all, the lack of closeness was just as much about my wavering commitment to Dan due to my growing anger at him. To cope, I stayed busy with activities that brought me joy and only missed Dan when confronted with trying to explain why he hadn't come with me. I was becoming aware that I didn't necessarily want Dan to participate in these things with me, but I wanted to avoid explaining why he wasn't there. I was becoming aware that while I wanted someone to be with and enjoy life with, that someone was probably not Dan. I was also aware that sometimes I preferred that someone be female.

I now faced the problems within my marriage with renewed vigor. After all, if my sexuality was part of the problem, I could solve this depression and emptiness. Additionally, I figured that my lack of interest in intimacy with Dan contributed to our drifting apart, whether or not it was because of my sexuality or anger at him. I could set aside my anger and initiate the closeness I longed for. So, I decided that what I needed to do was to put Dan first in my life and not allow my career to interfere, and then all those other questions about my sexuality that I was having would disappear. As I reflected on how I might reorient my priorities, I recalled remarks from a Christian counselor who once said that if you practice the behavior you want, your feelings will eventually follow. The comment was made on a Christian talk show after a guest explained to the Christian counselor that he wasn't in love with his wife anymore and wasn't sure what to do. The counselor responded to his story by advising him to act as if he was in love with her, and eventually, he would fall in love with her again. He told the story about how he dated his wife and set boundaries at work, ultimately finding that he was in love with his wife again. If it could work for him, I figured it could work for me.

On a long weekend in Petoskey with Dan, I tried to talk to him about how I felt we were drifting apart and not as close as we once were and how it contributed to my depression. I hoped for a supportive, understanding, honest conversation over dinner at a nice restaurant. Instead, the conversation turned into an academic exercise. After I laid bare my heart and soul to him, telling him I did not feel close to him, he explained that it made sense to him that I was feeling alone and disconnected because I had just spent the past three years deeply engaged in my doctoral studies and had little time for relationships or fellowship. He explained that I had disconnected from friends and family while pushing hard to finish my degree to keep my teaching job at the Christian college. He said that I just needed to be patient, and in time, I would feel close to my friends, family, and him again, and everything would be okay. He encouraged me not to change anything and to continue participating in the activities I enjoyed with people I cared about, and in time, the depression would go away. He tried to convince me that I wasn't depressed but experiencing a letdown after accomplishing a significant goal.

That conversation left me numb and bewildered. He gave me an intellectual answer when I wanted to be held, comforted, and affirmed. As we left the restaurant and got in the car, I suggested we drive to the overlook along the shore of Lake Michigan and watch the sunset. I still hoped to snuggle into Dan and feel close while enjoying a brilliant sunset over the lake. Instead, he turned the other way and returned to the cabin where we were staying. We drove back in silence. Inside me, the pain burned. Tears were welling close to the surface, and I beat them back. I felt another part of me dying. I was too afraid to push the conversation and ask for what I needed, and the weekend ended without any other attempts at reviving intimate discussions. Once home after the weekend, it felt like Dan worked even more. Was he avoiding the conversation, hoping that if he stayed away long enough, I would eventually give up on having those conversations? He was right; in time, I retreated and vowed to return to the routine that protected me from further hurt and pain. Each time I stuffed back the discomfort and pain, the deeper and longer the depression lasted.

That weekend, specifically that conversation at the restaurant, prompted me to call my pastor and seek advice about rekindling this marriage. I couldn't talk to Dan and needed to speak to someone who could help me reconcile what I was feeling with the sermons I was hearing. What wasn't clear to me was that I didn't want to press the conversation with Dan because what I needed and wanted wasn't something I would find from Dan. When I was honest with myself, I knew I wanted out of the marriage and wanted to pursue my life and career without Dan. I wasn't sure what that meant, but I believed that if I could leave the marriage, I would no longer feel the hurt and depression. I was at a crossroads.

I made an appointment to see my pastor. I was surprised he had time to see me because he led a church with over ten thousand people. I had heard that he didn't take counseling appointments any longer and that the extensive pastoral support staff were the only ones who provided counseling. Because I got an appointment with my pastor, I took it as a sign that I would hear what I needed to decide my next steps. As I waited for him to call me into his office on a hot Friday, I felt beads of sweat falling down my back. *Was it due to the heat of the day or my nerves?* He called me into his office. I had thirty minutes to get to the point. I briefly explained about my fourteen-year marriage and how we had drifted apart. I explained that my husband showed no interest in intimacy and closeness and that I, too, had lost all interest. I continued to share that I had tried for over thirteen years to keep the marriage together but was at the point of giving up. After a few questions and additional explanation, he paused to advise me. What he said next left me stunned.

"Based on what you shared, I believe that in God's eyes, you are not married. Your husband has failed to live up to his Biblical responsibilities toward you as his wife. Legally, you are married. You have a social contract. Deciding whether you want to continue working on this contract and make it a marriage is something you need to decide. However, I think God understands that your marriage is not following the biblical model and not fulfilling what He intends for biblical marriage. As the head of the household, your husband is responsible for ensuring the marriage follows the biblical model. He is not fulfilling his part. You have no obligation to stay."

I sat speechless. He continued to say more, but I heard none of his attempts at comforting my pain. He tried to assist by sharing information about a counselor who could help us address the problems, as he seemed to understand them. I told him I would call the recommended person to pursue that option. I left his office and went to a local trail to rollerblade, think, and pray.

As I skated along the trail, I thought. I started to get honest with myself. I retraced the journey that had brought me to this point. I reminded myself that even before my wedding day, I had doubts about getting married. Doubts, not because I didn't love Dan, but because I wasn't sure I wanted to be married, have children, or make a life-long commitment. Getting married was an expectation of my family. I heard this repeatedly from my grandmother, mother, and aunts. I recounted the story my mother often told me about how my grandfather cried when he heard I was born a girl. Puzzled by the story, my mom would explain that my grandfather knew how difficult life was for women, and he was worried I would have a difficult life because society held few opportunities for women. My grandmother always said the best any woman could hope for was finding a good man to care for her. Getting married was an expectation, and I knew it but didn't embrace it.

I told myself at that time that my doubts about getting married were because I was just young and conflicted about being alone and questioning my sexuality. I tried to tell myself that Dan was a wonderful person and would be a good provider. On the other hand, I wondered if getting married was my way of hiding who I was and avoiding what I feared: being alone. I asked if the real problem was that I didn't want to deal with my sexuality. I reminded myself how I was excited about being married and looking forward to being with a man. I figured my doubts would disappear once I was married. Though nothing like that happened, I didn't feel like breaking that commitment, so I stayed in the marriage, believing that if I worked hard enough, everything would be fine. However, I was not okay. I was depressed, and my depression was getting worse. I knew I wanted out of the marriage, maybe even out of life altogether. I started thinking about what my pastor said about how we weren't married in God's eyes. It would have been easy to blame Dan, and I was beginning to think that the counselor was right about Dan possibly being gay. I started to recall events and comments he had made that caused me to wonder about Dan's sexuality.

I knew that blaming Dan only for this empty marriage was untenable because marriage takes two people. I knew I had contributed to the situation and knew I no longer wanted to continue to work on the marriage because I felt like I was the only one who wanted it to survive. I also knew I was half-heartedly working on the marriage because I questioned my sexuality. I was taught to believe that divorce was a sin, but now, I was beginning to think that it was possible to get a divorce and not disobey God after my talk with my pastor. I decided that I needed no other reason to get divorced than to take care of myself because staying in the marriage was causing me to be depressed. As I neared the end of my rollerblading trip, I was pretty sure I was going crazy and needed to decide whether to stay or leave.

Weeks passed, and I continued mulling the conversation with my pastor. Finally, I shared with Dan that I had met with our pastor to discuss my depression and that we would talk on the way to Omaha to see our friend Karen. However, a new development interrupted my plans. Since Dan and I were going to drive to Omaha, Karen had decided to fly into town a couple of weeks before our vacation to attend her former school's graduation, visit her family and friends, and then ride back to Omaha with us to where she lived with her new husband. I was thrilled. I was looking forward to spending time with Karen. I could also avoid the inevitable conversation with Dan a little longer.

Karen and I met while teaching at a small Christian school. When I was first hired, the school comprised kindergarten through sixth grade. The year I started working, the school split from another Christian school that had founded this elementary school as a feeder program to the high school. I had just completed my student teaching at the founding school and knew about the opening. I applied and was hired during the summer of 1984. That fall, the school expanded by adding a 7th grade. The following year, the school added an 8th grade. After the first two years, the school decided to become a high school by adding one additional grade each year. As a result, the school needed to hire two new teachers to teach the other classes, resulting from adding a 9th grade. Karen and Joy were hired during the summer of 1986.

When the school year started in August of 1986, I was so busy preparing to teach new classes, setting into a new home that we purchased closer to the school, and coaching basketball that I hadn't even gotten a chance to get to know the two new teachers. Karen volunteered to keep score for my basketball team and help drive the girls to away games. I was grateful for the kind gesture. That is when our friendship started. Karen often told me that I was challenging to understand. According to her, I was distant. I was distant from most people because I questioned my sexuality and feared vulnerability. My marriage was ideal on the outside, but it was empty, lonely, and unfulfilling. I kept my distance to ensure no one could see what was happening in my life. As the year progressed, Karen and I spent more and more time together.

We were still close friends in the summer of 1997, but many miles separated us. With Karen now living in Omaha and it being summer vacation, now was a great time for me to put all my efforts into trying to be the perfect Christian wife for Dan. The week in Omaha, visiting our friends Karen and John, was fantastic. We visited the Omaha Zoo, caught a minor league baseball game, hung out, and got to know Karen's husband, John. When Dan and I had time alone, our conversations naturally flowed—the week made the relationship feel good again. The time flew by, and Dan and I were driving home before I knew it.

On the drive back from Omaha, I explained to Dan that my career kept me from giving more of myself to him. I explained that I thought we needed to prioritize spending time together. I asked him to consider ways to spend more time with me despite his growing law practice, which demanded more and more of his time.

I avoided telling Dan about the specifics of the conversation with our pastor, specifically that it was his responsibility as the head of the household to work toward fostering a biblical marriage. I wanted to ask for what I needed rather than come across as blaming him for what he wasn't doing. Indeed, deep down, I had to know I was avoiding asking for what I wanted out of our relationship: closeness, intimacy, and romance because I was beginning to understand that I had never received that from Dan, even before we were married.

After returning home from our trip to Omaha in June, I attempted to practice what we discussed. My first attempt at prioritizing time together with Dan and being affectionate was a disaster. My depression grew worse. Dan grew more distant. No matter what I tried, I was disappointed, empty, and hurt. The black hole of depression got deeper and deeper as the summer progressed, and it was becoming more apparent that Dan wanted nothing to do with being closer or spending time with me. I wanted to give up.

I decided I needed to escape this situation. I had finally reconciled in my heart that God would understand why I gave up on the marriage and left. However, I could not be divorced and teach at the Christian college where I was employed. I began to look for teaching jobs at other colleges and universities. However, I didn't think I would find a job at a college near Grand Rapids, and Grand Rapids was where I wanted to stay. My depression got worse. To keep my sanity, I kept telling myself that God had a plan and I needed to work hard to find another job, even if it was not in Grand Rapids. My self-doubt hinged on the fact that I was beginning to believe I was gay or bisexual. I wondered whether God would be there for me if I were gay or bisexual or whether he would punish me. My doubt was rooted in the question I kept asking myself, "How would I be obeying God if my life included divorce and homosexuality?"

While my pastor's words helped me reconcile divorce as an option for Christians, he didn't know that I believed I might be gay, and I wondered how that might have contributed to this dysfunctional marriage. The real question now was whether I would have the courage to take care of myself, which meant getting a divorce and facing head-on questions about sexuality or continuing to do what was failing. Little did I realize that the answer to this question was only four months away.

Chapter Two:
Growing Up Different

"I praise you because I am fearfully and wonderfully made; your works are wonderful, I know that full well"

-Psalm 139:14 NIV.

I was born in Ohio. The Midwest culture influenced my experience. My father worked as a regional salesman stationed in Columbus. My mom and dad had both grown up in Michigan. My mom was born and reared in Grand Rapids, Michigan, a rather large urban city with factories, most of which designed and built furniture. My dad was born and raised in a small town in northern Michigan, Boyne City. Boyne City was on the east side of a large lake and included a ski hill. It was known for tourism. My dad came to live in Grand Rapids after serving in the Pacific theater during World War II and a short two-week attempt at going to college at Michigan State College (now Michigan State University). He began working for General Motors after leaving college. After a short time at General Motors, he worked as a traveling salesman with Wolverine Worldwide. While he was in

Grand Rapids, he met my mother, and after a long courtship, they married.

I was born at the University Hospital in Columbus. I was a Buckeye from the start. My mother stayed home tending to me while my father traveled throughout the Midwest, drumming up sales for Wolverine boots. When I was older, my mom and I would watch the annual Ohio State/Michigan rivalry football game on television each fall. My mother often told me stories about living in Columbus. She would fondly recount living near the Horseshoe stadium, home of the Ohio State Buckeye football team. She would talk about how the city of Columbus would be transformed during the fall when the football team had a home game. She spoke of sitting on the front porch, holding me in her arms, and listening to the "Best Damn Band in the Land" at halftime. She talked about watching the Ohio State basketball teams at the arena and described the row house they rented. Her fond memories of Columbus made me want to visit Ohio. Little did I know that I would eventually move to Ohio for a job later in my life.

Our family of three moved from Columbus to Grand Rapids when I was two. I have no recollection of living in Columbus, only memories of the stories my mother would tell. My memories of living in Grand Rapids are snapshots. Those memories are of being very active as a child. I can only imagine how difficult it was for my mom to keep up with me. Most of my memories are of spending time with my mom. I was told that was because my dad traveled a lot as a salesman until he took a job with Meijer Thrifty Acres, a family-owned growing grocery store chain. I remember learning how to ride a bicycle, playing on the outdoor swing set at a local park, and taking walks with my mom.

One of my favorite activities was playing with the laundry basket. If I wasn't sitting in the basket, I was trying to figure out how to get our dog to sit in it. I would also hide under the laundry basket. I was just fascinated with it. Mom would be ironing, and I would make some annoying noise replicating a car that she would try to extinguish with little success. When the basket failed to capture my attention, I would head to the kitchen to empty the cupboards of pots and pans. Somehow, I frequently managed to slip off to the kitchen without my mother noticing, only to be found once the banging began. Then my kitchen fun would be cut short.

I spent many days outside. I remember swinging on swings, but I don't remember having a swing set. I remember playing in the sandbox with a neighbor boy. The sandbox was in his yard. One day, while we played in the sandbox, he hit my finger with a hammer. My response was to grab the hammer from him and hit him back; the only problem was that I hit him on the head. I wasn't going to tolerate being hit by anybody. My independent spirit showed up early. No need to go home crying to Mom about that; I will take care of the problem myself. As an adult, I would learn that an independent spirit was a two-edged sword, both good and bad.

My only childhood memory involving pain or punishment was an accident. I am still not sure how it happened. I was outside on one fabulous, crisp, sunny day. I was wearing a nice coat and bonnet with an elastic chin strap. Somehow, I managed to snap that chin strap right across my eyes. I sure don't remember any pain, but I do remember crying. My mom, outside with me playing catch, was just as startled by the whole episode. She just held me until I stopped crying. I don't remember being spanked as a child, but I remember getting a good "talking to" every now and then. My parents seemed to have adopted Dr. Benjamin Spock's approach to parenting in The Common Sense Book of Baby and Child Care (1946).

I don't have many memories of playing with my dad. I remember he got a job at Meijer, and my mom and I accompanied him to a grand opening for a new store on Plainfield Avenue. After showing us around, he took me to the toy department. We went up and down aisle after aisle of toys. I had never seen so many toys. I recall that he and I picked out plastic cowboy and Indian figures, and he told me I could have them after we paid for them. My love of the Zorro, the Lone Ranger, and Buck Barry affected my choice of toys. When I got home and proudly showed them to my mom, she was surprised and asked me why I hadn't picked out a lovely doll. I recall she mentioned that those were toys for boys.

One Christmas, I got a cowgirl outfit with a toy gun. I would run around outside pretending to shoot at things. I don't remember what I was shooting at, but the television shows I watched influenced my selection of toys and what I pretended to do. Early in my life, my mom wondered about me. This sweet little girl with long hair and pigtails was active, tumbling around in laundry baskets and sandboxes, standing up to little boys, and playing with what mom called "boy toys." I had my Barbie doll, but even then, I had Barbie riding bicycles and playing football. Mom called me a "tomboy." I was not like my mom. My mom had been a model for Westinghouse. She was thin, pretty, and feminine. I believed I had disappointed my mom because I wasn't the girl she had hoped for. I'm unsure why I thought this, but it was a clear memory.

On rare occasions, my parents would take me to McDonalds to celebrate a special occasion like my birthday. I was a precocious child, walking up to families sitting at tables around us where I would say hello and begin a conversation. My mother or father would often take my hand, apologize for the interruption, ask me to sit at the table, and remind me that people were having a family dinner and I was rude by interrupting their supper. I learned early on that children were supposed to be seen and not heard.

After a couple of years living on Suburban Shores, we moved to Comstock Park. I don't remember the move, but I remember walking into the house for the first time and asking if we could keep it. My memories of living in Comstock Park are pleasant. I had the perfect place for a child who liked being outdoors and active. We had three acres, a big circle driveway on a short, out-of-the-way street. I remember playing baseball until all hours of the evening. I often engaged in foot races with the neighborhood boys. We were always bragging about who was the fastest. Several of us were equally fast, so the races were very competitive. When we weren't playing baseball or running, we were riding our bikes. I was in a constant state of motion. Because I loved playing sports with the neighborhood boys, I was labeled a "tomboy" by their parents. As a child, I didn't understand the label. I just knew I enjoyed playing sports and being active. I was me, and no one seemed to indicate anything was wrong with being me.

When I was eight, my parents purchased a rundown cabin on a lake about an hour north of where we lived. We would drive to the cabin on summer weekends. I vividly remember the first day Dad took us to see the cottage. As I approached, it seemed old and run down. It was certainly not something I imagined when my dad told me he had purchased a cottage. My mom would often comment about the musty smell when she entered. I remember the place constantly feeling cold and damp, even on hot summer days. In time, I understood that my father purchased the cottage to remodel it into something suitable. He spent one summer gutting the inside so that only the structure's frame remained. Dad would ask Uncle Ed or Tim to come up with him on the weekends to help with a project. Over several summers, the run-down structure slowly transformed and felt like home.

I always wanted to help my dad while he was remodeling the cottage. I thought what he was doing seemed fun. My curiosity got the best of me, so I would sit and watch him work. I would pick up the tools I saw him using. I would then try to imitate what he did with the tools. To keep me from causing chaos, my dad would redirect my efforts toward helping him. He would ask me to bring him things, teaching me the names of the various tools. He would ask me to help him measure things before he would cut them. He would teach me to measure twice and cut once. After cutting two by fours, he let me have the wood scraps and asked me to think about how to use those scraps to build something else.

Once the cottage became a livable structure, my cousins would come up with Uncle Tim and Aunt Sally, and we would spend the weekend enjoying the water. We would go swimming and fishing. In time, my dad purchased a rowboat, and we would row out from the shore, throw an anchor, and fish. In time, Dad got a small motor for the fishing boat, and I learned how to operate the motorboat. After many lectures from my mother about safety, I was finally turned loose to drive the boat. In time, I would wander farther and farther away from the cottage until I was exploring the entire lake.

Spending weekends at the lake house in the summer was fun. I couldn't wait until the following weekend to visit my cousins, fish, and swim again. In time, I made friends around the lake. Some lived there year-round, and others would visit on weekends just like us. Life was carefree. I just ran from one outdoor activity to the subsequent activity, spending every minute I could outdoors. One of the friends I looked forward to seeing each weekend was Ervin. He and I loved baseball. We each collected baseball cards and would trade them back and forth. We would play catch, often simulating a pitcher and catcher routine, calling balls and strikes, switching roles each time we struck out three pretend batters.

Eventually, my Aunt Sylvia and Uncle Ed purchased a cottage on the same lake. They were only about a half-mile down the road from my parent's house. When my cousins came up, we would walk down to Uncle Ed and Aunt Sylvia's house. They didn't have children, so we acted like their children. I enjoyed visiting them. Aunt Sylvia was a great cook and always had fresh home-baked bread, cakes, or cookies. Uncle Ed enjoyed fishing. Often, he would take me fishing and show me how to bait hooks and take fish off the hooks if I was lucky enough to catch one. I always wanted to keep every fish I caught. That was great unless you were my dad and had to clean them all or my mom who had to cook them all. While I liked catching the fish, I wouldn't say I enjoyed eating them. Whenever I would catch a small fish, I wanted to keep it like the goldfish I saw in the fish tanks at Meijer's. My dad had to explain that these fish weren't like the goldfish, so I couldn't keep them in a fish tank. In time, I learned about the different fish species in Michigan lakes.

My first summer living in our new house in Comstock Park was fantastic. I don't remember getting to know any neighborhood kids, yet we all still knew each other. We had a big backyard, so I always explored the three acres. I climbed every tree that I could find. My favorite was an apple tree in the middle of the yard atop a hill. It was perfect for climbing. I could take one step on a tree knot, place the other foot a couple of feet above that, and pull myself into the crook of the tree where I would sit and see everything going on in our yard and around the surrounding two houses. I would climb up in the apple tree's crook every day and try to climb higher, only to be yelled at by my mom, worried I would fall and break a bone. On hot summer afternoons, I would climb into the tree with a book and a lunch that I had packed and sit and read in the shade, lying in the crook of the tree.

Every day was a new adventure. One day, I found grapes growing along the yard's edge. Eventually, I learned when they were ripe and good to eat. Before they were ripe and still hard, I found they were good for throwing. So, I'd set up a make-shift target and throw the grapes that would fall to the ground because I knew they would already be wasted. Another day, I found a path that crossed the back part of the yard. I kept asking my mom if I could walk that path. She kept saying no. Every day, I would sneak back to the trail and walk just a little further until one day, I reached the end of the path that came out along another road north of where we were living. I quickly jogged home, hoping Mom hadn't noticed I had been gone for a while. In time, the path would become a familiar bicycle trail that allowed me to ride through the backyard, on the trail to its exit point on the road north of the house, and back to the house along the road. Each day, I would time myself and see if I could ride the route faster and faster. I wasn't aware of it then, but I now realize how much I enjoyed competing against others and myself. Eventually, I realized that the route could be ridden in reverse. In other words, I could ride to the trail from the road and then take it to our backyard. I found that if I rode my bike down the hill in our backyard, I could go fast, even though the yard was bumpy. I would record my best times riding the route from either direction.

Another one of my favorite things to do at the house was sit in my dad's lap on the riding lawnmower and ride with him while he mowed the three acres. I never remember my parents mowing the lawn at Suburban Shores, but I knew that each Saturday, my dad would cut the grass on the property at the house in Comstock Park.

I counted down the days between Saturdays and yard mowing. Eventually, he would let me steer. Then, he would let me mow a small area by myself. I didn't realize that mowing would become my job as a teenager. It is remarkable that what was fun as a child turns into work as we age.

The August after we moved into the house, I turned five. When September arrived, I had to go to school. I had been in preschool the year before, but that was only for two or three hours a day. The preschool was by my grandparent's house. My mom would drop me off each morning and then head back home. I remember preschool being fun. I remember that the area was small but included an outdoor play area. The room had different sections that provided us with various tasks or toys. I doubt I even realized I was learning. I remember meeting new friends and often working in pairs. When preschool was over, my grandfather would pick me up, and I would play in their yard until Mom came to get me.

Consequently, after we moved and my mom told me I would attend school, I looked forward to attending every day because I figured school would be fun. After all, when I asked my mom how school was different from preschool, her description made it sound just like preschool but for a more extended period and every day of the week. I didn't have brothers and sisters, so I had no one to tell me about their experiences; I had to rely on my understanding based on what my parents told me. Consequently, everything was a new adventure with no preformulated ideas. My mom and I visited the school a few days before I was to attend. Greenridge Elementary School was small, with a fantastic playground. I met my teacher, Mrs. Oaks. She reminded me of my grandmother. I learned I would only attend school in the mornings and then ride a bus home at lunchtime. I was okay with that because I knew I could play when

I returned home. My mom didn't work, so I knew she would be home when I arrived.

I remember that first morning of school. I was all decked out in a light blue dress. My long blond hair was combed and put into pigtails. I was nervous about riding the bus but was open about attending school. I hadn't remembered riding a bus before. I was worried about knowing when to get off, where, and which bus to return to when coming home. I had just started meeting more neighborhood kids, and they told me to follow them, so I did that. The sun shone brightly on the first school day, and my mom fussed over me. She wanted to take a picture and walked me to the bus stop. Other mothers were waiting at the bus stop, too. The bus stop was in our neighbor's yard next to our house. So, I stayed with all the other kids, got on the bus, and began my school career. I came to enjoy riding the bus. The bus driver was pleasant. I would sit in the front seat and talk to him. As an only child, I spent most of my time with adults, and I found it easy and comfortable talking to them. I suspect the other children thought I was different.

I don't remember much about kindergarten other than recess. I loved the swings. It was something I could do alone. I was used to playing alone as an only child. I quickly learned to anticipate when the recess bell was about to ring. As soon as the bell rang, I would run out the door as fast as possible to get to the swings before anyone else. There were only so many swings, and all the kids wanted them. I used to get reprimanded for running in the hall. I hated being disciplined. I would feel so embarrassed and ashamed. I don't remember getting yelled at much at home, so being yelled at by my teacher at school embarrassed me.

Being called back into the classroom from recess was a two-step process. A warning bell would inform the students that they were supposed to line up. When the first bell rang, I'd run to be in line. I always wanted to be first. I can see now how competitive I was very early as a child. Most kids weren't in such a hurry to get in line and would stay and play until they saw the hall monitor come out the door to ring the bell again. When the first bell sounded, I would jump off my swing in mid-flight and run to the line. One girl, Kim, would always be in line before me. I wouldn't say I liked this because I wanted to be first. That meant I was the fastest. So, if I was second, I lost.

Kim would check out a big red ball for recess and play with it in an area near the door to reenter the school. Consequently, Kim was often the first person in line simply because she didn't wander too far away from the door. The swings I used were closer to the door than other playground equipment. I was unlikely to be first in line unless Kim did something different than her usual games using the red ball. I quickly discovered a way that I would get to be first in line when Kim would beat me to the front of the line. If Kim were there first and Kim was holding the red ball, I would rip the red ball from her arms and throw it so she would have to get it. When she would go get it, I would move to the first position. I didn't realize how mean I was to her. However, I didn't see it as mean then; I saw it as a game. I would always give her cuts behind me so I didn't see the harm in what I was doing. Years later, Kim became the assistant editor for the yearbook during our senior year in high school when I was the editor. We developed a good friendship. She would remind me of my mean stunts when we were both in kindergarten. As a high school student, I was embarrassed about my actions in kindergarten. She didn't bring it up to me to embarrass me or get even. But I couldn't help but wonder if my actions still hurt her. Kim wasn't the type to hold a grudge, but she certainly had the right to. However, even today, I feel bad for how I treated her.

I don't remember being friends with anyone in kindergarten. However, I seemed to know everyone. When I had my 6th birthday party the summer following kindergarten, my mom invited several girls and a couple of boys to the house to celebrate. I felt like I was friends with everyone, but I preferred to play alone. I did enjoy playing marbles with a couple of boys, and I remember trading baseball cards with Tom and Steve. Tom was a Johnny Bench and Bill Freehand fan, just like me. I loved baseball, including watching, playing, and reading about the game.

I don't remember much about first grade. Mrs. Rush was my teacher. I remember thinking she was mean. But now that I'm a teacher, I realize many kids believe teachers are mean. I remember going to the zoo with our class. My mom was a chaperone. The students in our class were divided into several smaller groups, and we went through the zoo in small groups accompanied by a parent. I was in a small group with kids I liked, and my mom led us through the exhibits, pointing out things we should notice. When we returned to school, I wanted to go home with my mom rather than take the bus. By the time we returned to school, there were only about thirty minutes before school let out, and I would board the bus to go home.

Consequently, I wasn't happy that my mom told me to stay at school and take the bus home like I usually did. My parents didn't want to treat me as unique or different from other kids, even though I was their only child. I can look back now and appreciate how my parents didn't spoil me but made me accountable.

Second grade was a traumatic year for me. When school started in the fall, my mom decided to babysit to make a little extra money for the family. One day, she introduced me to Shelly, a three-year-old she would watch every morning while I was at school. I was jealous. I couldn't tell my mom I was jealous. I'm not even sure I understood that I was jealous or even understood what I was feeling. I remember having a lot of headaches and stomachaches that year because I didn't want to go to school. Mrs. Brigham must have figured out something was wrong with me because she wanted to talk with my mother one day after school. The day Mrs. Brigham was going to meet with my mom, she kept me in at lunch to talk to me. She asked me why I didn't want to be at school.

I told Mrs. Brigham that Steve, whom I sat in front of, was picking on me. And he was nothing like I described to Mrs. Brigham and my mom later when she came to meet with Mrs. Brigham. So, the next day, I went to school, and she had moved my seat. It just so happened that she put me closer to the front of the room. Then, Mrs. Brigham made another discovery. I paid more attention and did better in my work. It took her a little while to figure it out. It made sense to her when she changed the seating arrangement again. She moved me to the back of the room, well away from Steve but far enough away from the blackboard to realize I couldn't see. I was off to the eye doctor, and in no time, I had glasses. I wasn't worried about what kids would think of my glasses. I was concerned about what wearing glasses would do to me when playing sports. Wearing glasses didn't deter me from playing hard or going all out. I often broke them diving into second base or for a ball in the outfield.

Wearing glasses was even more challenging in the winter. During the winter months, we were simulating Olympic bobsled and skiing events. The hill in our backyard was excellent for sliding, so we would build ramps and see if we could jump farther than one another. There was no guarantee that the sled and rider would land together or upright. Sometimes, I would land face-first in the hard-packed snow. We rode on or behind a snowmobile while not sliding down the hill. The Wingate boys had a snowmobile, and we would tie a sled behind it and take turns riding the sled. Of course, the driver would do everything possible to throw the rider off the sled. I constantly broke a bow of my glasses, making my parents furious. I had no idea how much fixing my glasses cost and didn't appreciate the challenge I was creating for them. I also don't recall ever being disciplined for breaking my glasses. I do remember many conversations about "acting more like a lady." I didn't know what "acting like a lady" meant.

My third-grade teacher was Mrs. Hathaway. She was challenging and demanding, much like Mrs. Rush. I liked her. I remember doing plays in her class. I remember a Thanksgiving play about Pilgrims and Indians. I quickly learned I didn't care to act or get up in front of my classmates. The other thing I wouldn't say I liked to do was read out loud. I think my struggle with reading out loud gave her the impression that I wasn't an excellent reader. But I was an excellent reader. My dad always read, and he taught me to enjoy reading. Before I could read, he would have me sit on his lap, and he would read the comics in the Sunday paper to me. I wouldn't say I liked to read aloud because I was afraid to make a mistake. I was shy and self-conscious. I preferred to read to myself. When we read aloud in class, I would read ahead and not pay attention because the reader would read slower than I could. I got in trouble a couple of times for not paying attention. I thought that was unfair because I was paying attention to the story; I wasn't paying attention to the person reading aloud and where the class was in the story, but it wasn't like I was misbehaving.

In third grade, we were introduced to a monthly book club. The club would offer us books to purchase. Even though we were going to the school library for one hour each week, we were encouraged to be an active member of the book club. At first, I didn't understand why anyone would want to buy books when they could borrow them from the library, but eventually, I realized that the books offered for sale were newer than the ones in the library. Dad told me I could order a book only if I read the book. I wanted to order two books the first couple of times I brought home the flyer, but he only let me order one. He told me he would allow me to order two books if I showed him; I read the one we ordered. Being able to buy books through the book club, I grew to love books and reading even more. I read every book I ordered. We would get them on Friday before going home, and I would finish them during the weekend. As soon as I finished the book, I would run to my dad and tell him I had finished the book. He would take the book and quiz me on what I read. I could usually answer every question he asked me. Soon, he would let me order two books from the book club. I was always amazed that my dad seemed to know the story as well as I did. I often wondered if he read the book before he quizzed me. In time, I realized he would read the books sometimes, too. That was just another bond I shared with my father.

Despite being an avid reader, I couldn't spell. Spelling was so hard for me. Each day in class, we did activities using the spelling words for the week. The teacher would hold a spelling bee on Thursday, the day before the spelling test. The spelling bee included words from that week and previous weeks. I wouldn't say I liked the spelling bee, even though it was a competition. I hated participating in things that drew attention to me more than I enjoyed competing. Knowing that I disliked standing up front waiting for another word, I devised a strategy to misspell the first word I was given on purpose so I could sit down. Mrs. Hathaway had a rule for us: whoever misspelled a word had to sit down. She told us we needed to sit down and study the spelling list for Friday, and after we felt we were ready for the spelling test, we could read.

Misspelling the first word allowed me to sit down quickly to study the spelling list. That would save me time when I got home because I had already memorized the spelling words at school. On Thursday, when I got home, my mother would quiz me, and if I spelled nine of the ten words correctly, I could go out and play. There were more advantages for me dropping out of the spelling bee than staying in until the end. This might have been the one time I wasn't as competitive as I usually would have been. I know Mrs. Hathaway noticed because, during parent-teacher conferences, she mentioned to my mom that I was always the first to sit down during the spelling bee, but I always spelled all the words correctly the next day.

Recess was always fun for me. In the fall, I'd play kickball or baseball with the boys. In the winter, I would go sliding down the hill with the boys and some girls. We didn't use slides to slide down the snowy, icy hills; we slid on our knees with just our snow pants on. I would go through two or three pairs of snow pants a year. My mom put patches on the knees of my snow pants when they were new before I even wore them, but I would manage to wear them out faster than she could go out and buy more patches. I know I frustrated her. She kept asking me why I couldn't be more like a girl. It was simple; I liked doing the things the boys were doing more than the things that the girls were doing. In hindsight, it was clear that she labeled some activities as boys' activities and some as girls'. The roles for boys and girls were evident to my mom but held no meaning for me. I understand today that gender roles were culturally defined while growing up. They were ridged, yet I don't remember having gender roles pointed out to me by other adults.

In fourth grade, I was placed in Mr. Anderson's class with a different set of kids than the ones I had been with since kindergarten. It was this year that I first realized that we students were grouped based on some unspoken metrics. I didn't have a label for it then, but I kept thinking that I was in the wrong group of kids the first week of school and that the kids I was supposed to be with were in another classroom. I believed I must have done something to be ousted from that group, but I didn't know what or why. After a few weeks, I realized these kids were just like me, and I felt like I was fitting in. Having studied to become a teacher, I now realize the elementary school was tracking us into academic groupings based on our performance. The group I was initially with performed better on educational measures than I did. As a result, I was grouped with another set of kids. While today I have no way of understanding what happened or how decisions were made, I can confidently state that changing up groupings of students did impact the friendships the kids made or didn't make. As an only child who naturally defaulted to doing things by myself, the school only reinforced that nothing was permanent, so don't get too attached to anything because changes always happen.

I soon realized that I was one of the top kids in class. My grades were higher than most of the others. I was competitive in some school activities despite my performance in spelling bees the previous year. Tim was the one kid I competed with all the time. He was good at math. He often got better scores in math than me, but only by one or two points. We became friends, and in time, we realized we had several other things in common. I loved playing chess, and so did he. I don't remember ever learning to play chess, but somehow, I had learned. I learned more by watching him and a couple of other boys play during recess when it rained or was too cold for us to go outside. We were both pretty good chess players, so we often enjoyed playing each other because the matches were competitive and usually lasted through recess periods and sometimes extended into lunch, where we had to pick up where we left off after recess. He would beat me sometimes, and sometimes, I would get the better of him. Generally, people would gather around when we played and watched. I didn't mind that type of attention when competing.

Two things stand out to me about fourth grade. The first thing I vividly remember was a special Vietnam assembly. The second event I vividly remember was a talent show. The Vietnam assembly was held to acknowledge the ceasefire between the US and North Vietnam. I didn't understand everything about the war, but I knew it was on the news every night, which was a big deal. I was asked to read a poem for the opening of the assembly. I had never read well aloud, and I had never read in front of so many people before. I was nervous. I remember reading the poem but didn't know what it was about. I remember that my voice sounded shaky and loud. I felt like a failure even though Mr. Andersen told me I did a good job. I learned that reading a poem out loud was very different than reading a story out loud. I remember thinking that reading the poem was more difficult because the lines and punctuation were in places that didn't seem right. I was turned off to poetry because of that.

The talent show was held near the end of the school year, in the evening, and all our parents were invited. Tim and I were signed up to do something but needed help deciding what to do. We couldn't play chess. The only other thing we could think of was juggling. Tim knew how to juggle. I didn't catch on as quickly, but I was getting better in time. We decided to juggle several footballs while music played in the background. We picked out a Simon and Garfunkel song, "Mrs. Robinson," and practiced a juggling act. I never felt comfortable juggling more than one football, so I just juggled one. He juggled two most of the time but dropped them often enough. We practiced every lunch break and recess after deciding to juggle. When the night of the event came, we were introduced. I remember the song and, looking up into the lights, started juggling one football. Of course, now I ask myself how juggling one football is juggling or even a talent. I don't remember my parents coming to the event; I was thankful they didn't. I concluded that what we did was dumb and vowed never to do another talent show again. I figured I had no talent.

Fifth grade meant I was back with the previous group of students again. My teacher for the year was Mr. Baylace. He was hard. I remember the SRA reading box and reading time was immediately after lunch. I was one of the top readers in my class. We didn't read out loud anymore, so I loved reading time. While in fifth grade, I found out that I liked to draw. Students in his class would get to draw when they finished their work, so I would rush through my work to have time to draw. Mr. Baylace was a great artist. During recess or lunch hour, he would give me suggestions and show me different techniques for drawing. I found that I enjoyed drawing.

Fifth grade was uneventful except for being a Safety. I loved being a Safety, and I must have been good at it because I got to be a Safety for two periods, and during the second period, I got to be a lieutenant. Lieutenant badges were blue, and captains' badges were red. I wanted the blue badge because blue was my favorite color. My logic wasn't fully developed back then. Had I realized that captains were "higher" than lieutenants, I would have wanted a captain's badge because I was competitive. At the end of the year, students who served as Safety got to go on a field trip to the Grand Rapids Symphony, The Roger B. Chaffee Planetarium, and McDonald's. My mom was a room mother and accompanied our group on the trip. In fifth grade, it was still okay to have my mother along. Besides, I would hang with my friends and not her. I remember my classmates liked my mom. That made me proud of her.

Another event I remember was field day. That was one event in which I knew I could excel. I was good at sports. I thought of entering as many events as possible and winning all of them. It didn't work that way, but I won five blue ribbons that day. Two memories about that day stand out to me. The first memory involved my participation in the high jump. The Olympics were still at the forefront of my mind. The high jump required us to get a running jump and see how high a bar could clear. I didn't know how to jump high, nor had I tried before the day of the event. The only understanding I had about the high jump came from watching the Olympics. So, I just used the Fosbury Flop because I had seen it done in the Olympics. The trouble was that the school didn't use any pads on the other side of the bar like they used during the Olympics, so I just kept landing on my back on the hard ground. It hurt every time I did the high jump. The pain was just a price of winning, and winning was the goal.

The second event that stood out to me was the softball game between the two fifth-grade classes. I was asked to pitch for our team. Several of the first two batters, who happened to be girls, hit the ball back to me at the pitcher's mound, and I would run the ball over to the person playing first base. I didn't have any confidence in my teammate on first base. Also, I was used to running the ball to the first base because that was what we did in our neighborhood games. I wasn't much of a team player because I had never played team sports. Back then, I didn't think anything of it, but as I grew older, that memory stuck with me, and I grew ashamed, even though my team won. I don't ever remember having the opportunity to play team sports while in elementary school. After graduating from high school, I remember team sports became commonplace for girls; I often wished that such opportunities had existed for girls when I was growing up. I am happy for all the girls today who can play sports year-round, including summer leagues, traveling teams, and even pro sports. I grew up in a man's world.

During the summer between fifth and sixth grade, I discovered something that I felt was unfair. Some neighborhood boys could sign up to play on summer baseball or football teams. Some of them asked me if I would sign up and play. I asked my mom if I could play on a summer baseball team. She called the local recreation center and checked to see what was available. Sports teams weren't available for girls. They were available for the boys but not for girls. I was jealous of the boys who could play on football and baseball teams. I never thought about getting mad at the recreation center or society because girls' teams weren't available. After all, my mom, grandmother, and aunts kept telling me girls didn't play those sports. The only good thing was that I would play with the four boys in the neighborhood, and we would simulate baseball games at every chance possible because they wanted to practice more since they were now playing on summer teams.

Sixth grade meant leaving Greenridge Elementary School and attending the middle school closer to my house. The middle school was in the old high school building, now called the junior high. I had a male teacher again and was back with the less academically prepared kids. My favorite time in sixth grade was reading. I read as many chapter books as I could. I loved biographies, especially sports biographies. I read about Joe Namath, Johnny Unitas, Bill Freehan, Archie Manning, and other famous athletes of the day. I like dog stories such as Lassie and Old Yeller. I even loved reading about history. The American Revolution was one era of history that interested me. I even found a way to turn reading into a competitive sport. My classmate Tom and I constantly competed to see who could read the most books each marking period. We often finished tied, but then he and I would add the number of pages in each book to determine a winner.

Sixth grade still felt like elementary school. We were kept separate from seventh and eighth graders and had our primary teacher most of the day. We would only switch classes for social studies rather than having a different teacher for each subject area, like the seventh and eighth graders. By the time sixth grade was over, I was forming a solid sense of what I liked. I identified as someone who wanted to read, draw, play chess, and play sports. I had many friends, mostly boys, but I was just being me. I knew I was different from other girls, but I liked myself and didn't need to change. I didn't get teased; my classmates knew me as me. I found the girls were mean to one another and had clicks. I was not too fond of clicks. I liked everyone and didn't want to mistreat someone because the people I hung out with didn't like them.

My classmates saw me like the substitute teacher who asked me if my favorite cartoon character was Peppermint Patty. I said no and told her that my favorite cartoon character was Snoopy. After she heard why I liked Snoopy (the intelligent, quiet type with a good imagination and one close friend, Woodstock), she told me I reminded her of Peppermint Patty. Peppermint Patty was a tomboy who played baseball with Charlie Brown and the Peanuts Gang. So, I started to identify with Peppermint Patty while continuing to love Snoopy. My classmates often identified with performers, musicians, and famous people; I identified with cartoon characters.

Sixth grade ended, and I was looking forward to summer and spending time at the lake doing the fun things I enjoyed. We would leave on Friday night each weekend and travel an hour north to the cottage. The cottage had transformed into a comfortable place to be. My father wasn't spending all his time working on projects anymore. Now, he had some time to enjoy fishing and swimming. When my aunts, uncles, and grandparents visited, we spent time goofing around. I remember many water balloon fights on hot days. We would play lawn games, from darts to croquet. Everyone pitched in to help prepare supper. My father was the "grill master." While he did an excellent job grilling hamburgers and hotdogs, he was best known for his burned chicken. Everyone would bring a dish to share. I remember most meals ending with fresh watermelon. All the kids and I would clean up after supper, allowing the adults to spend time playing cards and telling stories.

Every summer, I dreaded when the calendar turned to August because I knew returning to school would soon follow. The August after the sixth grade was different. To get ready to return to school, I had to meet with a counselor to pick up my classes before the start of the session. I had never picked classes before and wasn't sure what that meant. I brought my drawing pad when my mom and I met with the counselor. I knew I wanted to request an art class, and I thought I might have to show the counselor my work to get my way. The counselor gave me a draft schedule that included English, math, social studies, and science classes I had been assigned. I could decide what elective courses I wanted to take for the other three hours. The counselor asked if I wanted to take one hour for study hall. I said no, explaining that I would prefer to take a class because I already had a study routine at home after school.

I picked a gym class and an art class because I knew I liked both. I wasn't thrilled when the counselor told me I had to decide between home economics, shop class, Spanish, choir, band, or public speaking for my third choice. First, I wasn't sure I would like any of those classes, and second, I wasn't sure I was good at any of those classes either. I knew the band class wasn't an option because I didn't play an instrument. I didn't think I was good at singing, but I was open to trying. I certainly didn't want to speak in front of people, remembering my experience in elementary school reading a poem before the entire school. Before the visit ended, I signed up for a shop class in the first semester and home economics in the second semester. I was happy I could take art and gym both semesters. As my mom and I walked to the car, she reassured me that both classes, shop and home economics, would be something I enjoyed. I wasn't sure she was right, but I was looking forward to school starting in a couple of weeks because I would have different classes than before, which would only last one hour. I didn't realize how much people would change between 6th and 7th grade. Some of the boys' voices were changing, and some grew tall. Some of my classmates got braces. I didn't know that the dynamics of the social structure would change simply because I would be taking classes with older, more experienced students. I didn't realize that my family life would change significantly, either. All these factors would introduce more turbulent times into my relatively peaceful childhood.

Chapter Three:
Storm and Stress

"Blessed are those who find wisdom, those who gain understanding"

-Proverbs 3:13 NIV.

Seventh grade marked a significant change in my life. I suspect seventh grade is typically difficult for most adolescents. Adults often joke about the raging hormones, mood swings, and personality changes. Most jokes are rooted in some truth about adolescent development. I don't consider my junior high experience atypical for me or my classmates. Much of my 7th and 8th-grade experiences were "normal," but I soon discovered that my feelings were not so "normal."

Like the previous six summers, vacation ended too soon, and I returned to school. Transitions from sixth to seventh grade for adolescents mean changing schools. However, in this school district, sixth grade was in the old high school building sandwiched by the high school building on one side with the middle school building on the other. Consequently, I had already become familiar with the school layout. I felt at home, being familiar with the buildings, so that took care of my worry about finding the location of my classes. The only significant change that occurred was our classes were in the more modern middle school building, which was much bigger than the other two buildings.

Consequently, I worried a lot about getting to my classes on time. I didn't think five minutes was enough time to get from one class to the next class. My parents taught me to be on time, and I guess that lesson was deeply rooted in my DNA. I was beginning to understand that I worried about many things. As things became more complex and extensive, and I had more choices, I worried a lot more. However, despite all my worries, I never remember being late to class.

As August turned to September, I was adjusting to middle school and began noticing that my parents were getting into arguments. I don't particularly remember them arguing much before this fall. My dad seemed to be working more hours and additional nights for Meijer. The store stayed open later at night and opened on Sunday for the first time. I know he would have to close the store at least twice a week and didn't get home until very late, long after I was asleep. A couple of late evenings he worked, I was awakened by shouting between him and Mom after he arrived home. It was clear something unusual was going on. Being awakened at night didn't help me feel ready to attend school the following day. My studies were a struggle for the first time in my school career. I wasn't particularly good at grammar and spelling because I was not fond of the subjects and didn't want to work too hard. I enjoyed my other classes, but I had difficulty completing my homework even in those classes because I couldn't concentrate.

Periodically, I would get a hint of the conflict between my parents at other times of the day. In my coming and going after school, I occasionally overheard my mom talking to her sister on the phone. I kept hearing about her suspicions that Dad was "cheating." I can't say I fully understood what I heard, but I had a good idea that it involved another woman. I remember thinking I wished I had someone to talk to, like my mom had her sister. I don't remember having anyone at school to talk to about my home life. My friends and I talked about music or our favorite television shows at school. We'd talk about other people at school and who were friends with whom and who was "in love" with whom. Sometimes, we would talk about our pets or try to figure out our teachers. No one seemed to talk about their homes or parents, so neither did I.

I didn't feel like I had any close friends. I knew everyone in school and could hang out with any group. I was never alone at school or without people to eat lunch with or walk to class. But I never felt part of any group or close to any one person. Many girls had "best friends." I don't recall having a best friend. There was one 8th-grade girl who I particularly liked. I wanted to get to know her, but she had her friends to hang with. I would occasionally show up where she was and try to strike up a conversation, but it was clear that I wasn't someone she wanted to hang out with at school. What troubled me the most was that I couldn't stop thinking about this girl. That bothered me. Had I acted the same way around a boy and found myself thinking about a boy as often as I had this girl, I would have recognized it as a crush. However, being in school in the '70s, there was no label for my feelings. Indeed, being "gay" wasn't discussed anywhere on television, in the media, in textbooks, or among people. Consequently, I didn't understand what I was experiencing, which added to my feeling about being different.

I didn't find a niche in seventh grade. I knew that many of my friends lived near each other so that they could do things together on the weekends or in the evenings after school. I lived in a different area, more rural, and far away from most of my classmates. On weekends, I hung out with the neighborhood kids, but most of them were in different grades than me. I knew I wasn't popular at school, but I wasn't disliked or picked on. However, despite struggling in school, I was smart and worked hard enough to be considered a good student. Everyone was friendly toward me, but I didn't believe anyone was a true friend. I didn't take this personally, but I knew I was different. So, I often retreated to a quiet hallway area at lunch and read or sketched. I was content with escaping to a setting in a book or creating my environment by drawing. After all, these were the activities I enjoyed when I was away from school.

Once fall turned to winter, the middle school sports season afforded girls an opportunity to try out for cheerleading. There were no other sports for girls during the fall or winter, so I decided to try cheerleading. I figured this was like summer sports teams: they were only for boys. I was a "Bonnie Blue Bell" when I was younger and learned how to twirl a baton. Only girls participated in Bonnie Blue Bell activities. That was fun, so I figured cheerleading would be fun. It wasn't. I found that I wasn't coordinated. Learning to clap, move, and cheer simultaneously was a struggle. I'm sure the adults in my life had a great time figuring out how an athletic girl wasn't coordinated enough to simultaneously move, chap, and cheer. I suspect it pained them to watch me show them the routine I was supposed to learn. Eventually, I realized that cheerleaders got attention and were always in front of crowds. I wouldn't say I liked that type of attention. I preferred to blend in and fit in rather than stand out and be watched. It didn't take me long to realize that cheerleading was not for me.

During the spring, both boys and girls could try out for track. I decided to give track and field a try. I had yet to learn what events were included in track and field, but I knew I had done well on the fifth-grade field day, and if the circumstances and events were the same, I would enjoy track and field. The practice was always outside on the football field next to the women's softball field. Periodically, I would peek at what was happening on the softball field. I knew I loved baseball, so I was much more interested in what was going on at the softball field than I was supposed to do on the track or football field during practice. I played neighborhood baseball games each summer, even if it wasn't on a formalized team and leagues, so playing softball was what I wanted to do. I learned that the softball team was only for high school students. Since I couldn't play softball, I decided that I could at least try track because I would be competing.

I tried several different events in track. Running long distances wasn't for me. I was reasonably quick in short distances, but I found that I had put on some weight during the school year and wasn't as fast as other kids. I had been teased once by a boy because of my weight. I was walking down the hallway one lunch hour when Paul commented on me being big. His comments hurt me. That was the first time I began to think about my weight and size. I had always been one of the tallest girls in the class, and that seemed to be okay. I hadn't thought about my height or weight before Paul's comment.

In middle school track, the one event I excelled in was the softball throw. Rather than throwing a discus like the high school track members, middle school track members threw softballs. I could throw the softball a long distance. I won most of the softball throw competitions that spring. I could also jump well, so I competed in the long jump. Between my sprinting and my ability to land and fall forward, I did well in the long jump. It took me a while to get used to jumping at the right time to get the most distance from my attempt. All in all, I came to enjoy competing in track events.

Late that spring, my mom talked with me one day after school and told me she and my dad were separating. I didn't know what separating meant. The next day, after my mom told me they were separating, my dad got home later than usual from work. My parents began to argue, which became very loud and woke me up. I had been asleep for a while, and the fighting caused me to become afraid. The fight continued longer than I remembered in the past. I tried to sleep with the covers over my head, hoping it would stop. When the arguing continued, I decided to go to the living room to see what I could do. I entered the living room in time to watch my dad push my mom onto the sofa. I ran to their bedroom and picked up the telephone. My dad noticed me and followed me. He grabbed the phone and told me to go back to bed. I retreated to my bedroom and pulled the covers over my head. I just wanted the fighting to end. I heard them shouting for another few minutes, which seemed like hours. Then I heard the slamming of the door. It was quiet. I listened for a while in case it started up again. I was relieved that the fighting was over, but I wondered what would happen next.

Finally, I thought I heard my mom crying in the living room. I wasn't sure what to do, so I just huddled under the covers of my bed and tried to fall asleep. Sleep brought relief. The following day, I awoke to watch my mom pulling two suitcases out of her bedroom and moving them toward the front door. I asked her if she needed help. She declined. She set the bags at the end of the carport. I asked her what was up, and she responded that she had told my dad to pick up his bags and not come home for a while. I was stunned; this is what separating meant. Questions swirled in my head, but I was afraid to ask. My mom didn't say any more about what was going on. I didn't have time to ask more questions because I needed to get to the bus stop to avoid missing the bus.

I don't remember much of the rest of that day. I remember going to my favorite apple tree in the backyard after getting home from school. I climbed into the crux of the tree and just sat there thinking. I don't remember my thoughts, but I remember feeling like my life had just ended. I didn't know what the events of the previous evening meant, but I knew I was in for some changes. I kept thinking my dad should be home soon but remembered that my mom told him to take his bag and not return. I wondered when I would see him again or whether I would ever see him again. I don't remember my mom sitting with me to explain what happened. I wasn't sure if I should even ask her all the questions swirling in my head. I just decided to take it one day at a time.

That summer, my mom and I lived alone. I learned that my dad was living in our cottage. That meant my time at the cabin was limited, and I missed the friends I had met up there that I would see each summer. I would see him one night a week and on some weekends. I eventually met Karen, his girlfriend. I resented her because she was old enough to be my sister. I also didn't like being at our cottage without my mom because it didn't feel right. Karen had a son. I liked him. He was a bit younger than me, but having him around when I visited my dad was lovely because I would rather play outside with him than be around Karen.

Visiting my dad while he was with Karen was awkward for me. Karen tried to be my friend. Looking back, I can see how she tried to reach out to me. However, she was doomed to fail from the start. She was the "enemy". I did notice that she had my dad drinking Diet Pepsi all the time rather than beer. I did think that was good. I thought my dad looked happy, something I hadn't seen in the last few months when he was home with Mom and me. In some ways, I did think that they might be good together, but I couldn't bring myself to believe that Dad and Karen being together was "right." My dad knew I loved baseball, so one weekend, my dad, Karen, her son, and I went to Detroit to see the Detroit Tigers play. The pitcher that day happened to be Mark Fydrich. I loved watching "The Bird" pitch. He was a rookie pitcher who was winning games and exciting to watch. The Tigers won. It was a wonderful day. However, I wished my mom had come with us rather than Karen. My mom and dad once took me to a doubleheader baseball game at Tiger Stadium, and we had much fun. I just wished that the old times were back again.

Another weekend, I remember my dad and Karen taking her son and me to Cedar Point. I didn't know what Cedar Point was, but it sounded fun when Karen described it to me. The idea of having all kinds of rides in one location, and I could ride them as much as I wanted, sounded incredible. Cedar Point was a long car ride south into Ohio. I knew we would drive to Cedar Point one afternoon, stay the night, visit the amusement park, and leave for home the next day. The drive seemed endless. We checked into the hotel, got dinner, and watched TV when we arrived. We got to the park early the next day and rode every ride as much as we could. I do not remember the ride home. I'm sure I slept most of the way. It was neat that we all did things I could never imagine my mother letting me do. Despite my anger toward my dad, I could see the positive things associated with my parents being separated.

I remember arriving home and saying goodbye to Dad and Karen. It felt awkward. It was the first time I remember Karen being at my house when my dad dropped me off or picked me up. I remember wondering what my mom was thinking. She didn't come out to say anything to my dad like usual. I figured she was avoiding meeting Karen. I walked to the door. My dad drove off. When I entered the house, my mom asked if I had fun. She talked to me about the trip and what I enjoyed. She never asked about my dad or Karen. I was relieved. I don't remember my mom putting me in the middle between her and Dad. As I aged, I came to appreciate this about my mom. It wasn't until I was older and some of my other classmates' parents split up that I realized my situation could have been worse.

During that summer, my mom began working outside the home for the first time I could remember. That meant I spent many summer days at home alone. It was funny; I never worried about having things to do all the previous summers when I was home, but now that my mom was not home and working, I felt like I had nothing to do. For the first time since I can remember, I was bored. So, I began to find different things to do. My mom didn't know how to start the riding lawn mower, and our three-acre yard needed cutting. I took on this task with great enjoyment. Besides, it gave me something to do during the day. Eventually, the house needed painting. We bought the paint, and I went to paint the house one warm summer afternoon without asking my mom. I wanted to surprise her when she got home from work. The only part I didn't like was climbing the ladder to get to the higher parts of the house. I was beginning to learn the self-reliance that would later be both a blessing and a curse during my adult years. I cannot deny that the skills I learned would later be of value. When my mom got home, she was surprised, and I got a good lecture over dinner. I blew off my mom's lecture, chalking it up to the fact that she worried too much, but I obeyed her request not to paint the rest of the house until we got more help. My Uncle Tim came the following weekend, and we finished painting the house together. He was shocked at how much I had painted and how well I had done. He said I had done an excellent job.

The long summer finally ended. It was the first time since I started attending school that I could remember looking forward to the school year because I didn't enjoy summer like I used to. I didn't particularly appreciate having my parents living apart. They would talk occasionally on the phone, but then they would eventually argue again. I didn't figure they would ever live together again. The first day of school came, and I felt more at home in middle school. I had a better academic year and improved my grades in almost every subject area. My performance in 7th grade was not that bad, but I did struggle. The distractions of home often crowded out my ability to concentrate. Somewhere during my eighth-grade year, my parents' divorce was final. I don't ever remember my mom making any announcement about getting a divorce, but I do remember that one Friday night, she, Tim, and Sally went out to celebrate that the divorce was final. By then, I had learned to live with the separation, so I figured this new family reality was now the new normal.

One day, I came home from school, and my mom told me I would attend Confirmation classes at the Catholic Church. My mom didn't go to church much while I was growing up. I remember attending church with her occasionally, usually on Good Friday or other holidays. Growing up in Boyne City, my dad attended a Free Methodist Church, but I don't remember him attending the Catholic Church at all. I didn't know what being a Free Methodist or Catholic meant. I had gone to the church he had attended in his youth whenever we visited his parents in Boyne City. I knew his church was different from my mom's church. I wouldn't say I liked either of the churches because I had to sit still, pay attention, and be quiet. I couldn't sit still and was bored because I didn't understand anything the person at the front of the church was discussing. I found that the things that happened at church were boring. My mom seemed embarrassed by my inability to sit still. From time to time, I at least remembered to bring a paper and pencil with me to church so I could draw and create scenes and imagine myself somewhere else.

I attended Confirmation classes on Wednesday evenings. My mom would drop me off at the church and then visit her parents, who lived nearby, during the hour or so I was in class. She would pick me up after classes, and we would head home. We started going to church on Sundays also. We'd drive over, pick up my grandmother, and attend church together. My grandfather was a traffic officer at the church every Sunday, so he would already be there when we arrived. I remember staying overnight many a Saturday night at my grandparents' house while my mom went bowling with Uncle Tim and Aunt Sally. During bowling season, my mom would pick Grandma and me up on Sunday and attend church. We'd drop Grandma off after church and then stay for lunch. I remember I loved seeing Grandpa in his police uniform. Church was becoming more interesting, but I didn't feel the same about the Confirmation classes.

Confirmation classes consisted of a priest meeting with eighth graders each Wednesday to teach us about the church's traditions. Many of those who attended this class also attended a Catholic school. Those attending mass regularly or the Catholic school seemed to understand the information already. Most of the time, I thought the teachings could have been more interesting; after all, teachers at my middle school could make subjects I didn't understand more interesting. Since I hadn't attended church while growing up, some things they talked about didn't mean much to me; the other kids, though, seemed to understand those things better. One Wednesday night, the priest began to talk about heaven, hell, and purgatory. I hadn't heard about purgatory before. I had some sense that I believed heaven and hell were literal places. But purgatory was a new idea for me.

As the priest began explaining the idea of purgatory, I listened intently. The thought that people went into this "waiting area" intrigued me as the priest explained it. I raised my hand and asked him how long people stayed in purgatory. He explained that they were in purgatory for as long as their sins were unatoned. I continued my query. "What would someone have to do to atone for their sins?" The priest explained that other people, like their family or friends, must pray for their souls. He even used the opportunity to demonstrate that many people often buy special masses in memory of their loved ones, hoping they would have prayed and worshiped enough so their loved ones' souls would enter heaven.

Now, I felt like I was getting somewhere. I was looking for the absolute. My hand eagerly shot up again. The priest hesitated for a moment and called on me again. "What must someone do to guarantee they will go directly to heaven and not purgatory first?" This question seemed like a reasonable question to me. I wondered whether I could be good enough to bypass purgatory and go directly to heaven. How would I avoid this waiting area and ensure I would go to heaven? However, the priest didn't figure this was a reasonable question. His voice got more profound, and he was relatively short and stern with me. He seemed impatient. After a pause, he looked at me and said, "By being a good Catholic. Are you through with your questions?"

I was a little stunned. I thought, *No, I am not through with my questions*. I wanted to know just how good I needed to be so that I knew what I had to do to be assured that I would go to heaven. I was competitive and wanted to know how to "win" and go directly to heaven. I also wanted to live up to expectations and sought concrete answers. I don't know why I found the topic so intriguing, but I did. I felt embarrassed by the priest's short answers, stern tone, and apparent impatience with me. I wondered if I was the only one who didn't know the answer to these questions. I asked a couple of the other kids who had been going to church every week whether they already knew the answer. They just blew me off like the priest did. I garnered from my exchange that I was the ignorant one and that I was making the priest mad and impatient.

I left Confirmation classes that day and committed not to return. When my mom picked me up, I was glad to see her. I was ready to give her an earful. As usual, my mom asked how classes went and what I learned that day. My response seemed to startle her. "I learned that there are no guarantees about going to heaven, and since that is the case, I decided there was no reason to go to church or continue with these dumb classes!" My tone of voice certainly conveyed my frustration. After a few minutes of silence, my mom tried to understand my declaration. She asked probing questions. I worked hard to duck by supplying one-word answers.

"So, you talked about heaven today," she remarked.

"Yup!" I retorted.

"What else did you talk about?" she probed.

"Hell!" I shot back.

"So, you talked about heaven and hell today."

"Yes!" I mumbled.

"What did the priest say about heaven and hell?" she asked, trying to get me to talk more about why I was so angry.

"Just like I said! THERE ARE NO GUARANTEES, and these classes are dumb!" I shot back angrily.

It was clear to her that this conversation was going nowhere. She changed the subject. I was not any more responsive, and she finally stopped asking questions. I was relieved when she dropped the subject of Confirmation classes. We rode home the short distance in silence.

The following Wednesday, as I headed out the door to catch the bus in the morning, my mom reminded me about going to church that night. As I flew out the door, I yelled back. "I'm NOT going!" Sitting in school that day, I replayed the previous Wednesday night and my conversation with the priest in my head repeatedly; I became more and more convinced that I wasn't ever going back to that church. However, I was still curious about my questions on heaven and hell and wondered whether our school library had a book with the answers. I don't know if that was when I realized that not all adults appreciated my curious nature. But, somewhere during middle school, I learned that asking questions wasn't well received by adults, even teachers. Like many other circumstances, I again learned to rely on myself. I realized that answers to my questions were available, and I may have to find them myself. I turned to books. This would become a pattern – rely on myself and find answers in books – this lesson remained with me well into adulthood.

I don't know why my mom let me off the hook that Wednesday night. When she arrived home after work at her usual five thirty, I was engaged in some activity. She was tired as usual. She asked me to get ready for church. I shot her a look and declared, "I'm not going!" I had learned long ago not to sass my mom. When my dad lived with us before the divorce, I knew he would not tolerate me talking back to my mom. After the divorce, I didn't defy her often, but this was going to be an issue that I had decided was worth whatever punishment came for taking a stand.

She tried to use the "reason with her" approach. My parents often talked with me about their reasons for rules and decisions. I guess I responded well to that approach or reasoning with me was the only approach they knew. I learned that everything has a reason. I realized I didn't have to agree with the logic if I eventually complied respectfully. However, concerning the issue of returning to Confirmation classes, I knew I wouldn't comply. That was a big decision for me. I had long learned that compliance would serve me well. When I conceded, adults responded favorably. I took those responses to mean that they liked me. However, this issue was more significant than complying, being liked, or obedient.

After a brief conversation, my mom relented. I didn't go to Confirmation classes on that night or any other night after that. When my mom and grandmother would talk on the telephone, I overheard many conversations suggesting that I should attend Confirmation classes. All I knew was that I won something I felt very strongly about. I learned that I could bring the desired result if I had strong convictions and stood up for those convictions based on logic. That lesson was empowering for me. I'm not sure I could articulate this lesson as clearly then as I can now. Still, it was clear that emotional responses and outbursts were inadequate, and talking things through generally resulted in good outcomes. However, I was greatly bothered by knowing that my grandmother told my mom she was damned to hell because I rejected the Catholic faith. I overheard her say that to my mom. I was mad. However, I was more puzzled by how my mom could be held accountable for my decision. Whether I was aware of my decision, my grandmother's pronouncement affirmed that I would never become a Catholic church member.

Did I think about being self-reliant and logical when I was an adolescent? I probably didn't consciously think about the lessons I was learning, but I was applying what I learned. I knew what I was learning wasn't always clear to me, but I knew how to navigate the adult world and did so when it benefitted me. Reflecting on middle school, I learned to be self-reliant, rational, independent, compliant, and determined when sticking up to my convictions. More than at any other time, the events outside my control shaped me into the adult I became. For good or bad, I became a strong, independent woman.

Eighth grade seemed to fly by. The class I hated the most was physical education. During the winter, we did units on gymnastics and dancing. I thought square dancing was dumb. When would I ever square dance? This was the 70s, and disco was the rage. Gymnastic routines were even worse. Tumbling was horrible for me. Somehow, rolling forward doing summersaults and backward doing summersaults seemed useless. When would I ever do summersaults outside of gym class? When we weren't working on our gymnastics "routine," we were learning to jump on a trampoline and walk on a balance beam. I hadn't understood the competitive value of doing gymnastic routines.

As the Olympics became more commonly televised and watched in my home, I began to see the competitive nature of the sport, but as an eighth grader, I saw nothing of value to gymnastics. All the girls in my class seemed to like gymnastics. I was afraid of the trampoline and the balance beam. I had horrible pictures flashing in my mind of trying a flip on the trampoline, landing on my head, and being in a wheelchair for life. Indeed, my mom's anxiety impacted my willingness to take risks. When I thought about the balance beam, I pictured falling off, as my balance and coordination weren't outstanding, and I didn't believe the spotters could catch me because I was often taller and heavier than they were. I wasn't lightweight and petite like the other girls. I had a stocky build, and I didn't think any girls would catch me if I fell. I coasted through gymnastics and dance. I liked my gym teacher and tried to do enough to get by. Besides, she was also the softball coach, and I didn't want to upset her in case I could play on the softball team one day. Thankfully, the next unit was on basketball, and I couldn't wait.

When spring arrived, our gym class moved outdoors. We were doing units on track and field, softball, and touch football. We began with track and field. I excelled in the softball throw. I improved over the previous spring when I tried out for the track team as a seventh grader. I enjoyed sprints and the long jump. I wouldn't say I liked the hurdles, but I did find them an exciting challenge. I immensely liked team sports when we moved into the touch football and softball units. These experiences confirmed that I enjoyed softball more than track and field, and I decided to try out for softball in high school rather than track and field.

I was excited about going to class when we began our unit on softball. Our teacher, Norma Orth, was the high school softball coach. One day, as we finished our physical education class and walked back to the locker room to change, Ms. Orth caught up and asked if I would like to join her high school softball team for practice after school. She mentioned they only had ten players on the team and that if I could join them for afternoon practices, I would give them another person to do drills and take the field during practice, allowing at least one person to practice batting against their pitcher. I felt so special. I couldn't wait to get home that night and tell my mom about the invitation.

My mom was a bit reluctant to allow me to stay after school to practice softball. I don't know that she understood how important it was to me to be invited to be a part of something. I'm sure I tried to tell her, but I don't think she understood because she was never an athlete. Knowing my mom, she worried about me getting hurt, how I would get home, or something else. She finally gave her permission, eventually telling me her biggest concern was picking me up after practice because the practice was from 2:45 to 4:30, and she didn't get out of work until five. She was worried about me walking home. I told her I could hang out at school until she could pick me up after work. She knew I would take a good book and wait inside the lobby until I saw her car pull up to the curb. After we worked out the details, I grabbed my glove, ball, and bat and headed to the backyard to practice hitting and catching. Tomorrow was going to be the best day of my life.

The next day at school, the hours dragged until the bell rang, signaling the end of the school day. The only thing I could think about was practicing softball. When the bell rang to dismiss class for the day, I went to the locker room to change. All the high school softball players were changing already. I didn't know any of them, and they didn't know me. It was common for many people to be in the locker room after school, so I figured they had no idea I was about to join them on the field. Now, I was starting to get a little nervous. I didn't know what to expect. I wasn't even sure where to go. I figured I would watch the high school girls and then follow a safe distance behind. As the girls started trickling out of the locker room, they stopped to pick up the softball equipment. I grabbed a bag, too, figuring it was a great way to fit in. Helping was always a welcomed behavior I had learned.

When we all left the locker room and headed to the field, Ms. Orth was already there and awaited her team. The team huddled up around her. I wasn't sure what to do, so I hung back. She invited me over and introduced me to the girls. She explained that I was a middle school student, and she had asked me to come and join the team for a few practice sessions to help them out. She instructed different players to take their places on the field. She sent me out to centerfield. I ran out and took my place.

For the next two hours, I was in heaven. These girls seemed to accept and welcome me to their domain. I dove for fly balls with a great deal of success. I even got to bat. I knew I belonged when I sent one pitch over the makeshift fence in left field and into the bus lot. Several girls watched with amazement and congratulated me on the hit after practice ended. I was sad when softball practice was over. I had finally found my niche. I was invited to practice with the girls twice weekly for the next few weeks. The end of the school year flew by while I enjoyed playing softball. I never got to go to the away games with the team, but I could sit on the bench for a couple of the home games. I would help with equipment and cheer on the players. I welcomed being part of a team.

As an educator later in life who specialized in middle-level education, I often read about the challenging adolescent years. I frequently wonder whether the middle school experience today is as bad for adolescents as adults anticipate it to be based on their experiences. As I talk with middle school students, their struggles for identity and belonging are still paramount. I found my niche by accident. How do adolescents in schools now find their niche? These early experiences shaped my desire to be a middle school teacher. Several of my classmates at Calvin who were also studying to be teachers wanted to teach elementary grades or specific subjects in high school. Several told me they wanted nothing to do with being a middle school teacher. For me, I wanted to be a middle school teacher because I hoped I was that teacher who could be supportive, understanding, and accepting.

In middle school, I experienced positive and negative lessons in my struggle for identity and belonging. During middle school, I learned I was different from other girls in my class. First, I was one of the few kids from a single-parent home. While times have changed and single-parent homes are more prevalent, having a different home situation from other children made me feel different regardless of whether my peers perceived it to be different. Second, I became aware that my feelings toward girls and boys differed from the other girls in my class. I didn't understand how or why I was different; I just knew I was different. This awareness would become more robust as I progressed through high school and college. Perhaps the challenges of dealing with my parent's divorce distracted me from becoming aware of my feelings toward girls earlier. Third, I came to realize that where one lived mattered. I lived in a very rural area of the school district, well away from the housing developments of many of my class members. As a result, I knew very few kids before school, and because of my distance from them, I never really became their friends.

As the school year closed, summer loomed. I wasn't looking forward to summer for the first time in a long time. I knew I would miss the camaraderie I found with the softball team. I knew that summer was different now that my mom had to work, and we didn't go to the lake house together on weekends as a family. I knew it would mean more time alone and restrictions because she was at work, and I didn't want to worry her about me wandering all over the area. My neighborhood friends were changing, too, as some of the families had moved. I wasn't sure how much I would see my dad during the summer either. For the first time, my somewhat predictable life was no longer predictable.

Chapter Four:
The High School Years

"Do you not know that in a race, all the runners run, but only one gets the prize? Run in such a way as to get the prize"

-I Corinthian 9:24 NIV.

The summer between middle and high school was exactly as I had anticipated: long and lonely. My main distraction was my new dog, Private. She was a black terrier and poodle mix that Ken, my cousin, gave me the previous summer as a birthday present. Private was a stray. She had wandered onto the army base at Fort Bragg, North Carolina, where Ken was stationed. He mentioned that his buddies wanted to use her for target practice, so he had befriended the dog. The dog was neglected because he often had to leave the base for several days on maneuvers. He decided to give me the dog when he learned my first dog had to be put to sleep.

I remember the first time I saw Private. I had returned after spending a weekend with my father and was excited because Ken was bringing Private with him. When Dad pulled into our driveway, I said a quick goodbye and ran toward the door. Upon entering the garage, I noticed her tied on a leach. I stopped dead in my tracks. My first thought was that she was ugly. Her hair was long, extending down almost to the ground. It was matted. She was dirty. I couldn't see her eyes. She was skinny and small. She needed love and care. I immediately fell in love with that dog.

From that moment forward, Private and I were inseparable. My summer routine involved Private; she was involved in everything I was doing. Every Thursday, I would put Private in a basket on the front of my bike and ride about two miles down the road to the little village of Comstock Park. We would stop at the drugstore. I would pick her out of the basket, tuck her under my arm, step inside the door, pick up my weekly copy of *Baseball Digest*, and quickly step to the cash register and pay. The store owner didn't want dogs in his store. Since the magazine counter was just inside the door and the cash register was directly across from the rack, he allowed my brief visit with my dog in hand. I'm sure it helped that I was his regular customer, coming every Thursday afternoon for a copy of the *Baseball Digest*. Eventually, the owner just placed a copy of the magazine at the cash register, facilitating a quicker visit.

After securing my copy of *Baseball Digest*, I stopped by the ice cream store on my way home and ordered a small sundae every week. I was becoming predictable. The clerks loved Private too, often making her a "baby cone." Private was fast becoming an ice cream addict. Next, we would head across the street to Mill Creek Park, where I would find an unoccupied tree, tie Private on her leash to the tree, lay on the grass enjoying the warmth of the summer days, eat my ice cream, and read about all the important events that happened the previous week in baseball. On the way home, I would stop by the library and check out some books to read over the weekend and early part of the following week. The library didn't want dogs inside either, but the librarian seemed to like Private, so she tolerated my brief visits. It helped that Private was small and rarely barked. People didn't even know she was in my arms until I checked out the selected books.

I spent Wednesdays with my grandma and grandpa during the summer. My mom would drop me off at their house on her way to work, and I would spend the day with them. Private would come with me, and she and their dog, Honey, could have a play day, too. My mom would pick me up on her way home. Each Wednesday, I would cut Grandpa's grass. I enjoyed helping them. On sweltering days when Grandpa would water his lawn, I would run through the sprinkler. Sometimes, he would need to go to the meat market, and I would go with him. Once at the meat market, he would buy Polish sausage. I learned to like pickled baloney and eggs, which he allowed me to try. I would accompany him from the meat market to the store, where each visit would yield a new pack of baseball cards. I loved collecting them. My parents would continue to tell me how I was wasting my money. Little did they realize that one day, in graduate school, I would sell those baseball cards and have enough money to buy my first computer. I earned a little money by cutting my grandparents' lawn that I would use on Thursday to buy ice cream and my copy of *Baseball Digest*. It was usually my grandfather who would buy me baseball cards. My mom always reminds me that girls don't collect baseball cards.

The other three days of the week were generally dull. I was told I could not leave the yard even though I did leave every Thursday and rode to Comstock Park. Since I couldn't leave the yard, I would play basketball and practice baseball with the neighborhood kids if they were home. We had a basketball hoop in the backyard in a grassy area where I would practice basketball. I couldn't dribble the ball because it was grassy and the ground was uneven, so I shot hoops until I got tired. If the neighborhood boys weren't home, I would practice baseball by pretending to be a pitcher and throwing a tennis ball against the wooden shed in our yard. I used tape to put a square on the shed door representing the strike zone and pretended I was pitching to a batter. I kept track of balls and strikes. Often, I would throw nine innings of a hypothetical game. When I wasn't outdoors, I would be inside reading. Television wasn't a big part of my life. Where and when I grew up, I only had three channel choices. I found that the television shows were for adults and were not interesting. I also wasn't someone who listened to the radio a lot. I found the kids at school had favorite bands or singers. Not me. I just had favorite authors and books.

While each week was routine and relatively dull, the weekends were more fun. I continued to visit my dad every other weekend, and we would spend time at the lake house. Once there, I could visit the friends I had met there and enjoy spending time with Karen's son. When I wasn't seeing my dad on weekends, my mom and I would visit her family and do things with them. Sometimes, we met at my grandparents' house for cookouts, fun, and games. My cousin Deb and I often played tennis at a local school near my grandparents' house. At other times, my mom and I would visit my Aunt Sally and Uncle Tim. They had a pool table, so my cousins and I would play pool whenever we went to their house. Weekends always flew by quickly, only to usher in another long week.

The summer routine and the accompanying boredom meant I was looking forward to school beginning in August. I was entering ninth grade, which meant moving into the high school wing of the same building where I attended middle school. I wasn't nervous about entering high school because I thought I was familiar with the building and the daily routine of school. I didn't realize that high school would allow me opportunities to get involved with more activities and meet new people. Early in September, while in gym class, my gym teacher approached me to try out for junior varsity girls' basketball. I asked her about the details like the time, date, and location of the tryouts. I was excited and eagerly shared the information with my mom, who knew after last spring how essential sports were becoming to me. She enthusiastically agreed to let me try out but also cautioned me not to be disappointed for not making the team. That was my mom, always trying to protect me. Little did she realize that I wasn't worried about making the team. Of course, I didn't know enough to be concerned.

The day of tryouts finally arrived. The bell ending the seventh period rang, and I headed to my locker across from the gym. I put my books away and grabbed my gym bag. I went to the locker room attached to the gym, changed, and walked out to the floor where several girls were gathering. I recognized some of the girls from the softball team. They recognized me, and we struck up a conversation. Two coaches came out of the locker room and walked to center court. One blew a whistle. The one who blew the whistle was the varsity coach, and the other was my gym teacher and the junior varsity coach. They explained that the varsity girls were here to help with the tryouts and that we would run through several drills during the first hour, and in the second hour, we would be divided up and scrimmaged.

The two hours flew by quickly. It was so much fun being able to dribble, shoot, and scrimmage. I didn't want the time to end. I don't remember getting tired. I do remember having to play defense against a couple of different girls. I couldn't practice some of my skills at home because we only had a hoop in a grassy area. At the end of the practice, we gathered at center court once again. Both coaches explained that they would decide which ten girls would make the team over the next twenty-four hours. I remember looking around and counting fifteen girls. I figured I had a pretty good chance of at least making the team. The coaches told us they would meet one-on-one to tell us whether we made the team. They told us they would inform us by the week's end. The coaches then said to us that tryouts were over and wished us luck.

I headed to the locker room to change. I quickly changed and headed to the lobby to watch for my mom. Tryouts ended at five, so I didn't have to wait long. I didn't take a shower before pulling on my sweatpants and sweatshirt. I didn't change back into school clothes because I knew I needed to save those for school. I remember having a couple of pairs of sweatpants and sweatshirts that were perfect for slipping over practice shorts and my t-shirt. I hated showering after practice in the locker room. I was shy. I was used to privacy. I avoided the shower any time I could. In middle school, they made us shower after gym class unless it was the day's last class, and I was not too fond of this rule. There were no rules like that in high school. I was happy that gym class was just before lunch, so I could take my time changing, thereby showering after most of the girls had left. Looking back now, I can't believe how much thought I put into avoiding situations where I felt shy or uncomfortable.

The next day, I was attending my second-hour English class when the junior varsity coach came to the door. She handed Ms. Poga a note. We were in the middle of a silent reading activity. Ms. Poga approached me and whispered that the coach wanted to see me. I was worried. Tryouts were yesterday, and she was already coming to talk to me. It couldn't be good that she was coming to see me so quickly. I thought it might take a day or two for the coaches to decide who made the team. I walked to the door, lost in thought. The coach greeted me.

"I was impressed with your basketball skills yesterday. I invite you to join the junior varsity team if you still want to play."

"Oh! YES! I want to be on the team!" I excitedly replied.

"Okay, then. Consider yourself on the team. Practice begins next Monday. At practice, I will give you a schedule of our games. We practice after school from 3:00 to 4:30 on days we don't have a game. For the first hour, we have the court alone. From 4:00 to 4:30, we share the court with the Varsity team. See you then."

"Thank you! Thank you! I will see you then!" I replied. I then walked back into class. Everyone was looking at me. Generally, when someone was called out, it was because they did something wrong. I walked in with a massive smile on my face. I was sure the class knew I hadn't been in trouble. I don't remember reading the rest of the hour as I thought deeply about what being part of the basketball team would be like.

I don't particularly remember much about my first year of high school. The most notable event occurred during basketball season while playing at our rival school. I came down with a rebound. An opponent and I had the ball in hand when she pulled hard to try to wrestle the ball from me. My foot was wedged between her and another leg, and the twisting motion, coupled with my secure grip on the ball, meant my knee twisted. I wilted to the floor in pain. I remember being helped off the court. After the game, I was helped to the locker room, where I changed. I iced the knee through the varsity game. I limped onto the bus and then limped off when we returned to school. I limped toward my mother's car and saw her grimace. The next day, we visited the doctor and learned it was a sprained knee. I was done for the season. Thankfully, the knee healed quickly, and I could play varsity softball in the spring. So began my high school sports experience.

During the summer, between my first and second year of high school, I did what every soon-to-be sophomore did: I took driver's training. I was excited about learning how to drive a car. I grew up driving the riding lawnmower and a small fishing boat. I figured driving a car couldn't be any more difficult. My driving instructor was a teacher I liked and my former shop teacher. He was very encouraging and complimented my driving. The class flew by, and I passed the written test at the end of the week. My birthday was the following week, so my mom promised to take me to get my driver's license. She was true to her word, and I was so proud to have earned my license.

One day, close to school, I received a letter about the beginning of fall basketball season. The letter introduced the new coach, Mr. Meyers, who replaced the former varsity basketball coach who had passed away during the spring. Ms. Ramsdale had been a popular teacher and a good coach. I was despondent when I learned about her death. It was hard to imagine a teacher that young passing away. I didn't know Mr. Meyers. The letter explained that the varsity and junior varsity players would begin practice together while the school finished hiring a new junior varsity coach. The JV coach I played for the previous year decided to take a year off.

The first practice began the following Monday at 10:00 am. I rode my bicycle to practice, excited to start. As basketball practice began, I looked around and recognized several of the girls with whom I had played varsity softball the previous spring. I noticed only a few girls from my sophomore class at practice. I recognized a few new girls I didn't know, so I figured they were first-year students.

Practices were way more intense than my first year. We also ran so much more. Each day after practice, I would ride my bike home. The next day, I would get up, ride to practice, play hard, and ride home. Friday came quickly. At the end of training on Friday, Coach Meyers called several girls into a meeting to talk to them about the new junior varsity coach and inform them when JV practice would start the following week. He didn't call my name. The juniors and seniors left the practice floor and entered the locker room. I hung around and sat near the locker room but away from the meeting. I was wondering if he had forgotten me. After the meeting broke up, I approached Coach Meyers.

"Mr. Meyers, can you tell me who the new JV coach will be and when our practice will be on Monday?"

Mr. Meyers looked at me quizzically. He smiled and asked, "Renay, why are you asking?'

"Coach, I am a sophomore and still want to play basketball, so I want to make sure I come to practice on time."

Mr. Meyers's smile broadened. "Renay, I didn't realize you were a sophomore. However, even though you are a sophomore, you will play for me on the varsity team this year. I expect to see you at practice on Monday after school at 4:00 pm sharp. Ok? See you then?"

"Thanks, Coach," I responded enthusiastically.

I began to walk to the locker room as joy welled within me. I would play with the varsity team and the girls I knew from the softball team.

I went to the locker room. Most of the girls had already left. Some girls were still showering, so I gathered my things, stuffed them into the backpack, and walked to my bicycle for the five-mile ride home. As I peddled home, many thoughts raced through my mind. First, I was so excited to be playing on the varsity. I knew some of the girls from the softball team and liked them. I wondered whether I would even play. I wasn't sure if I should ask if I was going to come off the bench or if I was going to start. I decided I didn't mind either way because I knew I liked to practice and was learning a great deal.

Then, I wondered how the juniors and seniors would accept me. Class ties were significant in high school, and I wasn't part of their class. Then I remembered how well they welcomed me during the spring softball season, so I figured it would be the same as a basketball team member this fall. I wondered how my classmates would respond to me playing on the varsity while they were playing junior varsity. I finally decided I didn't care. I knew I was just very excited to be on the varsity. It was another way I was different. But the difference was good.

The new school year began the following Monday. I couldn't wait until 2:30 when the school day ended. My classmates who were playing basketball headed down to the gym as practice began at 2:45 pm. The junior varsity and varsity teams shared the gym. One week, the JV would start training at 2:45 and have the entire gym until 4:00 pm when the varsity would come in. The teams would then share the gym until 4:45 pm, when the junior varsity would leave, and the varsity would have the gym until 6:00 pm. The JV team would begin practice this first week at 2:45 pm. My classmates walked with me down to the gym. They entered the locker room to change. I continued walking down to the library to read and finish my homework while waiting for practice. At 3:30 pm, I walked into the locker room to change shortly before 4:00 pm. I emerged from the locker room with the varsity girls waiting to begin practice. My classmates looked my way. I could see they either realized I was playing with varsity or were confused by my confusion.

At 4:00 pm, the junior varsity gathered at one side of the gym, and we gathered at the other. We began practice by running laps and then sprints. We used the half-court time for conditioning. I was sure my classmates realized I was on the varsity team by this time. At 4:45 pm, the JV ended the practice, and we began working on plays. I loved to practice. I was learning so much. The week flew by. When the weekend arrived, I was exhausted but looking forward to the following week when we were scheduled to play our first game.

Practice on Monday was less intense than in the previous three weeks. It consisted of a walk-through of our game plan. Coach Meyers included many different combinations of offense and defense. He wanted to ensure that we understood the offense and zone defenses he might use. He wanted us to be familiar with our teammates as he explained that many different combinations of girls might be on the court during the game. Near the conclusion of practice, he called us over to talk to us about our game day schedule. It was a home game. The JV would play first. He explained that he expected us to attend the JV game and cheer on our fellow students. He explained that at the end of the third quarter, we should enter the locker room and be ready to go through our warm-up drill as soon as the JV game ended. Next, he revealed his starting five. He called two juniors and two seniors. Next, he called my name. I wasn't sure I heard him right. I think he just said I would be starting at center. As he talked a bit more, I realized he did identify me as the starting center. Could this be real or a dream?

Next, he handed out uniforms. Once we each had our uniforms in hand, we were free to go. He reminded us to dress up for school on game days and attend the JV game before it started. We then headed to the locker room to change out of our practice clothes. As I stood by my locker, opening the lock, several girls congratulated me on being named a starter. They made me feel part of the team. I didn't change out of my practice clothes but carefully put my uniform in my bag and left the locker room. As I walked to the front of the school, where I expected to meet my mom for a ride home, my heart swelled with joy. Tears came to my eyes. I was so happy to be playing basketball and so happy to be starting. I couldn't wait to tell my mom the fantastic news.

Chapter Five:
Meet My New Friend

"I lift my eyes to the mountains – where does my help come from?"

-Psalm 121:1 NIV.

Friday night was a varsity football game. The high school typically fielded a good football team, fueling the hopes and expectations of the residents and students of winning a conference title. The game was at home this Friday night; I attended and cheered on the team. After home football games, many juniors and seniors left the stadium and headed to different houses throughout the little village to celebrate the win. One of the houses that typically received a group of people was Pastor Gordon's home. Several of my high school friends gathered at Pastor Gordon's home after every home football game. One of those people was my basketball teammate, who invited me to join her at Gordon's home after the first football game this year. The gathering at the Gordon house was known as the 'Fifth Quarter' because of its proximity to the high school football field and because it always occurred after the end of the game. The location was at most two blocks from the high school field, an easy walk for our group of high school friends who attended the football game. The short walk ended in a warm house, serving refreshments suitable to teenagers who had just spent the past three hours outside cheering on their friends and classmates. We visited, ate, and waited for several of the football players we knew to join us.

This was my second time attending the Fifth Quarter gathering. I would not call it a party, but it was a social gathering. There was no alcohol, but I would not have expected alcohol to be available because that was not part of this group's activities. Most of the people attending were schoolmates, juniors, and seniors. Brenda had invited me to the event. Brenda was a varsity basketball member and a starter with me. I am not sure at the time I understood the significance or uniqueness of this opportunity to play varsity basketball nor how it would open a whole new world of friends beyond my classmates. I was happy to play basketball and enjoyed meeting new people at the high school.

As I circulated through the house, I saw several classmates attending the gathering. At that moment, I realized that these classmates knew each other very well and saw each other often on weekends while attending the local Bible church in the village. Many of these classmates lived near the housing development surrounding the school and little village. I live further out in the country, farther away from these friends, limiting my opportunities to see them outside school. I lived in a very rural area, and we only had a few neighbors because most of us had several parcels of land to farm. My parents didn't farm, but several of our neighbors did. These classmates saw each other often and knew each other well. They were welcoming of me. I loved living in the country and taking advantage of the three acres to enjoy the outdoors, but I realized there was an entirely vast social experience I had never known about. My mind was reeling with a mix of excitement at meeting new people and nerves because I was afraid of making a mistake. There seemed to be rules about who sat with whom and who talked to whom that I was observing. I was new to the group, and I wanted to fit in.

Lost in my new world and thoughts, I was brought back to reality by the clapping that started, signaling the arrival of the football players who had just won an important game. As we all said our hellos, the players grabbed their first helping of food, and an older man made his way to the front of the living room to gain our attention. Someone else had done this last week. The person who spoke last week was a fellow student who talked about the difference Jesus, as a person, made in his life. I had never heard someone talk about God and Jesus as a person, let alone having a relationship with them. While I was confused by this student's words, I was drawn to what he had said about how that relationship made a difference in his life and how much the relationship meant to him. He talked about a constant friend with whom he spoke through prayer. He described the peace and confidence he had because of that relationship.

My parents had divorced two years earlier, and I had felt little peace and confidence since then. Due to the divorce, my mom had to go to work, leaving me to spend much time alone at home. I wasn't old enough to drive yet, and visiting friends was more difficult because we lived several miles north in the country. The only way I could see anyone in town was to get on a bicycle and ride five miles into the village. While Mom was at work, she forbade me from leaving the house. She said if I did, I might get hurt. My mom worried a great deal and, as a result, tried to shelter me. I was raised to respect my parents' wishes. So, the idea of a constant companion caught my attention.

The group had quieted down, and Pastor Gordon introduced Bob Donaldson. Bob began to speak, and I listened, hoping to hear more about this Jesus person. Like my classmate said the week before, Bob spoke about his relationship with Jesus. He talked about how this relationship had changed his life and how that relationship meant everything to him. He shared his life story, which I felt was like mine. I kept thinking that I wanted to talk to him after he spoke to the group; a thousand questions were running through my mind. The first and foremost question was how one has a relationship with this Jesus. I remembered my experience at Confirmation classes and wondered if this Mr. Donaldson would dismiss me as the priest did.

As Mr. Donaldson finished his story, he said he had just one question for us. He asked us to bow our heads and close our eyes to answer his questions without our friends seeing us. He asked us to respect one another and not look around while he asked us to respond to his questions. Next, he asked those of us who had a personal relationship with Jesus to raise our hands. I was so tempted to look but afraid of being caught. However, I felt a movement beside me where my friend Brenda was sitting. I sensed that she had raised her hand. I was relieved because if she had a relationship with Jesus, maybe she could answer my questions if Bob couldn't or wouldn't. Next, Mr. Donaldson asked if we wanted to know more about having a relationship with Jesus and, if so, to raise our hands. Finally, someone was asking the question I was asking. I raised my hand. Next, he told us to put our hands down.

Mr. Donaldson then told us we could look up and open our eyes. Mr. Donaldson began to talk more. He wanted to share how one could invite Jesus into our lives. He asked those who had already asked Jesus into their lives to pray while he talked to those of us who wanted to ask Jesus into our lives. He explained that many people wanted to have a relationship with Jesus, but sins get in the way.

Further, he said that God sent his only son, Jesus, to this world to live as we do and to die on the cross as atonement for our sins. My mind was just reeling. I thought it was cool that Jesus was an only child. But what was atonement? I concentrated more and more on Mr. Donaldson's words, wanting so badly to understand. I realized I had missed some of what Mr. Donaldson was saying because my thoughts were rampant.

Next, I heard Mr. Donaldson say that if someone wanted to invite Jesus into their life, they just needed to ask. To ask, he said you just needed to pray this prayer. He asked everyone to bow their head again and close their eyes. He said anyone who wanted to invite Jesus to be their Saviour to pray this prayer as he prayed.

Mr. Donaldson began, "Jesus, I realize I am a sinner, and that sin is keeping me from a relationship with you. I acknowledge that the wages of sin are death. I understand that you died on the cross to pay for my sin. I believe that whosoever believes in you will have salvation and everlasting life. So, I pray now to ask you to come into my life and forgive me of my sin so I can enjoy an everlasting relationship with you. Amen."

I thought, "Is that it?"

I tried hard to remember what Mr. Donaldson said as he prayed. I just listened when Mr. Donaldson prayed. I didn't pray as he prayed. I attended church with my mom off and on, and when we prayed, they taught us to pray while kneeling. I wondered if my priest had previously discussed a relationship with Jesus, and I wasn't paying attention. So many thoughts kept rushing through my mind.

After the prayers, Mr. Donaldson dismissed the group. We all began to scatter through the house to talk and socialize with our friends. Some people started to leave. I tried to find Mr. Donaldson, but whenever I caught up with him, people surrounded him and spoke with him. I was afraid to interrupt. I didn't want my classmates to hear my conversation with him. What if I was the only person who felt the way I did? Suddenly, Brenda tapped me on the shoulder and said they were leaving for home. I had ridden with Brenda because she lived in the country a few miles from me, and she passed my house on the way from school to her house. Before I knew it, we were pulling into my driveway. Brenda asked if I was okay because I was relatively quiet while we drove home. I wanted to talk to her so badly, but her brother and girlfriend were in the car with us, and I was afraid of what they'd think if I started talking with Brenda about this Jesus person. I told her I was fine, tired from a busy week, and would see her Monday at practice. I exited the car, walked to the house, and greeted my mom, who was relieved I was home.

Chapter Six:
A Restless Night

"How long must I wrestle with my thoughts and have sorrow in my heart day after day? How long will my enemy triumph over me?"

-Psalm 13:2 NIV.

I awoke around two in the morning and could not get the story and prayer Bob Donaldson shared Friday night off my mind. "I acknowledge my sin" was a phrase that kept coming to my mind. I am not a bad kid, I thought. "Died on the cross to pay for sin." I remember that every Good Friday, the priest talked about the death of Jesus and how he had suffered on the cross. I do not remember the priest discussing why he died on the cross other than the Romans didn't like Jesus as he was a threat to their rulers. Mr. Donaldson said he died for me. I wasn't alive when Jesus was on the earth, so how could he die for me? I did not understand all this and was frustrated because I knew I wanted a relationship like the one Mr. Donaldson and my classmate described. Still, I didn't think I could have a relationship with Jesus without understanding sin, atonement, and dying on the cross.

Two became three in the morning, and I was still not asleep. Finally, I decided to get on my knees and talk to this Jesus like I heard Bob Donaldson talking to him. If I spoke to this Jesus person, I thought I would begin to understand. I kept thinking about what I might say to Jesus. I wondered how Jesus would speak to me or how I would know that Jesus was listening to me. In my church, the priest would always pray, and we would respond to the priest by saying specific phrases. I slipped off the bed and onto my knees, facing my door. I didn't want my mom to hear me because I didn't know what I would tell her if she came into the room while I was on my knees. My mom slept poorly and often sat in the living room at night, so I figured there might be a chance of her hearing me and coming in to ask what I was doing on my knees. I thought she wouldn't understand if I had to answer that question. Of course, I wasn't sure I would be able to explain what I was doing either.

As I kneeled, I decided to talk to Jesus like I was talking to my friend. I began by telling him I didn't completely understand what Bob Donaldson said tonight, but I wanted him in my life and to be a friend like Bob and my classmate described. I explained that I believed he was real even if he were in heaven, and I wanted a relationship with him even if I didn't understand what that meant or would be like. I explained that I didn't understand all this but wanted to trust him to be my friend. I asked him to come into my life and make me a better person who doesn't sin. I concluded by saying Amen because I thought that was how one talked with Jesus. I knelt there for a minute with my head bowed and my eyes closed. I was still determining what I was waiting for. I finally looked up and said, "Are you here, Jesus"? After a long pause, I crawled back into bed and stared at the ceiling. I felt calm and tired but wondered what I should expect to happen next. Finally, I fell asleep.

I awoke the following day around noon. I went to find my mom to see if I was in trouble for sleeping late. I found her in the basement washing clothes. She greeted me pleasantly and remarked about how late I slept in and how unusual that was. I explained that I hadn't slept well. She asked about the football game and what we did after the game. I started to tell her about the Fifth Quarter meeting and what Bob Donaldson had shared. She said she was glad I had fun but didn't say anything more about what I had shared about Jesus. I knew she was glad I hung around 'good' friends and had returned home before my curfew. Mom told me what she wanted me to do before I headed out for the day. We cleaned the house together on Saturday morning so that the work was completed quickly, allowing each of us some time to relax. Each Saturday, I cleaned my room and often helped my mom with tasks she couldn't do without my help or ones she thought I could do while she did things I couldn't do around the house. Sometimes, I washed windows, vacuumed, or cut the lawn. Today, I moved the furniture in the living room so she could clean and dust under and behind the furniture. The only thing I was ever asked to help with that I hated doing was ironing clothes. I don't know why I hated ironing because I would always iron in front of the television, which would help me pass the time quickly.

We had a modest, three-bedroom house. The living room and kitchen were small. We had one bathroom, but that wasn't a problem because we each went to work or school at a different time. Each Saturday, I quickly cleaned my room to do what I had planned for the day. This Saturday, I helped Mom move the furniture back in place after she had cleaned. Then, I was free for the day. I went into my mom's bedroom to find the white Bible I was sure she kept there. She walked in and scolded me for invading her privacy. She asked what I was looking for, and I explained that

I was looking for the white Bible I once saw on her dresser. She was curious as to why I would be looking for the Bible. While I explained I wanted to learn more about the Bible, she looked through her drawers. She explained that it was my grandmother's Bible and had been in the family for a long time. After searching a couple of drawers, my mom found it. She gave me a quizzical look and asked, "So, what specifically did you want to learn about?" I replied that I just wanted to read it. She made a face that looked even more puzzled. She handed it to me, told me to take care of it, and put it back in the drawer where it came from once done.

I went to my room and jumped on the bed. I lay back against my pillow, opened to page one, and started reading. I found that it made no sense. It was written in a type of English language I needed help understanding. Each sentence contained way too many "thee" and "thou" and "shall" and "shalt not" words that seemed old-fashioned. I expected the Bible to read like many books I was accustomed to reading. Finally, I closed the book, set it on my bed, jumped up, and headed for the door. "Where are you going?" Mom asked.

"Heading to Brenda's," I yelled as the door closed. I jumped on my purple Schwinn and peddled north up a large hill. I loved heading downhill but not going up. I had peddled up this hill so many times that I tried to push harder and faster each time. At the top, I was breathing hard but turned left down a Six-mile Road. A brief flat stretch and I was turning into Brenda's driveway. I knocked on the front door. Brenda's mom looked surprised when she opened the door and saw me standing there breathing hard, but letting me in. I asked if Brenda was around. She came out and was surprised to see me. I had never stopped by Brenda's house before. We had only been friends for a couple of months, and whenever we had gotten together, it was after school. Generally, we talked to each other during first-hour study hall. I considered Brenda a friend, but I was unsure what she thought of me.

"Can I talk to you about last night?" I asked.

After a pause, she responded, "Sure."

Glancing at her mom, she had me follow her to her bedroom. I remember her house feeling bigger than ours. I followed Brenda down a hall toward her room, growing increasingly nervous. We entered her bedroom, she sat on her bed, and I sat on her floor. A moment of silence passed. Brenda finally said, "What did you want to talk about?"

There was no turning back. I was so nervous. I liked Brenda, but I wasn't sure if she liked me or even considered me a friend. She had always been friendly toward me, however. I felt so awkward. She patiently waited. The silence seemed to last forever. Finally, I spoke.

"Last night, when we had to close our eyes, and Mr. Donaldson asked us if we knew Jesus, did you raise your hand?" I sat, anticipating Brenda's response. She paused and looked at me. I thought I was going to throw up. Maybe I shouldn't have asked her that question.

Finally, she said, "Yes, I did."

Now, what do I say? I thought.

"Cool!" I said quickly. "So, when Bob Donaldson had us pray last night...." I paused, unsure of what to say.

"Did you pray?" Brenda asked eagerly.

"No!" I replied.

Brenda looked crushed.

I quickly said, "Well, not then, anyway."

Brenda looked puzzled.

I told Brenda about my sleepless night and how I eventually knelt and prayed. I explained to Brenda that I had yet to learn if it had worked. Brenda sat listening and smiling. I felt like a blabbing fool. I didn't know Brenda well and was spilling my guts to her. Was that normal?

Finally, Brenda interrupted me. "You're saved!" she exclaimed as she reached to hug me. A thrill of excitement passed through me that I had never felt before. So, this must be what it means to have Jesus in your life. It must mean someone is "saved." I couldn't help but wonder what I was saved from.

We talked a bit more, and I asked a few more questions about my prayer. She then had me meet her parents and explain that I had "accepted Jesus" last night. Brenda, her parents, and I talked for a while, and I told them about my prayer. Everyone seemed so happy for me. I enjoyed the attention and conversation. Soon, I felt I needed to get back on the bike and head home before my mom started worrying about me. I was still on a high as I peddled out of their driveway and turned onto Pine Island Road. But I didn't know why I felt so good.

The weekend passed quickly; before I knew it, it was Monday morning, and I was getting ready for school. I was looking forward to seeing Brenda in the first-hour study hall. I liked Brenda. I wished she was my sister and could have her in my life. After graduating from high school, I knew many of us would go our separate ways and never see each other again. I figured if she were my sister, we would see each other all the time because families always spent time together. I didn't like being an only child and wished I had brothers and sisters like many friends.

We both got to study hall; Brenda's friends were hanging around at our usual table in the cafeteria. I hoped to talk to her more about my prayer asking Jesus to be my friend and save me, but I didn't want to discuss it with her friends hanging around because I was afraid they would think I was silly. I was also getting to know her friends and didn't want to embarrass myself. The day passed quickly; the next thing I knew, we were gathering to practice basketball. Monday practices were a bit more intense than the rest of the week. We reviewed our game plan for the game on Tuesday. We were learning another new offense and reviewed it repeatedly. Finally, practice time was over. We all headed for the locker room. Some of us changed and then headed home. I generally donned sweatpants and a sweatshirt. I preferred to shower at home. Brenda went her way, and I went to sit and wait in front of the school for my mom to pick me up after she got out of work. It always felt like an eternity waiting for her to arrive. I couldn't wait to have a car and drive to school like my other teammates. Finally, I saw my mom's car coming up the hill.

Once home, I changed, ate, and finished my homework. I had a little time to watch television and talk to my mom about our day. I often enjoyed going to my bedroom about an hour before I wanted to turn off the light and sleep so that I could read. Reading usually helped me put my mind at ease and let me turn off all my thoughts. I fell into bed and read for about an hour but didn't fall asleep. Most days, I can fall asleep anywhere and sleep through anything. But apparently, I wasn't sleeping quickly tonight. Not good, I thought. We have a road game tomorrow, and I need to sleep. I was haunted by the thought that I didn't know whether Jesus was in my life.

How would I know if Jesus was my friend? I tossed and turned, mulling over how I might now or how I might find out. Finally, I slipped out of bed, knelt, and prayed. "Jesus, are you real? Are you here? If you are real, can you help me know when you are here or when you hear me?" I was quiet for a while. "Jesus, if you are real, can you help me get ten rebounds tomorrow night?" I had no idea how to know whether all this was true. How would I know that what Mr. Donaldson and my classmate told me was true or at least valid? Not sure how to proceed, I started throwing out ideas to Jesus so he could reveal himself to me so I could know that he was now part of my life and with me throughout each day. I figured getting ten rebounds was how He could show me He was helping me. So, I prayed and challenged Jesus to help me play well and secure at least ten rebounds to confirm that he was now in my life and part of my life.

I crawled back into bed. I thought about what I had asked Jesus. Ten rebounds seemed like a lot. I was only five-eight, and I knew tomorrow night I would be guarding someone who was a five-eleven senior, and my coach just wanted me to box out my opponent and keep her off the boards. I figured getting any rebounds would be impossible, but if Jesus were all-knowing, all-powerful, and everywhere, he would show me He is with me if He helped me do something I didn't think I could do for myself. As I contemplated what I had just prayed, I fell asleep.

Tuesday morning came, and I was excited to go to school because I knew we had a game that night. I generally enjoyed attending classes, and since I moved to another class every hour, the school days passed rather quickly. My favorite class was still history though I enjoyed English as well. Geometry was challenging, and science was interesting, but there were many terms and facts to memorize. While history class required us to learn terms and facts like my science class, memorizing facts and terms in history seemed easier because they seemed to connect through the narrative of history. The facts and words in my science class seemed unconnected to me and, therefore, seemed more challenging to remember.

The school day ended, and I had to wait until 5:00 pm to board the bus to travel to the high school across town where we would be playing. Because I didn't have a ride home and then back to school for the games, I typically stayed there between the end of the school day and game time or the time to board the bus for away games. I passed the time between the end of the day and needing to board the bus or be in the gym to cheer on the JV team by finishing my homework. Thankfully, the school library remained open until 5:00 pm, allowing many of us who stayed after school to wait for bus rides, games, or practices, a place to study or hang out while we waited. During home games, once the library closed, I could usually find a quiet spot in the locker room where I could continue studying, drawing, or reading after completing my homework.

The JV game was fun to watch, and the team played well. It was now our game time. As I warmed up by running through our layup line, I kept talking to Jesus. I reminded him of my request. Despite being five-eight, with my opponent being five-eleven, I was the person who jumped the ball and would be defending this senior opponent. The game started with me winning the tip against my foe. We scored the game's first points; then our teams settled into a nice flow. We seemed to trade shot for shot, rebound for rebound, and basket for basket. The first half of the game was over, and we were still within striking distance of winning. We were down by just six points. During half-time, the coach reviewed our assignments and game plan. He reminded me to box out and keep her off the board. He said I had accomplished what he wanted so far in the first half, and I just needed to duplicate that same effort in the second half. He explained that to win, we needed to keep our opponents from getting easy second-chance shots under the basket. Then, we needed to keep making a higher percentage of our offensive shots.

We emerged from the locker room and warmed up during the remaining minutes of halftime. The second half of the game began with a jump ball. I again jumped the ball to start the second half and won the tip. Just like the first half, we scored the first points. Gradually, our opponent pulled away from us because our offense couldn't sustain the outstanding effort we executed in the first half. As the fourth quarter wound down, it was clear we wouldn't win. I kept scrapping and boxing out, hoping that if we at least kept them from making easy second-chance points, the margin of their victory wouldn't be large. The rest of the team didn't give up either. Our team managed to make better shots near the end of the game. However, when the final buzzer sounded, we lost by ten points.

The locker room was quiet as we showered and prepared to board the bus. I put my sweat suit on and skipped the shower. This was my usual routine. I felt so awkward taking a shower with people. I always felt like people were staring at me. Conversely, I worried people thought I was staring at them. However, I was always curious whether people felt as awkward as me in these situations. It never seemed like it. I grabbed my bag and headed out of the locker room. I boarded the bus and picked my seat carefully. I generally sat alone. I was the lone sophomore on the team. Everyone else was a junior or senior and had known each other for a long time. They were all friends, and I could tell who would sit with whom. All fall, I had been sitting by myself. I didn't mind. I just figured it was because I was a sophomore.

I was replaying the game and what I could have done to help us win. Suddenly, I realized that Brenda had slid into the seat next to me. She had never sat with me before. She generally sat by herself. My heart leaped. Wow, I thought Brenda was my friend, but this was unexpected. We talked all the way home. We got off the bus and into her car, and she took me home. I cherished every minute with her because I could ask her all the questions about Jesus and the life I wanted. After all, it was just me and her riding home. She always seemed eager to answer my questions; time seemed to fly by quickly when we were together.

Brenda dropped me off at home. I opened the door, entered the living room, and talked to my mom briefly before heading to the shower. After a long, hot shower, I said goodnight to my mom and fell into bed. I couldn't stop thinking about Brenda sitting next to me on the ride home from the game. I replayed our conversations in my mind repeatedly and decided to pray and thank Jesus for my good day. The next thing I knew, I told Jesus how much I wished Brenda was my sister so I had someone to talk to daily. While praying, I thanked Jesus for helping me play a good game. After praying, I was reminded about my request to Jesus. I began to wonder how many rebounds I had during the game. It was customary to talk to Jesus for one minute and have other thoughts swirling in my mind simultaneously. I wondered if he knew what those thoughts were when I was talking to him and thinking.

As I drifted off to sleep, I wondered if I had ten rebounds, so I began to try to recount each play I was in and whether I had come up with a rebound. I had been so focused on how great it felt to have Brenda to talk to on the ride home that I never asked the coach to see how many rebounds I had. The next thing I remember was my alarm going off, waking me up for school.

Chapter Seven:
The Test

Jesus answered him, "It is also written: 'Do not put the Lord your God to the test'"

-Mathew 4:7 NIV.

As I got ready for school, I couldn't help but think about Brenda. I couldn't wait for the first hour to see her even if I knew we wouldn't be alone and accompanied by her other friends whom she knew from the band. As usual, Brenda and her friends were in the cafeteria before me. They were saving me a seat. Many of her friends had become my friends, and I was starting to feel like I belonged. Several of her friends also attended the Fifth Quarter event after each home game, so now I spend more time with them by attending other events together as they invited me to more and more things. Because of my time playing on the varsity team and hanging with Brenda and her friends during study hall each morning, I was starting to feel more comfortable making friends, especially with older classmates.

The football game was away this week. I knew I could not go to away games. Brenda and her friends asked if I wanted to go. I made up some excuses about why I could not go with them on Friday. They were disappointed, but my reason for visiting my dad made sense. They knew my parents were divorced and my father didn't live in town. They understood I wanted to see him whenever he was in town. But, telling them I would see my dad on Friday was a lie. I didn't want to tell them my mom didn't like me going to the away games because she worried so much about bad things. I was ashamed I lied. My feelings led me to wonder: was that what Jesus died for? I didn't particularly appreciate lying, and my parents raised me to be honest and tell the truth, but I didn't want to tell them that my mom wouldn't let me go because she worried too much. I used to ask her early in the year to go to away football games, and she would say no, and I would get frustrated because I thought her worrying was ridiculous. I didn't want to argue with her, so I stopped asking about going to away games. I had long learned not to press the issue because the answer wouldn't change. I figured she didn't appreciate me when we were fighting, and sometimes she might remind me that this arguing and debating was why she and Dad were no longer together. I didn't understand why the divorce happened. Before the divorce, my parents had never fought. We all seemed to get along so well. The mystery worried me, so I kept the peace and avoided conflict.

Study hall ended, and we all headed to our second-hour class. That Wednesday went fast. I couldn't wait to get to practice and see Brenda again. What was wrong with me? I used to want to practice because I loved basketball, and now I wanted to practice so I could see Brenda. As the bell rang to signal the end of the day, I headed for my locker to put away my books and school things, grab my gym bag, and head to the locker room to change. My school locker was directly across from the gym, so I was typically one of the first players to arrive and change. Once changed, I would grab the basketball rack and roll it out to the area in the gym where we kept them. I would grab a ball and begin warming up, stretching after a set of shots I usually practiced while waiting for the team and coach to gather at center court to start our official practice.

Coach Meyers entered the gym. He signaled to us to gather on the bleachers as we did each day after playing a game to debrief the game and plan for the next game. Coach explained that while we didn't meet our goal of winning the game, we did meet many of our in-game goals. The coach pointed out that we had lost to an excellent team expected to win the league that year. They were in first place, and we made them work for the victory. He went on to say that this was still early in the season and likely we would continue improving and to remember that we would see them again later in the season on our home court. He praised us, saying that last night, we demonstrated that we would be one of the top teams in the league despite being picked to finish in the middle of the conference.

Coach Meyers continued his debriefing, mentioning the leading scorer, the player with the most assists, and the player with the most steals. Then he said we had one player who met and exceeded our expectations in rebounding. I knew he was talking about me, but I just wanted to know if Jesus was real; in other words, did I get ten rebounds? Coach Meyers had the team guess the number of rebounds I secured. "Ten," one teammate said. "Twelve," another teammate said. "Fourteen," another called out. Coach looked at me and asked how many I thought I had grabbed. I had no idea but knew my goal, so I said, "Ten." A big smile came to his face, and he said, "Would you believe you had 18 rebounds last night?"

"No way!" I exclaimed. My teammates clapped, and some began slapping my back and hugging me. I loved the celebration of accomplishments despite our loss. We all understood that achieving an overall team victory happens when we each have little victories throughout the game. It was a short celebration as we went into our fast-break drill, which always got our blood pumping. Before I knew it, I was dripping with sweat and sucking wind. Next, the coach began reviewing our offense and showing us where he thought we would have opportunities to take advantage of our opponents' defense and size. We simulated in-game situations like inbounding the ball at different locations on the court. Before we knew it, practice was over. I went to the locker room, grabbed my bag, and headed to the front of the school to wait for my mom. All the others were in the locker room for a while. I assumed they showered before going home.

Within the school's entryway was an open foyer that led directly into the library; a left turn led you to the middle school wing, while a right turn led you into the high school wing. Along the front of the library was a row of chairs for people to use while they waited for rides. I took one of the seats where I could easily watch through the windows on each side of the double door for my mom to arrive. Once seated, I pulled out my sketch pad.

"Hey, you need a ride?" Brenda asked as she appeared in the entryway and walked toward the front door. I wanted to say "yes" but stopped short when I realized my mom was coming, and I couldn't tell her before she left work that I had gotten a ride home.

"No thanks, I have a ride, but thank you for the offer," I responded.

"See you tomorrow in study hall. Home game tomorrow, too," Brenda replied. She walked out the front door. I watched her walk to the parking lot, wishing I was riding home in her car. A horn brought me to consciousness, only to see my mom waiting in her car by the curb. I walked to the car, thanking Jesus for the 18 rebounds. My natural skepticism took over.

"So, Jesus, how do I know you helped me get those 18 rebounds, and it was not just me trying to prove to myself that you are real? You know, there is something I could improve at, and that is scoring points. I am not a scorer, and our offense doesn't even include me in the scoring plan. Scoring many points is not something I control, so if you are real, Jesus, I will score twenty points tomorrow."

As my prayerful thoughts ended, I opened the car door, entered the passenger seat, and said hello while shutting the car door. I asked my mom how her day had gone. While she talked about her day, I watched out the window, thinking about Jesus and Brenda. I managed a few short comments and head nods in response to my mother's questions about my day, but I was more in tune with the thoughts running around my head. I struggled to believe Jesus was real because I needed something concrete and tangible as evidence. I felt no different, but He had passed the first test. Let's see if he can deliver tomorrow with something far more unlikely than accomplishing what is expected of me. I had yet to stumble across the truth in Hebrews 11:1, *"Now faith is the substance of things hoped for, the evidence of things not seen"* (KJV).

Chapter Eight:
I Like Dreaming

"I praise you because I am fearfully and wonderfully made; your works are wonderful, I know that full well"

-Psalm 139:14 NIV.

As I drifted to sleep, I once again talked to Jesus. I spoke to Him about my day or something I thought about before falling asleep. I had always reflected upon my day as I fell asleep, so this seemed like the same thing I did before, but now I made it more conversational with Jesus. When I was very, very young, I recalled making up pretend friends and involving them in my play. Was this the same thing as that? The only way to find out was to put this Jesus to another test. I likened it to experimenting like we did in science class. As I prayed to Jesus this time, I explained how important the Thursday game was to us. We were playing my self-proclaimed rivals. I asked this Jesus as I prayed, "So if you are real, enable me to score twenty points tomorrow night." I didn't see it as a selfish request because it would benefit the team. I wasn't looking for credit or fame; I just wanted assurance that Jesus was a real being, not an idea like Santa Claus or make-believe friends.

I needed Jesus to demonstrate his genuine nature by asking him for something I thought I couldn't control or do myself. I had previously scored at most six or seven points in a game this season. I was not the scorer within our offensive game plan. Generally, I averaged five points per game when I secured offensive rebounds and could shoot it immediately or whenever I made free throws because I was fouled while rebounding. My role in the offense was as a weak side forward whose primary responsibility was to rebound on the offensive boards whenever the shooting forward or guards missed their shot. In other words, I was to mop up. On the defensive end, it was a similar assignment. I was to box out the weak side forward and ensure the opponents' offense would not get a second shot. These assignments did not afford me many opportunities to score.

While I fell asleep quickly that night, I woke up several times during the night. Finally, the alarm screamed for me to wake up and start my day. The school day consisted of my usual class routine. During game days, the cheerleaders would make locker decorations the night before and tape them to our lockers. The decorations would wish us luck or contain encouraging words. These decorations also signaled to those with lockers around mine that I had a game that night. They would then see me either at my locker or in the hall, wish us luck, and say encouraging things. Thinking about the game throughout the day was easy because of these traditions. Since tonight was a home game, which meant we had to be in the gym at six in the evening for the start of the JV game, most of my friends went home after school and returned later for the game because there were three hours between the end of school and the start of the JV game. During away games, my teammates typically hung around after school because there wasn't much time between the end of school and the time to board the bus.

So, during home games, I had to find additional things to do in and around school because I couldn't get home and back in time; I didn't have transportation. One of the things I found to do required walking down the hill from the school to the main street in the little village. Besides the post office and library that anchored each end of the main road, there was a park that I often played in or hung out at, which was situated between the eighth-of-a-mile stretch that made up the village. The park faced several buildings, including an ice cream shop, barber shop, store, pharmacy, beauty shop, restaurant, bar, and pizza shop. That was all there was to the little village. Thankfully, two restaurants lined the east side of the street, affording me a place to grab a bite to eat and study before heading back up the hill to school for the junior varsity game. The little village felt like home to me. Everyone seemed to know or at least recognize each other. Walking four blocks from the school to the downtown area, I always felt safe. It was early October, and the weather was fantastic. Fall was in full splendor and beautiful as leaves turned from green to vibrant red, orange, or yellow colors.

For every home game, I would go to the family restaurant, select a booth, and spread my books on the table. The same waitress was there every time I went. I would order supper and work on my homework until the waitress brought my order. She often talked to me and asked about my day, the team, and our season. I am sure she was just being nice, but I appreciated her friendliness. She said she started following the girls' basketball team because I frequently stopped in. If other customers came in, she did her job and ensured they were served. She would check in with me often to ensure I had all the milk, soda, or water I wanted while I passed the three hours between the end of school and when I had to return to watch the junior varsity team. I always finished enough homework so that after the basketball game, I could focus on visiting with my mom and going to bed once I arrived home. After finishing my meal and paying, I said goodbye to the waitress, left, walked up the hill to school, dropped off my books at my locker, and headed to the bleachers to cheer on the junior varsity.

The junior varsity team was comprised of first and second-year students. The sophomores were my classmates. I would have been playing with them had it not been for my opportunity to play on the varsity. As a result, I didn't have many chances to hang out with them. The juniors and seniors I played with were closer friends to me than my classmates. They treated me well and were as inclusive as they should be, but it was clear that I was not wholly one of them because I would never see them in classes. After all, they were in courses typically taken by upper-class members. I felt like an outlier. I was part of the team but not part of the group. I was part of my classmates playing junior varsity, but there was some distance between us. Sometimes, I wondered whether my classmates were jealous. I wasn't sure because they treated me fine when I saw them in class, but I didn't hang out with them after games because they finished before my games. I knew in my heart that I wasn't part of any crowd. I was unsure if I wanted to be part of the crowd, but I would have at least wanted to make that choice. But for now, I didn't feel like I had a choice.

After the third quarter of the junior varsity game, I headed to the locker room to change before our game. I was always the first one in the locker room, hoping I could change before everyone else got there, and began changing. I was the only child and didn't need to share space with siblings at home, so I wasn't comfortable sharing space with others. I hated changing in front of the other girls. I felt shy. I hurried and changed, then headed to the bleachers to watch the fourth quarter. I sat along the side of the gym near our locker room and cheered on my peers who were ahead in a close game. They were not winning many games but were competitive in every game. When the buzzer sounded, they had lost by three points, but they played well, and it was clear they were improving every game.

Our game tipped off twenty minutes after the junior varsity game ended. The game's pace was steady as each team sprinted back and forth. We were within four points of the other team during most of the first half despite our shooting guards seeming off their mark tonight. Because they were missing more shots than usual, I had many opportunities to secure rebounds and even had the chance to put a few balls in the net on the offensive end after securing a rebound. We should not have been trailing in this game. This is a team we should beat easily.

During the second half, our opponents came out with a full-court press. On a full-court press, I was usually set up near half-court when taking the ball out from under the basket we defend. Ball handling was not my specialty, so I was the last option in the press. During a press, I was to drift backward toward our basket as the guards passed the ball up the court. The idea was that the defenders would leave me unattended near our basket to double team the guards bringing the ball up, or the guards would drop back and deny a pass to the natural shooting forwards, leaving me open because of a mismatch having a guard defending me but inching away to double team a pass to the shooting forward. This would create situations that would allow me to score. We successfully broke their press, and I even received several full-court passes heaved down the floor when the player inbounding the ball struggled to get it to one of the guards. I secured the ball on a full-court pass and headed directly to the basket. I scored on the first two presses before our opponents returned to a half-court press.

The coach called a time-out and reviewed our half-court press option. I would set up near the baseline and sideline and again become the last option. Like in the full-court press, I saw the ball coming my way the first few trips down the floor. I grabbed the ball and headed straight for the basket. A side layup is not the easiest, but somehow, I delivered. The next trip down the floor, I again had the ball. I made a move to the basket, but the defense had adjusted. I pulled up and shot a jumper. The crowd cheered as the ball ripped the net and tied the game.

Our opponents dropped the press. We settled back into our routine, ran our offense, and gradually pulled away for a victory. Our coach came into the locker room for a few remarks before we changed and headed home for the night. He praised our adjustment to the press. We responded well. He quickly reviewed a few of the statistics related to the in-game goals we had focused on. We had improved in all areas and, most importantly, committed fewer turnovers. We gave up fewer second chance points, and then the coach surprised me by pointing out I had scored 24 points, my personal best. I was numb. I knew I had shot the ball more than usual because of the press. I had what was becoming my regular double-digit rebound game, but I was not expecting a twenty-point game.

As I grabbed my clothes and looked for Brenda for a ride home, I prayed to Jesus. "Thank you for helping me have a good game. I am beginning to believe you are real".

Chapter Nine: The Journey Begins

"Do two walk together unless they have agreed to do so?"

-Amos 3:3 NIV.

I lay in bed after the game, realizing I was getting more and more certain that Jesus was real. I decided to learn more about him and what the Bible says about my faith. This Friday was homecoming, and the first-hour study hall was empty. Many people in the study hall were off working on homecoming activities and putting the finishing touches on their class floats. The usual gang was not there. I was delighted to discover Brenda and I were alone, sitting in familiar places. This allowed me to ask questions about Jesus and my new faith in God. Brenda also told me about church on Sunday and invited me that Sunday to check it out. She explained that Pastor Gordon taught from the Bible on Sunday and that I could grow in my faith by attending church and Sunday school. She also mentioned that the church held events on Wednesday evenings, and a high school group met on Wednesdays. She said I would know most of the people who frequently came. After learning more about how Brenda's church worked, I decided to go that Sunday.

Saturday night, I asked my mom about going to church. She was puzzled but supportive. Brenda called and told me when they would pick me up. Come Sunday, I was ready thirty minutes before Brenda and her family were to pick me up. I was eager and nervous at the same time. I sat with Brenda, who sat with her family. The church service was not like anything I had experienced before. It was much less routine and more casual than what I had experienced when going to church with my grandmother. I enjoyed the music, and the songs were in a hymnbook that I could use to follow the words and participate. When Pastor Gordon asked us to turn to a passage in the Bible, I did not have one. Brenda shared hers with me. I was able to read the Bible verses that Pastor Gordon talked about. I took notes.

After the service, I saw several people from school. They all seemed happy to see me. Many asked me to come back to church Sunday night and explained about the "youth group." I did not commit, but I did tuck the information away in my mind. After several conversations with other church members, Brenda's family headed out, and I joined them. They dropped me off at home, and I went to my bedroom and changed. My mom and I then headed to my grandparents' house for Sunday dinner and an afternoon of watching football games. Sunday was always family time, so I knew not to plan anything on a Sunday. That is one reason I was surprised my mom didn't mind that I went to church with Brenda. I realized my grandparents went to church too, so it worked out well that I could go to my church and then come home and go to my grandparents' house with Mom.

This pattern would repeat itself for the remainder of the school year. Brenda's family seemed to have adopted me and made me part of their family on Sunday. I also began to join them from time to time on Sunday nights for youth group and then again on

Wednesday nights. I loved learning from the Bible. I found it very interesting. I also found that I prayed to Jesus periodically throughout the day. Often, I would pray unconsciously. Perhaps this is what the Bible meant by "pray without ceasing." One thing I loved about attending on Wednesday nights was singing. The songs were modern and contemporary. Brenda played the guitar along with the youth pastor. Brenda was musically talented.

I was enjoying my newfound faith, church, and friends. I was also enjoying my sophomore year in high school. I volunteered to help produce the yearbook and was selected to be one of the official photographers. I learned how to use a SLR camera for different types of photographs. I learned that each type of photograph may need different lighting or film speed. My favorite types of photographs were action and sports photos. The challenge with capturing a sports moment included anticipating the moment, using the correct film speed, and knowing what angle would produce the best-stopped action frame. Part of being a photographer for the yearbook included being able to attend school events to take pictures. I was quick to volunteer for events because that allowed me to go and be involved but not worry about being asked to dance by a boy or be included with a group of friends. If I showed up to an event alone, no one questioned why I was alone because they saw the camera in my hand and knew I was working the event. In addition to being involved on the yearbook staff, I was also inducted into the National Honor Society because of my grades and involvement at school. The National Honor Society met monthly at lunch to plan service activities within the community and at the school.

The fall semester flew by between basketball and all I was involved in. I was sad when the semester ended and wasn't looking forward to ten days off for Christmas break. I knew I would not see my school friends because I lived so far out in the country. I hoped to see people at church but was unsure if I could attend because I wasn't sure if I could talk my mom into taking me to church. I also knew I would have to spend some time with my dad over Christmas break. If I had to visit my dad in Mount Pleasant, I knew I didn't know anyone around his house, and likely, we would have to work, so I feared spending time alone with nothing to do. I looked forward to seeing my father, but I resent what he did to break up our family. Deep inside, I blamed him, believing his affair had broken up in our family. My resentment kept me distant from him now.

I had been learning about forgiveness in my youth group. I remember God forgave our sins and sent his son Jesus to pay the consequences of our sins by dying on the cross. God's forgiveness of our sins and our faith in Jesus allowed us to have a relationship with God through Jesus. As I learned these ideas in youth group, I could not help but think about my dad. He had sinned. He had an affair. I needed to forgive my dad. I was hurt and angry. I wondered if God felt that way about my sin. I also realized that to receive God's forgiveness through His Son Jesus Christ, I had to invite him to forgive me and accept, by faith, that the blood of Jesus paid for my sins. I wondered if my dad would ever ask my forgiveness for breaking up our family and hurting Mom and me.

As school closed for Christmas break, I learned from my mom that we would spend Christmas Eve at my grandmother's house. She then told me I would spend a long weekend beginning on Christmas Day with my dad. While my mom still had to work while I was home from school, he asked me to wrap the Christmas present she had bought or made for her family. There were not many presents to wrap, but I enjoyed the opportunity to wrap them. I learned how to make bows and added them to the presents to make them festive. As I wrapped each gift, I would place them under our Christmas tree that was set up in the corner of the living room. My mom loved Christmas. She loved decorating the house and the Christmas tree. She hated taking the tree down on New Year's Day because the pine needles would fall off. After all, the tree was on display in the living room over the month; the tree would dry out. We always had a real Christmas tree. I don't remember when artificial trees became an option, but I don't remember ever having an artificial tree until I was married. Our family tradition includes picking out a live tree each Thanksgiving weekend and decorating the tree. That allowed us to enjoy the tree for at least a month during the holidays.

As Christmas Day neared and I knew I would be going with my father for a long weekend, I kept praying that my anger and bitterness would disappear. I kept asking Jesus what I needed to do to stop being angry. I remember thinking that forgiveness was what I needed to do. I needed to forgive my father just like God forgave me. By this point in my walk of faith, I had learned how to do a word study using the Bible and a book called A Concordance. At the church library, Brenda showed me a concordance and then proceeded to show me how to use it to do word studies or find verses that further explained stories in the Old Testament. On the Wednesday night before school, I would go on break for the holiday and go to the Church library and ask to check out a concordance. The library let us check out books for a week. I explained that I would go with my father over the holiday and asked permission to check it out for two weeks. Thankfully, the church librarian was very understanding. She let me check the concordance out for two weeks because there were other copies of the concordance available should other people want to check one out.

One day on Christmas break, anticipating going with my father over Christmas weekend, I remember praying to Jesus, telling him that if God was indeed God and all-powerful, as I have been learning about, he could do the impossible. So, I asked Jesus to do the unthinkable and reunite my parents. My mom had been dating for several months. The guy she was dating was nice; his son was three years younger than me. I liked him, and he was like a brother to me. I often thought about how cool it might be to have a younger brother. However, I often wondered if my mom married this person, would I have to call this person "dad." I remember thinking, "Jesus, you could fix this problem and confusion by just getting my parents back together." I knew what I asked was impossible, but if I talked to Jesus like a friend, I would share from my heart. It was easier to pray than to keep a journal like I used to do. Besides, I did not have to worry about anyone reading my thoughts like I worried about them reading my journal. My request was no longer anchored in determining if God and Jesus existed. This request was now rooted in the belief God and Jesus did exist. As I was learning more and more about the character of God, I came to believe that while he allowed certain events to happen in people's lives, he could use those events to accomplish good things that he wanted to happen.

Christmas morning arrived. I had a stomachache as I anticipated my father picking me up and going with him for the remainder of the Christmas break. Mom kept on me all morning to ensure I was packed and ready to go when my father arrived. She was in the kitchen making coffee and sweet rolls when he came. I was still throwing things into my suitcase. Since I was not ready, she invited him in for coffee and rolls. She was a bit annoyed at me for not being prepared. Despite being divorced, my parents still got along, or at least in my presence. They argued a great deal before the divorce, but afterward, they seemed friendly to each other. Why couldn't they just get remarried, then? Until many years later, I didn't realize how rare it was that my parents seemed to get along after the divorce and even while they were dating other people. As more of my classmates and other friends I met after high school shared their experiences living with divorce and being shared between two parents, I realized that my situation was excellent.

I finished packing. Breakfast was not ready yet, so I sat in the living room and talked with my dad. He asked me what I wanted for Christmas. I responded, "Let me show you." I left the living room while he looked a bit puzzled. I am sure my father was thinking I would get a picture of the newest thing that captured my imagination. Often, the holiday season meant we would comb through the Sears or Montgomery Ward catalogs and circle things we wanted. Instead, I found my mom's jewelry box in her bedroom. I knew she kept her wedding ring from Dad in her jewelry box. I grabbed it and returned to the living room. I walked up to my dad and handed it to him. He looked at the ring and looked at me. He looked confused.

"Dad, what I would like for Christmas is for you and Mom to get married again."

I could see something in his look. He paused and asked, "You would like that?"

"Yes," I responded. "You both still love each other and belong together."

"I don't know if that is possible," he said. "Mom might not...."

Mom interrupted by calling us to the kitchen for breakfast. Dad put the ring in his pocket.

"We will talk later," he said.

We then went to the kitchen for breakfast. I ate slowly. That was unusual for me because I was a fast eater, typically because I wanted to get away from the table as fast as possible so I could go outside and play. But now, I didn't want this moment to end. It reminded me of the old times when my parents were married. We all eventually finished eating, no matter how hard I tried to drag out breakfast. Before long, I was saying goodbye to my mom and Private. Dad and I drove off. I choked back tears. I didn't want Dad to think I didn't want to be with him, but I wanted all of us to be together in one house for Christmas. I was still angry. I believe it was because of my dad's sin that I was hurting so much. The drive north to his house felt endless.

Chapter Ten:
I Believe in Miracles

He replied, "Because you have so little faith. Truly, I tell you, if you have faith as small as a mustard seed, you can say to this mountain, 'Move from here to there,' and it will move. Nothing will be impossible for you"

-Mathew 17:20 NIV.

My dad showed me around once we arrived in Mount Pleasant. Before returning to his mobile home, he drove me around the small town. Mount Pleasant was a college town I had never visited before. It was fun discovering a new place. He showed me Central Michigan University and took me to the Meijer store where he worked. He also took me to their Sagebrush store, a small fashion store specializing in Levi brand clothing, popular amongst my classmates. I loved the Sagebrush store. Dad turned me loose and told me to pick a pair of pants and a shirt for my Christmas present. I was excited to be able to pick out my clothes. He visited with the workers while I tried on numerous items. Finally, after what seemed like hours, I brought the things I had selected to my dad. I couldn't decide between two shirts, so I asked his opinion. He liked them and said he would get me both shirts and the pair of pants I selected. I knew I could use them for school in January, so I was thrilled. All my classmates wore Levi's clothing, which was another way to fit in and feel part of the group.

After my father finished what he needed to do at work, we left and returned to his house. It still seemed strange that my father had his own house, and I lived with my mom in what I considered the family house. He lived in a mobile home on the outside skirts of the college town. The mobile home seemed dark but well-kept. I couldn't imagine my father cleaning the house or living alone. Nothing about the mobile home seemed memorable. My father started dinner. I never remember my father cooking when he lived with my mom and me except for grilling burgers, hot dogs, or chicken on the grill whenever we entertained family during the summer. While he cooked dinner consisting of baloney and potatoes, he asked me whether I wanted to go north to Boyne City to visit Uncle Mike and Aunt Sally and their three girls. I loved my cousins, so I was entirely in favor of going. We agreed to go north and began to plan a time to leave in the morning. Perhaps this Christmas visit wouldn't be as bad as I thought. I was so worried that I would have to hang around Dad's house alone while he worked. The idea of visiting my cousins thrilled me. I thought that my prayers to Jesus changed my attitude. That night, I gave thanks for the answers to my prayers.

We left for Boyne early the following day. The weather in northern Michigan this time of the year was hard to predict. We had to call Mike and Sally to tell them we were coming and check if the weather was safe to travel. They said they were getting snow and the weather was expected to continue for the next few days. Given what we heard from Mike and Sally, we didn't know whether we would run into much snow on the way, but we figured the ride north might be challenging. Dad always carried a couple of bags of salt and a shovel in his trunk this time of year in case the road became terrible, or he got stuck in the snow somewhere. Surprisingly, the streets were clear, and we arrived at Mike and Sally's by noon.

After unloading the car, visiting, and catching up, my cousins and I decided it was time to play outside. They had much snow, so Terry, Ginny, Cindy, and I donned our winter coats, hats, mittens, and boots. As we dressed, we talked about what we wanted to do. There were so many great sliding hills across the road from their house. We boarded the snowmobile and headed across the street with the sleds. Between sled rides, snowball fights, building snow forts, and riding the snowmobile, we returned to the house, thoroughly exhausted. As my aunt heard the door open, she ushered us to the basement to change. Once we had pulled off our outdoor gear, we headed to the kitchen, where we helped with dinner. While we were outside playing, our Uncle LG arrived. There were seven of us at the dinner table. This seemed overwhelming as an only child and not used to having more than three people at the dinner table. As we ate, I listened to everyone telling stories about past winters when my aunt and uncles were kids our age. Dinner was so enjoyable. After eating, the cousins and I cleaned up the kitchen and headed to the bedroom to listen to music and talk. Mike, Sally, LG, and my dad played cribbage and talked most of the evening. We played various games and talked about our experiences in school, comparing stories about our classmates, teachers, and basketball games.

As the night wore on, we girls finally went to bed while the grownups continued to play cards. Lying in bed, she asked me about my mom and how things were going. We talked for a long time about life. I told her I hated that my parents had divorced and that I was angry with my dad because I blamed him for causing the divorce. I shared with her about my discovery of Jesus. To my surprise, she knew about Jesus. She shared with me what she believed. As we talked, the pauses between our responses to each other grew in length. Finally, we both fell asleep.

The next day, after breakfast, my cousins and I headed outside to play. We spent the day outside and played again until we were exhausted. I didn't know winter could be so fun. We didn't have as much snow in west Michigan as they got in northern Michigan. When we did get snow, I would play with the neighbors, but there were many more options for things to do where my cousins lived—the day passed quickly. Sunday came quickly, and it was time for Dad to take me home. Our trip back to my house was three hours long, depending on the weather. The roads were known for being snow-covered this time of year, as lake effect snow fell daily while the winds blew the newly fallen snow across the streets.

The drive from Boyne to Grand Rapids seemed endless. Dad helped me carry my things into the house when we arrived home. I took them to my bedroom. Mom and Dad sat at the kitchen table and talked. As I put things away, I heard them talking. I took my time, hoping Dad and Mom would keep talking. It seemed like old times; I didn't want that feeling to end. I also hoped Dad and Mom were talking about reuniting again, but I knew that was just my fantasy. While I hoped they would get back together, I didn't necessarily think that would happen. I didn't know anyone whose parents divorced had ever gotten back together again.

Finally, Dad came looking for me. "I have to go," he said. We walked to the door, and I hugged and kissed him and said goodbye. I thanked him for my Christmas presents and a great weekend. He said goodbye to Mom and explained that his day off this week was Thursday, and if she didn't mind, he would like to come down to see me earlier so we could spend the day together since I was still on Christmas break. Then he left.

Mom asked me about the weekend. I told her I needed to put some things away, and then I would come out and talk to her. I just wanted to cry but didn't want her to see me cry. I didn't want her to think I missed Dad more than I had missed her. I went to my room, cried, and then composed myself. I remember telling Jesus how much I wished my parents would reunite. I shared my heartache with him. The more I shared my hurt through prayer, the better I felt. I was slowly learning the value of prayer to Jesus.

When I returned to the living room where my mom was sitting, I brought my new clothes to show her. She seemed happy with what I had picked out and surprised by how many items I had gotten. We talked and talked about what I did when we visited my cousins. She asked me how Mike, Sally, and LG were doing. I was glad she didn't ask me anything about what Dad or others might have asked about her. My mom was always good at avoiding conversations about Dad. I just never knew why, but I was glad she did. She told me about spending Christmas Day with her parents and how special it was because it was just her and them—the rest of the day passed quickly. It was always lovely being home. While we didn't have much, the house was comfortable, light, and warm. It felt like home, something I didn't sense at my dad's mobile home in Mount Pleasant.

Thursday came, and Dad was at our house by noon since I was still on Christmas break. Mom had left for work that morning, so Dad and I headed to the shopping mall for lunch. I didn't get opportunities to go to the mall often because it was so far away. After wandering the mall for a while, we decided to see a movie. This was my first time going to a movie with my mom or dad, so this was a special treat. The day flew by. When we returned home,

I expected him to drop me by the door and kiss me goodbye like he usually did. Instead, he parked the car and followed me into the house. Mom had just arrived home from work and hadn't started dinner yet.

Consequently, Dad offered to buy dinner if I would walk down to the pizza shop, pick up the pizza, and bring it home. I happily volunteered because I did not want to cook, and I loved having Mom and Dad together, even if I knew it was only for a short time. Mom was constantly tired after work, and I cooked while on vacation or not playing basketball. I discovered I enjoyed cooking, but after a full day with Dad, I realized why my mom didn't like to cook after work. I bundled up and walked to the pizza shop. We lived just a quarter of a mile from a convenience store and gas station. Recently, a pizza shop opened in the area where a car repair shop had once closed. One would never know that the building had once been used to fix cars.

The walk was short. The weather was relatively mild. Snow was all along the side of the road where the snowplow had put it earlier in the day. Once I arrived at the pizza shop, I ordered a large ham and cheese pizza and played pinball while waiting. Once the pizza was done, I paid and walked back home. When I arrived home, my parents were still talking in the kitchen. Boy, did this feel like the good old days! We had dinner together, and then Dad prepared to leave. He said that his day off was Wednesday as usual next week and would be here after school to pick me up. I visited him every other weekend and Wednesday, as we had been doing since they separated and divorced three years ago.

Chapter Eleven:
For Everything, There Is a Season

"...give thanks in all circumstances; for this is God's will for you in Christ Jesus"

-I Thessalonians 5:18 NIV.

Christmas vacation was over, and I was going back to school. I generally enjoyed school and even more recently since I met new people and saw them on Wednesdays and Sundays at church. The days at school didn't seem to go as fast as they had during the fall when I was playing basketball. That was because I had nothing to look forward to after school except going home. Volleyball was the sport for girls in the winter. I did not play volleyball. I played volleyball in gym class and thought I might like to play. Because of all the demands on the gym during the winter, volleyball practices were held at different times, including after junior varsity and freshman boys basketball games. Since volleyball practices began so late and weren't immediately after school, my mom wasn't willing to drive me back to school and then home again, only to have to return to pick me up. She discouraged me from playing volleyball. So, I opted to be on the bowling team because we bowled twice weekly, and there was never practice. Mom bowled every Saturday night with her boyfriend, sister, Sally, and her husband, Tim, so I had become familiar with bowling and thought I might enjoy it. I found bowling interesting, and it was something my mom and I could discuss. My mom and I didn't have much in common, so I was excited we could share this experience even though we were not bowling together on the same team.

Because I was on the school bowling team, Tim and Sally suggested to my mom that I go with them to practice on Saturdays before the adult league began. Uncle Tim was an excellent bowler and always tried to help me get more consistent with my delivery. He also wanted to help me realize that bowling was not like pitching a softball, and I didn't need to throw it as hard as possible down the lane. Bowling kept me busy during the cold months of winter that often seemed to drag by because of the shorter days and longer nights. It helped me pass the time until softball season began in March. Softball was my favorite sport of all.

I bowled on Tuesdays and Thursdays and spent every other Wednesday with my dad, who took me bowling from time to time because he, too, enjoyed it. He picked me up every other Saturday around noon. A pattern was emerging. Each time he would pick me up or drop me off, he would linger around the house a bit longer. I didn't mind. I was finding that I was becoming more and more forgiving of my father as I learned more about the forgiveness of God. I prayed more and more that God would work a miracle and that my parents would remarry. I held out little to no hope. Oh, me of little faith.

The third weekend in January came, and Dad called Mom to explain that he had to work on Sunday, so he would come down for the day on Saturday and leave early Saturday night. I didn't mind because then I wouldn't have to miss church, and depending upon when Dad left, I could go to the bowling alley with Mom and her boyfriend, Curly. I felt increasingly comfortable at church and didn't want to miss it. I was learning about the Bible and was soaking up everything I could while listening to Pastor Gordon and Pastor Mike. I liked learning. Church felt a lot like school, but the subject was the Bible. I felt like I was learning about history because the Bible taught much about society and the world long ago. I liked history. The more I learned about Biblical history, the more I thought I was getting to know Jesus. American history was my favorite subject in school. When I learned about America's history in school, I felt like I was learning about people essential to our country. Church felt similar, except I didn't pray to historical people from America's history.

As the week progressed, I kept thinking about Saturday and trying to drum up ideas for things Dad and I could do that day. I would listen to my classmates talk about what they would do with their families on the weekends and file those ideas away in my mind to consider as opportunities for Dad and me when he came down to visit. Mom and I didn't do much on the weekends. First, we didn't have a lot of money to do things. Mom had only begun to work three years ago when she and Dad divorced. Because of the divorce, we had just enough weekly money to pay the bills and buy groceries. Besides helping her clean the house, we played board games occasionally. We also enjoyed similar TV shows. My mom was not a reader, but she periodically asked me to share information about the book I was reading. We would also cook together. My mom didn't think she was a good cook. However, I thought she was a good cook. When we decided what to make, I would go to the basement and get the needed ingredients. Most of the time, those ingredients we had canned together over Labor Day weekend while we watched the Jerry Lewis Telethon.

During the summer, I would help the farmers near our house pick their crops in exchange for bushels of tomatoes, corn, beans, or cucumbers. Mom and I would then freeze or can the vegetables. We would eat the things we froze or canned throughout the winter. I was always so proud to uncork the tomatoes when making chili. I knew I had helped can the tomatoes and felt pride because I was helping feed us during the winter.

When Saturday arrived, I had three ideas about what my dad and I could do. When Dad arrived, he knocked on the door. Mom invited him inside before the two of us took off. This was becoming routine. He would come earlier and earlier. My mom must have been expecting him because she had brunch ready for us. We sat down for breakfast and talked about the previous week. Dad asked about what I had planned for us, and I shared with him a few ideas. We settled on going to the zoo to see the winter exhibits. He said he would give that some thought but wanted to talk to my mom for a while and asked if I could give them some time alone. Everything was normal, or at least the new normal, since Dad started coming inside the house when he picked me up. However, he had never asked me to leave and give them some time to talk before. I wasn't sure what to make of this development. I left the kitchen and headed to my bedroom. I turned on the radio so they didn't worry. I was listening to their conversation. After some time had passed, Dad knocked on my bedroom door and invited me to join them in the kitchen.

Then Dad said, "I have something to tell you. I think you will like it." He then told me that Meijers would transfer him back to a store in Grand Rapids. He explained that he would manage a new Sagebrush store that Meijers would build at a local store where Mom and I shopped. I was cheering inside. I wish I could tell you that it was because Dad was coming back to Grand Rapids, but it was because he would manage a Sagebrush store. I could imagine the benefits. Then, Mom awakened me from my fantasy when she chimed in.

"We have something else to tell you." I looked at her and waited.

Then Dad said, "I have asked your mom to marry me."

I then looked from him to Mom and then back to Dad. I can't imagine what my face looked like. Indeed, I never expected to hear this. I think my silence worried them.

"Are you ok with that?'" Mom asked. I was still speechless.

After a long pause, I gained control of my thoughts and emotions.

"Sure!" I exclaimed. "But...what...how? Yea! You made my day! No, my life! I don't know what to say." I began to cry. Tears of joy and not sorrow this time. I was overwhelmed. I had so many emotions at once that I didn't even know what to say, think, or do.

The things I had planned for the day never materialized, and I was okay with that. Dad explained that he would be transferred to Grand Rapids early in February. Mom explained that the three of us would visit my grandmother today because they wanted to tell Grandmother and Grandfather the news. We all piled into my dad's car and drove a short distance across town to my grandparents' house.

When we arrived, they were just as surprised at our arrival as I was by the news earlier that morning. We all sat in their living room, and I witnessed their reaction to the information that my parents had decided to get remarried. My grandparents were more stunned than me. I learned that my parents had already settled on getting married by a judge. They asked my grandmother and grandfather to be the witnesses. As I sat in my grandparent's living room, I couldn't help but wonder if I was dreaming all this. I would have been in denial had I not just witnessed my parents telling my grandparents. This was real.

We returned home, and I said goodbye to my dad. My mom then started getting ready to go to the bowling alley. Curly was supposed to pick us up in thirty minutes. Wait, I thought. What about Curly? My mom had been dating him for over a year now. He was a nice guy, and he treated me very well. I liked his son, and we had some fun times together. I wondered if Curly knew. As I got ready for the bowling alley, I concluded he couldn't have known. I wondered when my mom would tell him. I wondered how he would feel when he learned my mom was marrying my dad. I wondered if Uncle Tim and Aunt Sally knew. I couldn't imagine that Aunt Sally didn't know because she and Mom talked every night on the telephone.

Curly picked us up on time. I tagged along and spent the night watching them at the bowling alley. They had been teaching me to keep score, so I became the unofficial scorekeeper. Curly, Tim, Sally, and my mom were a pretty good team. They were hot tonight. That just meant I had to work harder at keeping score. We all had a lot of fun. Afterward, we headed home. Typically, I would go to Tim and Sally's house and stay there while the four of them went out. This Saturday was different. Curly, Mom, and I went straight home. Mom told me I had to go to bed as I had an early morning on Sunday. I started to plead for a few more minutes but then realized she was dropping a hint. I headed to my room, pulled out a book, and tried not to listen. I turned on my radio so I couldn't hear. This was one conversation I was sure I didn't want to overhear. Mom might feel better talking to Curly if she thought I couldn't hear the conversation.

After a long time, I heard the door shut; a car started and drove off. I lay contemplating whether I should go out and see how my mom was doing. About that time, she opened my door and whispered, "You awake?" I didn't answer. I didn't know if I wanted to know what Curly and she talked about. She quietly shut the door. I was relieved. Then, I prayed before falling asleep, as had become my nightly routine.

"Jesus, thank you for today. Thank you for dying on the cross for my sins, coming into my life, and giving me eternal life. Thank you for being my friend, father, and strength. You have shown yourself to be real over and over now. You have delivered on every test I have challenged you with, including this one, which I couldn't imagine would ever happen. Forgive me for doubting you. You are a God of miracles. How can I ever doubt that you are real and in my life? Forgive my sins. Amen."

I lay there for hours, dreaming of what life might be like again. I felt like I was living in a Disney movie.

Chapter Twelve:
Until Death Do Us Part

"Husbands, love your wives, just as Christ loved the church and gave himself up for her"

-Ephesians 5:25 NIV.

February 9, 1978, my parents remarried. Standing in a courtroom before a judge, they were surrounded by my grandparents, mom's sister, Aunt Sally, Uncle Tim, and me. I heard the judge proclaim them man and wife; my family was complete again. We returned from the court to our house to celebrate. Dad hadn't moved back into the house yet, but that would happen this weekend. Having everyone there and talking about the ceremony and memories from before their divorce was so special. I couldn't have been happier.

Dad moved back into the house the following weekend, and life settled into a familiar and comfortable rhythm. I made sure to be as good as possible. I still wonder whether my sin and misbehavior as a kid contributed to my parents' divorce. I figured my newfound faith made this miracle possible and promised Jesus that I would behave and do everything my parents asked me so I wouldn't ever cause problems between them. I kept my room clean, set the table and did the dishes, and was home on time. I was very compliant. I am sure my parents must have wondered where the real me was and when she was coming back. However, I was committed to ensuring not to be the reason for my parents getting divorced the second time, assuming myself as the reason for their divorce in the first place. After the divorce, whenever my mom was mad at me, she would yell at me, saying that THIS was why my dad and she divorced. Whether I was the reason or not, I believed I was, I had no intention of screwing up the miracle God had just given me. I didn't want to disappoint my mom, and certainly not Jesus.

Shortly after my parents' remarriage, softball practice began. Our sessions started in the gym, given the chilly conditions in late February and early March. Games usually started in the third week of March, immediately after Spring break. Practices were held directly after school. We shared the big and the little gyms with the baseball team. The little gym in the middle school was set up with two batting cages made from nets. One of the teams would use the little gym for the first hour and work on hitting, pitching, and catching, while the other would use the large high school gym for infield and situational practice. Outfields were generally out of luck until practice could move outside. During the second hour, the softball and baseball teams would switch gyms. This situation wasn't ideal, but spring weather in Michigan was unpredictable.

Having practice every day until the games began helped me to be more disciplined and focused on getting my homework done. I worked harder at my studies to make my parents proud of my grades. Being compliant and well-behaved was one of many ways I would ensure I didn't contribute to another divorce. My aim was to show them I was not a mistake, and they could be proud of me. I was going to do this by being the best student and the best athlete

I could be, just being the best person I could be. I prayed daily to God to help me be my best. A Bible verse became my life mantra during this time. It said, *"Know ye not that they who run in a race run all, but one receiveth the prize? So run that ye may obtain"* (I Corinthians 9:24 KJV). I memorized the verse and then saved it in my heart. I also wrote it on my locker door and softball glove to be reminded all the time.

The remaining months of the school flew by. Softball season was too short, but I remember having to pitch during one game when the weather was so cold that I couldn't keep my pitching hand warm. It was hard to squeeze the softball. Yet that was probably my best-pitched game all season. Of course, it might have been my best-pitched game because the batters were too cold to swing. I remember getting a hit that game, and my hands stung so badly after the bat contacted the ball that I wasn't sure I'd regain feeling in my hand soon enough to go back out and pitch. As you might imagine, it was a low-scoring game. After the game, we ran to the bus, where the bus driver had kept the bus running while he waited for us.

As a softball team, we were competitive. We finished near the top of the league. I pitched most games, though we did have other pitchers on the team. When they pitched, I played first base. My strength as a player was my hitting. I was strong and could hit a home run if I contacted the ball well. Not every softball field we played at had an outfield fence like our home field. Consequently, a few of my home runs came because I hit the ball between the left and center fielder, and it rolled a long way before one of the opponents could catch up to it and relay it to the infield. I was quick enough to run around the bases and score. In general, we had a good-hitting team, and as a result, we were very competitive.

As the softball season ended and the final week of school arrived, I wondered what type of summer I would have now that my parents were back together. Would we go to the lake each weekend like before the divorce? My mom had already told me she would continue to work even though she and Dad were remarried. She explained that she liked working and appreciated being out of the house during the week.

The first weekend after school ended, we went to the lake on Saturday to open the cottage up for the summer. That required us to clean the inside area because the dust had accumulated over the winter months when no one was there to do the cleaning. We tested everything to ensure appliances, electricity, and plumbing were working. We only spent Saturday there and then returned home. On the drive home, we all discussed spending weekends at the lake. Mom asked me to pick up more responsibilities around the house during the summer to make it easier for us to be away on weekends. I was happy to have something to do during the weekdays, so I welcomed this news.

We were a family again. I prayed and thanked Jesus every night. I knew what had happened was unusual. None of my classmates who were members of a divorced family ever had their parents remarry each other. There were more kids in my class now whose parents had divorced than when my parents had divorced. Most of the time, they would tell me stories about how their parents would fight when one dropped them off at the other parent's house. Many of those kids recounted stories to me about the times they felt one of their parents would use them to hurt the other parent. I was an unusual teenager in so many ways. I didn't fit in with a specific group, hence, I could be part of every group. I didn't see my school friends much during the summer because I lived in a different part of the school district. I didn't go to church as much during the summer because we spent weekends at the lake, so I couldn't see my friends at church as well.

Therefore, the distance between my peers and me remained. However, I took comfort in the Bible verse, *"A man who hath friends must show himself friendly; and there is a friend who sticketh closer than a brother"* (Proverbs 18:23, KJV). I knew that no matter what, my best friend was Jesus. As the summer progressed, I grew closer to my family and Jesus. I might not have gone to church every Sunday, but I prayed a lot and did "devotions" every morning. I learned the importance of reading the Bible while attending the youth group. I kept learning because I wanted to catch up with my peers who had been attending church for a long time. I had no time to waste. The crowd I tried to fit in with was my Christian friends.

June quickly became July. We celebrated the Fourth of July at the lake. We watched as all the boats around the lake participated in a boat parade. Each boat was decorated for the day. I couldn't believe how many boats passed by. There were so many kinds of boats. I sat at the end of our dock with a couple of the neighboring kids and pointed out the boats that were our favorites. That night, each cottage put flares in the ground along the lakeshore. Someone then shot off fireworks over the lake. It looked beautiful.

Being at the cottage each summer weekend allowed me to enjoy even more of the great outdoors. I loved catching catfish because they would fight more than other fish. Catfish was more active at dusk, so I wanted to go fishing each evening because that was the best time to catch. I used to release them after getting them off the hook because I didn't want to clean them. I knew how to clean fish and enjoyed eating them, but that was so much work. I was very selective about the fish I would keep, clean, and eat. Most of the time, I was satisfied with catching them and letting them go.

Uncle Ed and Aunt Sylvania often visited the lake early on Saturday morning. When they would drive up early to visit, we would all go fishing for an hour before Uncle Ed would help Dad with a project. He and Aunt Sylvia taught me how to troll for northern pike. I learned that I had to be patient and keep my bait moving to attract them to attack my bait. Northern pike was the most challenging fish to catch. I vividly remember the day I caught my first largemouth bass. That fish sure did fight. Before securing the fish at the surface, I kept imagining how big it was. While my imagination was way off the mark, the fish was still the biggest I had ever caught. The most common fish I would catch were perch and sunfish. I was learning about all the different fish species in Michigan's inland lakes.

July became August, and I began training for the upcoming basketball season. I was now a junior and expected to contribute more to this team because I had gained experience during the previous season. We returned four seniors to the starting lineup in addition to me, so we were expected to do better than the year before. I readied myself for this reason by running every day. My favorite time and place to run was at the lake. I had set the goal of running around the lake by the first of August. I had been running different routes all summer and had yet to learn how far it was around the lake. My parents and I would drive around the lake from time to time to visit my dad's brother, who lived directly across from us on the other side of the lake.

August's first weekend arrived. I got up and dressed for a run. I told my mom and gave her an idea of the direction I was running. However, I didn't tell her I wouldn't be turning around and retracing my route as usual. I put on my headphones and took my cassette player. I played my favorite Don Francisco tape. Don Francisco was a Christian artist who sang ballads. He was one of my favorite Christian artists, along with the Imperials. I had come to enjoy listening to Christian music.

I was never into music before, but after discovering Christian music, I enjoyed it, especially while running. That morning, I walked out the front door and started jogging to run the entire distance around the lake. I ran and ran and ran. When I got close to the other side of the lake across from our cottage near the home of my dad's brother, I knew I was halfway to my goal. I flipped over the cassette tape and started the player to listen to the other side. I was surprised at how good I felt. I HAD A SLIGHT DOWNHILL STRETCH once I passed my uncle's house. The slight descent helped me feel stronger as I had to exert less effort.

Soon, I was turning left near the public boat launch. Once I took that turn, I knew I could make the mile back to the cottage. This landmark was my first goal at the beginning of the summer. I knew running from our cabin to the boat launch and back was at least two miles. Now, with each step, I seemed to get stronger. Perhaps it was because I was realizing a critical goal. Soon, I coasted into the driveway. Exhausted but happy I had accomplished my goal. Now, I was ready for basketball practice to begin.

School started after Labor Day, and September turned into October. I felt like my life was more like everyone else's. I truly believed that having Jesus and the church as a foundation in my life made a difference. Basketball season was less successful than we had hoped. We finished third in the league and were defeated in the first round of the district tournament. Toward the end of the season, we were playing a game on the road. We were winning, and the flow of the game was quick. Both of our teams were playing a fast-break offense. On one play, I caught an opponent from behind and knocked the ball out of their hands. I dove to keep the ball in play and slid into the bleachers. I kept the ball from going out of bounds, and a teammate was able to secure the ball. I was hustling to make a play. Our coach called a time-out to draw up a play as the game was nearing the final minute. As I went to the huddle, I patted a couple of teammates on their rear end and cheered their effort to secure the ball I had kept from going out of bounds.

The outcomes of the league hadn't been decided yet, and I knew that if we won and got some help from a couple of other teams, we might end up in a three-way tie for first place. The coach drew up a play to isolate one of our best scores. We broke the huddle after the time out and inbounded the ball. We worked our office, trying to take time off the clock, hoping to get our scorer an open shot. As our opponents tried to double-team our point guard to force a turnover, they left our scorer open. The guard saw the opportunity, passed the ball, and our forward scored. We were now ahead by three points. This was important before the three-point shot was introduced to high school basketball. The opponents quickly inbounded the ball after our basket and rushed to the other end of the court but missed their shot. I secured the rebound, passed it out to our guard, and we ran out the clock.

The game ended with another win. I felt good about my effort, our team's effort, and the final score. Now, we had to hope that we would get help from other teams in the league to defeat the two teams with one less loss than we had. We headed for the locker room, grabbed our gear, and headed for the bus. I was generally one of the first players back on the bus. I still couldn't bring myself to shower after the game. I got on the bus, picked my seat as usual, and sat in the middle. I usually sat alone just like last season before Brenda had begun to sit with me, coming and going to games. I was one of two juniors on the team, and even with another classmate playing on the same team, I didn't feel like I had any close friends. I did miss Brenda, who had graduated the previous year. Most of my friends were not athletes, so I didn't have them to hang around with on road trips. I always appreciated them coming to the home games to cheer us on.

Suddenly, Jill stopped by my seat and asked to sit with me. I was a bit surprised but said sure. We talked briefly about the game. "Nice job on the boards again tonight," Jill said,

"Yeah, thanks; nice game yourself," I replied.

"There is one thing I want to tell you. You need to stop slapping us on the butt, okay. Are you gay or something?" Jill asked.

I paused a minute, a bit stunned. I was not even sure I realized I was patting anyone on the butt. I replied, "Sure. Yes, sure. Sorry. I guess I didn't realize I was even doing that."

"Well, just don't do it anymore, okay," Jill said as she got up out of the seat and went to sit with someone else.

I was glad it was dark, and the lights on the bus were off because I was burning red with embarrassment. I hadn't realized I was patting people on the butt. Perhaps I was imitating the boys' basketball players I often watched on TV. I don't know. However, right then and there, I vowed to never do that again. I also distanced myself from my teammates for the rest of the year. I didn't want them to think anything wrong or untrue about me, and I had to figure out what she meant by being gay because I didn't remember hearing that term before. And I didn't sense it was anything positive by how she said it.

Chapter Thirteen: My New Best Friend

"Though one may be overpowered, two can defend themselves. A cord of three strands is not quickly broken"
-Ecclesiastes 4:12 NIV.

After the basketball season ended in late October, the time until Christmas vacation passed quickly; I was worried about being bored during Christmas break. My dad was back home and my mom was still working, so I knew I would be home alone daily. However, I was assured of at least meeting my friends during the break because I now attended church consistently on Wednesday night and Sunday since I was allowed to drive to church. I was thankful to have my license. I used to vacuum my mom's car and wash the inside windows on weekends to show my appreciation for being permitted to use it occasionally. During the summers, I used to wash the outside of her car, but not in the winter months. I had finished an art class in which I learned how to use acrylic paint, so I asked for some books and supplies as Christmas presents to start painting. One important skill I learned as an only child was how to entertain myself alone. Little did I realize how important that skill would be to me throughout my life.

As the final week of the fall semester was about to end, my mom came home one night after work and asked me if I was interested in making some money while on Christmas break by working with her at the collection agency to help them catch up on some work. She explained they were behind in filing at work and would pay me hourly if I came in and helped them get caught up. The plan was that I could go to work with my mom in the morning and work until noon, and then she would bring me home on her lunch break, or she could pick me up at lunch and work all afternoon and then come home with her after work. I asked her a few questions about what to expect, what to wear, and whether she thought I would be good at the job. She was reassuring and asked me to think about it and let her know in the morning. I told her I didn't need to think about it anymore and agreed to work during the morning hours. I was happy to have something new to try during the break. I had been to my dad's work a few times but never to my mom's, so I thought this would be an excellent opportunity to see her work life. I was also happy to have some time to myself because I hoped to have time to read or go cross-country skiing and ice skating.

The first day I went to work at the collection agency, I met all my mom's coworkers. Everyone was so lovely and seemed very happy that I had decided to come and help. They all were dressed more casually than I expected. I wasn't sure what to wear so I wore my best school clothes. The office manager showed me how the file system worked and then watched me as I began the task. Once she was sure I understood what needed to be done, she returned to her desk; the four hours passed quickly. I had never worked at an actual job before. I had only shoveled snow or picked crops. While those tasks were considered work, and I did get paid for them, typically with the produce I gathered, this opportunity seemed like a real job. I enjoyed my first day. At noon, Mom took me home. We grabbed lunch on the way home so she could eat and return to work by one o'clock. She dropped me off at home, and I passed the afternoon cross-country skiing on the trails around our house.

I returned to the collection agency on the second day. I met a new worker, Julie, who was hired part-time to help with typing and answering phones. The workers wanted me to get the filing caught up in a week's time so Julie could keep it current when she worked three or four hours daily. Julie was a student at the community college. She had graduated from high school the previous year and was from the northern part of the state. She came to the city to live with her father and stepmother and pursued a program at the community college. Julie seemed quiet. I figured she was nervous like I was on my first day on the job. She also seemed nice.

I stayed a few extra hours that day as my mother gave Julie an orientation. She introduced Julie to all the workers at the agency and explained what each of them did. When she got to me, she introduced me to Julie and explained that I was her daughter and that I was trying to help the office get the filing done so she wouldn't be overwhelmed. She seemed nice, but my shy personality kept me from interacting with her.

I finally said, "Hello, Julie, it is nice to meet you."

Before I knew it, I was clocking out and heading home for the afternoon. Mom dropped me off at home and explained that she would be late getting home because she had a couple of things to finish at work that she couldn't get done during the day because she was providing an orientation to Julie. I was happy to be able to work a few extra hours because I was putting the money into savings. Since I was learning about photography at school, I have been trying to save for an SLR camera. Once home, I retreated to my bedroom and a good book. I had given no thought about meeting Julie. I also didn't mind that Mom would get home later than usual because it gave me an excuse to skip making dinner.

The week went fast because working at the collection agency kept me busy. I divided my day between work and cross-country skiing and sledding. I enjoyed the winter season. I loved being outside no matter what season, but more so in the winter because each day seemed fresh and beautiful. It seemed like it snowed overnight, almost every day. The fresh inch or two of snow would cover up all signs of life from the previous day, providing a new opportunity to leave an imprint. Living in the county had its advantages. While my high school friends lived in the suburbs and could see each other frequently, they had to wait for someone to take them to a park to enjoy winter sports like cross-country skiing, sledding, or snowmobiling; I could just walk out the back door and engage in most winter outdoor activities I loved. The only activity for which I had to leave the house to enjoy was ice skating. The pond in the park in the center of the little village always froze over and provided opportunities to ice skate.

One of the more complicated outdoor activities I enjoyed required working with the neighborhood boys to build our equivalency of a bobsled run. We would pile snow into parallel rows wide enough for a sled to fit between them. Those rows would extend down the hill in my backyard. At the end of the hill, we would build a ramp with plywood and logs. We would then pack snow on the ramp to ensure the sled would keep going once it reached the ramp at full speed and then be launched into the air at the end of the ramp. The goal was to see who could jump the farthest. We would spend all day building a masterpiece. The boys would use their three-wheelers and snowmobiles to haul water to the bobsled run. We would pour water along the route and create an icy top layer to ensure a quick ride to and up the ramp. Three or four hours would pass before we realized, and I would hear my mother calling me in the distance to return to the house. The neighborhood boys and I would plan to come back after supper to engage in sled races. I would run off, leaving them to finish up what was left to complete before they went home for dinner, too. This project occurred every winter; looking back, it taught us much. Because we spent so much time building the sled run and ramp, we learned to set rules because we respected each other for all our work to develop our sled run and ramp. One rule we all agreed upon was that whenever we used the ramp, we had to fix anything we broke before we went home. That way, we knew we could use the ramp for sledding any time. I had no idea these moments would teach me essential skills and lessons to help me in my future career.

I entered the house and went from the door directly to the basement to take off my wet and snowy snowsuit. The three steps between the door and the basement door were a blessing to my parents. After a day of acting like an engineer building the incredible sled run in the neighborhood, I was caked with packed snow in zippers with dripping wet knees from kneeling on the wet snow. After changing and re-emerging at the top of the stairs, my mom informed me she was cooking, so I quickly headed for a shower to be ready for dinner.

During dinner, Mom and I talked about our day. It was Friday, and I loved Fridays. My father worked until midnight, so I had my mom to myself. We had become closer during the divorce and remained so even after my parents remarried. I had come to cherish my time with my mom. She would come home from work on Friday, and we would decide whether I would cook dinner or we were to work together. After dinner, we would watch various television shows. Between them, we would talk about our day or the storyline of the previous show. We were big Dallas fans and enjoyed watching Archie Bunker and the girls on the Facts of Life. I didn't appreciate or understand the importance of my relationship with her before the divorce, but I was beginning to appreciate her more and more.

She didn't understand me very well before the divorce, either. I was a bit of a tomboy; she had been a girly girl as a teenager and early adult. I didn't mind the occasional dress but was much happier in jeans and a T-shirt. My mom had been a model for Westinghouse, and I am sure she was hoping for the girly girl who would take after her. Instead, she had me. I took after my dad. Before the divorce, I was "Daddy's girl." After the divorce, the playing field was leveled, and I was just as close to both, with the edge going to my mom. But I knew I was not the girly girl she wanted me to be. I enjoyed having my dad back because he let me do more than my mom would even consider letting me do. He wasn't as nervous and anxious as she was, so having him intervene when I wanted to do something that worried Mom was helpful. However, I could tell he didn't know me as well as Mom. He missed some critical times in my life, and I was a different person now than before the divorce.

The dinner conversation tonight was interesting. Mom explained that Julie had asked if I could join their family on Saturday as they were going to the theater to watch a movie. She told me I needed to call Julie tonight if I wanted to go. She mentioned that Julie's brothers and sisters were coming down from a city up north to visit their dad and would also go to the movie. Mom told me what movie they planned to see, but I wasn't familiar with it and didn't remember my friends talking about it. The only other two films I had ever watched at a theater were one when Mom was dating Curly and the other when my dad had taken me to a movie; so, we didn't often go to the theater. I didn't realize other families went to the movies so often.

I was very surprised by this news. My mom would never let me do things with friends, people, and families we didn't know. I had only met Julie once, so I didn't even know if I would enjoy watching a movie with her and her family. Maybe Mom knew Julie and her family better than I thought. Mom told me that Julie's sister was my age and played sports in high school, just like me. She said Julie and her thoughts were similar to mine, and I might want to meet her. Mom handed me Julie's phone number. I took a minute to contemplate what I would say. I didn't understand why this was so hard for me, but meeting new people was always hard.

I was excitedly nervous. I took a deep breath and decided to call Julie after I cleared the table. This would give me more time to rehearse the conversation in my head before I called. Once the table was cleared, I picked up the telephone and dialed the number. The phone only rang once. Julie answered.

"Hello, may I speak to Julie," I said.

"Hello, Renay, this is Julie. Are you going with us tomorrow?" she asked.

"Yes, I would like to go tomorrow. What time?"

We arranged for the time they would pick me up because the theater was closer to my house. I explained how to get to our house. I was surprised when I realized that Julie and I had talked for over an hour. She was telling me about her sister Theresa and her brothers and sisters. We talked about so many things. I finally had to tell Julie I had to go because my mother kept walking into the kitchen, and I figured she wanted to use the phone.

I hung up, and Mom said, "You two talked for a long time."

"Yeah, I guess so."

"So, what did you talk about," she asked.

"You know…things," I said illusively.

"Are you excited for tomorrow?"

"Kind of," I responded with a smile.

"Just kind of. Is that all I get?" my mom asked.

"Yeah. I don't know what to say. I am a bit nervous but excited too".

I then explained that I wanted to watch a television show and headed to the living room. Mom called her sister and had their usual long chat. That gave me time to watch TV, contemplate Saturday, and how I might navigate going to the movies with people I had never met and one person I had only met once. My shy side had me terrified.

Chapter Fourteen:
How Do I Build a Friendship?

"A man that hath friends must show himself friendly, and there is a friend that sticketh closer than a brother"

-Proverbs 18:24 KJV.

As a kid, I never really thought about how to be someone's friend. I had grown up in the country, and the five other kids in the neighborhood and I were just friends. I don't think we ever declared ourselves as friends. We only had each other to play with, which made us friends by default. We would argue and take sides. We never made up but would move on and start playing together again. It happened because you could never play football, baseball, or basketball by yourself, so we always needed each other. That meant life was simple, and we realized we needed each other because we were all we had. We also had a lot in common and enjoyed doing things together. As my world grew, I lost that simple lesson about friendship and began to overthink navigating relationships.

Saturday morning dawned bright and cold. I was awake early as usual. Mom and Dad were sleeping in as usual. I pulled my sleeping bag out to the living room and crawled in. My dog, Private, crept in too. She loved getting inside and staying warm. I spent the morning watching cartoons. This was my usual Saturday morning routine. Mom and Dad arose and went through their morning routine of reading the paper over coffee and breakfast rolls. Mom kept me on time, ensuring my chores were done, my shower taken, and appropriate clothes put on, so I was ready when Julie came by to pick me up. Julie drove a yellow Volkswagen, so I watched for her vehicle in case she missed the house. I sat in the living room reading, or at least pretending to read, while I watched out the window for her to arrive. I was nervous. My stomach was doing somersaults. I just wanted Julie to get here so I could get on with this because I knew once we started, I would stop thinking about how I was feeling and enjoy the time. I wasn't aware of my shyness, but this event helped me realize that I needed to become comfortable with new social situations.

Julie pulled up in her yellow VW bug. I thought the car was incredible. She came into the house and said hello to my parents. She met my father for the first time. He was about to leave for work, so I was glad he finally met her. After a few minutes of small talk, we left. Julie lived with her stepmom and father in a housing development about ten miles south of our house. That was relatively close compared to most of my high school friends. She explained we would return to her house before going to the theater. She told me who I would meet as we drove and what to expect once we arrived. I had not been to her home before, so my nerves were high.

We pulled into the driveway and went into the house. Things were so hectic compared to my house. I met her father, Jim, and stepmom, Jane. I met her younger sisters and brother. Then I met Therese, her sister, who was my age. I realized why Julie and my mom thought we would hit it off. We had much in common, including our love of basketball and softball. Theresa seemed nice, and we hung out in the living room and talked while everyone else got ready to go to the movie. Therese was easy to talk to. I didn't feel as shy around Theresa as I did around Julie the first time. Before I knew it, we were leaving to go to the movie. Julie asked me to ride with her and Therese—the other kids rode with Jim and Jane in Jim's car.

After the movie, we returned to Julie's house. Once there, Jim and Jane started making dinner. While they cooked, we all went to the living room and played a board game. The movie, dinner, and game time flew by. Before I knew it, Julie had to take me home. I had a great time. I liked Therese and wondered when or if I would see her again. She was heading home to northern Michigan the next day, and I was sad we hadn't met earlier in the week so we could have spent more time together. We had exchanged addresses and promised to write. Calling was long distance, and we knew we could not do that often. I was excited to have met a new friend I felt was a lot like me. We had a lot in common. I also discovered that I enjoyed spending time with Julie and that she was fun to be around. I didn't think I would like Julie initially because I thought she was more like the cheerleading type of girl. However, I discovered she was not the cheerleading type I had originally thought of. I found that I hoped to see Julie again soon.

Julie dropped me off and headed back home. I entered the house and shared my day with my parents. They were happy that I had a good time at the movie. My mom seemed delighted that I had enjoyed meeting Therese. It was almost like she felt a sense of accomplishment. Before I knew it, I was getting ready for bed. As usual, I picked up a book and tried to read. I found I couldn't read. I kept thinking about the day. I liked Theresa but felt a sense of competitiveness. That was cool. What surprised me was that I kept thinking about Julie. I had come to appreciate her. I found I couldn't wait to see her again. I wondered how to find ways to hang out. I asked if she was just being nice to me because she was hoping Theresa and I would hit it off since Theresa came down every so often to visit, and I could be a friend for her when she came to town. All these thoughts swirled in my head as I drifted off to sleep.

Christmas vacation was over, and I was back to school. The winter months were spent hoping for snow days and longing for summer. I was not involved in sports during the winter, so I'd just come directly home after school. Once home, I had a similar routine, which began with completing my homework. After finishing my homework, I would go cross-country skiing; I returned from skiing in time to start dinner. After dinner, I would clean up the kitchen, do the dishes, and go to my bedroom to draw, read, or study the Bible. This routine would occasionally be interrupted when I decided to attend the boys' home basketball games on Tuesday or Friday nights. Our boys' team was not so good, and I wasn't a close friend of any of the players on the team. However, I knew most of the players, and I wanted to go and cheer them on because they had come to our home games to cheer us on.

On Thursday night, I was finishing dishes and thinking about meeting my neighborhood friends outside on the hill where we had built this excellent sliding path and ramp when the telephone rang. I figured it was Aunt Sally, who usually called to talk to my mom about this time of night. I was lost in thoughts about how to build the jump higher at the end of the sliding hill. That was our goal this winter, and so far, all the different ways we had tried to build the ramp higher had failed. The next thing I knew, Mom was handing me the phone. It was Julie. I was surprised Julie was calling me. I hadn't summoned my courage to call her; now she was calling me. A thrill and excitement flashed through me.

"Hello, Julie."

"Hey, Renay! How are you? I have been waiting to hear from you since vacation. What are you up to?"

"Not much. School is school. I started pitching practice last week with the coach. Been just hanging around here. How is school going for you?"

"Good. I talked to Theresa earlier, and she asked how you were doing. Her volleyball team is in first place." As Julie talked, I couldn't help but think she called only because she wanted to speak to me about Theresa. I wasn't sure what I thought about that because I wanted to see Julie. Then, I suddenly realized she had changed the subject. "How would you like to go roller skating Friday night?"

"Oh, sure...well, let me check with my mom quickly just to make sure we didn't have something happening." I didn't want Julie to think I had to ask my mom for permission, but I knew I had to. My mom was happy and surprised by my question. She asked whether I learned how to roller-skate. I blew it off and said it couldn't be much different than ice skating, and I did know how to ice skate. I was an athlete, wasn't I?

"Hey, Julie. I am good to go. What time?" We talked a bit longer and finalized our plans for Friday. I was excited. It was Thursday, so it would be Friday before I knew it. I went back to finishing the dishes. Mom called her sister, and the night settled into the routine. After I finished the dishes, I headed out to go sliding with the neighborhood kids. Soon, I was lying in bed, tired from being outside. As I drifted off to sleep, I only thought about seeing Julie. A few times, I wondered whether I could roller skate. The last time I went roller skating was in junior high. I figured it had to be easier than ice skating because roller skates had four wheels.

Chapter Fifteen: Falling

"There hath no temptation taken you but such as is common to man: but God is faithful, who will not suffer you to be tempted above that ye are able; but will with the temptation also make a way to escape, that ye may be able to bear it"

-I Corinthians 10:13 KJV.

Friday night arrived, and Julie picked me up from my house. It was six thirty, and the roller rink opened at seven. It was open until eleven. My parents were allowing me to stay out until midnight. That was a first. Generally, I had to be home by eleven. They liked Julie and trusted her. Whatever persuaded them to give me another hour, I was happy for the extra time.

We arrived at the rink, paid our entry fee, and exchanged our shoes for skates. We grabbed a table and a couple of cokes and changed our shoes. The lights were low, with various strobe lights flashing around the rink. The music was loud. Once we both had our skates on, we moved toward the rink, where we merged in with the people. I hadn't skated in a while and was surprised it came to me naturally. I wasn't smooth on my feet, but I was not embarrassing myself yet. Julie was an excellent skater. I admired her ability to move quickly. I hoped I would be smoother and quicker by the night's end. The music changed, and the announcer called, "Couples skate."

I made my way to our table to get a swig of coke. Julie followed. She recognized a few people, said hello, and chatted briefly with them as she made her way to the table we had claimed for ourselves. Soon, she stood beside me so we could talk despite the loud music. We talked easily and waited until the couples-only song was over. Soon, the music changed, signaling it was time for everyone to skate, and we returned to the rink.

As the night progressed, I grew more comfortable skating with Julie. She was fun to be with. This time, when the music changed, the announcer called, "Backward skate." I made my way to the table. Julie quickly skated up next to me and asked me to try it. I explained that I wasn't very good at skating backward. She persuaded me to try it because that was the only way to improve. We made our way back to the rink.

She naturally began to skate backward. I stopped and tried to skate backward. It was clear to Julie that I was not getting the hang of it. She skated beside me and tried to talk me through how to push off my skates sideways. I began to move slowly. At least I was moving in the right direction. Suddenly, I fell. Julie held her hand down to me smilingly. I gingerly got up and grinned. The song seemed to go on forever. The music switched, and the announcer called, "All skate." I was relieved that my practice session was over. However, part of me was hoping for another opportunity to try it. I figured Julie was correct. If I practiced skating backward, I would eventually get the hang of it.

After several more songs, the announcer called for a couple's skate. I was headed off the rink when a hand grabbed my arm. It was Julie.

"Let's skate." She smiled.

I was still trying to figure out what to do next, but Julie seemed to get it. She spun backward and grabbed both my hands. She told me to skate forward, and she would face me while she skated backward. It took me a bit to figure out how to turn smoothly while pushing Julie, but we seemed to do just fine. As the song ended and Julie stopped, I hadn't expected it. The next thing I knew, I was sitting on the rink. Julie grabbed my waist and helped me to my feet as I attempted to get up.

"If you keep falling like this, you will be sore and bruised tomorrow," Julie proclaimed.

"The only thing that will be bruised tomorrow is my ego," I replied. We both laughed and began to skate again. After another couple's skate where Julie led and I tried to skate backward, I mastered the backward skate. I also found I enjoyed the couples skating more and more. I wasn't sure if it was because I was getting more comfortable skating, less self-conscious, or just like being with Julie, but whatever the reason was, I was enjoying it.

We took the next song off. Julie looked at her watch and asked, "Do you want to grab a snack before heading home?"

"Sure," I replied. We began to take off our skates and put on our shoes. I found myself growing sad at the realization that my curfew was growing closer. We headed to the car. Julie asked about where to go, and we settled on McDonald's. We drove through the drive-through, sat in the car, and ate our food. I was glad for the time to talk. It seemed like we always had things to talk about. After a brief bite to eat, Julie took me home.

It was quarter to twelve when we pulled into the driveway. Julie turned off the car. That surprised me. "I don't want to wake your parents up," she said. We faced each other and talked for a couple of minutes.

"I should get in," I said.

"Yeah, sure. What was your week like?"

"Not too bad. Why?"

"Let's go skating or to a movie next Friday, OK?" Julie suggested.

"Absolutely!" I responded. "I will call you this week, and we can decide then. How about Wednesday?"

"Sure, Wednesday would be good. Dad and Jane are at church, so give me a call." Julie responded. I pulled the door handle, and the door clicked and opened.

"Hey," Julie said. I stopped and turned back and faced her. A moment of silence passed between us. My stomach flipped. She reached to hug me. I removed my hand from the door and welcomed the embrace. As she slid her arms along the top of my shoulders, I felt a warm wave of excitement wash over me. While embracing, I hoped the moment would never end. Suddenly, I became very uncomfortable. My discomfort made no sense, and I moved to pull away. Julie held on and resisted my back peddling. She whispered. "Tonight was fun. Thanks for going!"

I reluctantly pulled back and looked her in the eyes. "It sure was! Thanks for asking me to go".

"Talk to you Wednesday."

"OK, Good night, Julie."

I left the car, shut the door, and walked to the house. When the house door closed, I heard Julie's bug starting up. I stood by the door and listened until I could no longer hear the car. When my mom wasn't in the living room waiting for me to arrive home,

I quietly walked to my parent's bedroom to say good night. My mom responded, acknowledging my arrival. I knew my mom would still be awake. She only slept once I got home. She was quite a worrier. I didn't know why, but I knew she was worried. I figured she was less anxious tonight because she was already in bed when I got home. Usually, she sat in the living room, in the dark, waiting for me.

I headed to bed, underdressed and pulled on my pajamas, and thought about the night. I was so proud of myself for learning how to skate backward. I didn't want to embarrass myself. I examined a few bruises on my legs that were appearing. I fared well, given a few falls. As I turned off my light and crawled into bed, I remembered thinking that Julie never fell or stumbled. I also remembered she hadn't laughed at me when I did. Thinking about Julie and the evening brought a warm feeling. Lying in bed, I remembered how it felt when Julie held my two hands on the first couple's skate. I closed my eyes and relaxed, slipping into sleep, but I kept seeing us skating together. My last thought was how great it felt when Julie hugged me and held me briefly when I started to pull back.

Before I knew it, it was Wednesday, and I counted the minutes until I called Julie. I cleared the table after dinner and called Julie while washing the dishes. I dialed her phone number and prayed that Julie would answer rather than her dad or stepmom. I wondered if she wanted to talk to me as much as I wanted to talk to her. Jim answered. After some small talk, he called Julie. We talked for an hour as I finished washing the dishes and noticed Mom walking into the kitchen occasionally. That was generally a signal to end the call.

Julie and I had agreed to go to the movie Friday night. We also decided on what movie we planned to see. I hung up and retreated to my room because I knew my mom would be calling her sister now. I picked up an excellent book to read. I read almost every night before turning off the lights and lying in bed until I fell asleep. Reading often helped me clear my mind. I never had difficulties falling asleep and figured it was because I read before turning off the lights. Tonight, I found myself reading the same sentence repeatedly before realizing I couldn't concentrate. I was replaying my telephone conversation with Julie. I thought about the movie we were going to see. Eventually, I picked up the book again and began to read. Finally, I fell asleep, knowing that Friday would come soon.

Since Julie had a car, she often volunteered to drive. I appreciated that because I was never sure how my mom felt about me using her car. Julie came to pick me up early this Friday. She arrived at our house about an hour after I had arrived home after school. Julie and I were still home when my mom and dad came after work. We all sat at the kitchen table and talked for a while. Before long, we decided we needed to get to the theater. We would catch a matinee and perhaps the last half of the varsity boys' game at school.

After a short drive to the theater, we parked and entered the theater. We purchased our tickets and carefully selected our seats. The theater was surprisingly empty, which could be because of the varsity boys home basketball game at the high school. The previews began before the movie. Before entering the theater, we secured a large serving of popcorn and a soda for each of us. After a couple of brief previews, the movie began. A couple of times during the film, we each reached for the popcorn simultaneously, only to clasp hands. Those innocent moments were very awkward for me. Julie never seemed too rattled by it. Maybe I was overthinking the situation, but I almost thought it was intentional on Julie's part. I figured it was my wishful thinking or desire to be close to someone.

After the movie, we decided to go to Fables, our favorite restaurant, for dinner. We had thought about attending the home basketball game, but then the conversation turned fun, and we decided to hang out at Fables for a while instead. We were the only ones in the dining room for the longest time. Gradually, more and more people began entering the restaurant, and the dining area was filling up. We figured we were starting to annoy the workers by occupying the booth some people needed, so we decided to go for a ride and continue our conversation. It was a nice spring-like day in late February. At least there was a hint of spring in the air. We drove for a while and found a place to park alongside a creek.

"What a beautiful spring-like night," I observed.

"Yeah, I love this time of year!" Julie exclaimed.

Julie and I sat silently as the hum of the VW bug garnered my attention. Shadows fell across the road as the moon showed brightly, silhouetting the leafless trees. We both seemed to be looking outside, trying to see what was making the sounds we were hearing. In time, we began to run out of things to talk about. We also noticed that time had passed more quickly than we realized. We both looked at the clock on the dashboard at about the same time.

"I don't want to go home," I protested.

"Me either, but I need to study tonight," Julie said. She reached for the glove box, lightly brushing my leg.

"Hey, don't be getting grabby there," I said with a wishful, teasing tone.

I thought the touch was beautiful but too brief. I couldn't believe I was so aware of that little innocent touch. With that realization, panic welled within me as I became aware of the longing I now had simply because Julie brushed my leg, reaching for something. The hope quickly turned to shame that now lingered deep within me. Time seemed to pause. I was becoming aware that I wanted to hug Julie. I decided to break my silence.

"Do you have to get home to study?" I asked.

"Well...I should study...but...it's not like I have a test 'til next week," Julie replied.

Looking for a way to extend our time together, I searched for an idea.

"We aren't far from the park, how about a walk?" I said with a pleading tone.

"Okay, but I know a better place to walk along the riverbed."

I was puzzled when Julie hit the turn signal, indicating a right turn.

"Really, where is this place?' I asked.

"Just a mile down this road. When Dad was here at Christmas, he took us cross-country skiing, and we ended up on a trail near the river along this road. I think there is a place we can park and pick up the trail from there."

A comfortable silence existed between us, and Julie drove down the road. The VW bug rolled to a stop. I looked around. I then glanced at Julie.

"Are you sure we can park here?" I asked. The area was just off the road behind a row of trees. It appeared by the tracks in the gravel that other vehicles had parked there before.

"I'm sure. I always see cars pulled off here", reassured Julie.

The VW bug was canary yellow—a classic VW bug with one exception: a sunroof. Julie had installed the sunroof shortly after she got the car. She loved the sun by day and the stars by night. As I looked up through the sunroof, a canopy of leafless trees engulfed the vehicle. I wondered if the trees I saw above also hid the bright yellow image I was sure everyone could see from the road as they passed. I was worried someone would see the car pull off the road and pull off to see what was wrong. I didn't want anyone to surprise us on our walk.

We didn't get out of the car right away. I was taking my lead from Julie, who didn't want to get out of the vehicle. We started another conversation. I was getting a little warm and rolled the window down a bit, letting in some cooler night air. I could smell spring in the air. Even though the sun had set, the night air still had a hint of warmth. The night was cooler and would soon get colder. Julie cracked open the sunroof, and the sweet smell of the season flooded the cab. Julie looked out over the river with rapped attention as the glimmering moonbeams cascaded through the trees, bouncing off the river's ripples as it ran through its banks. The absence of leaves invited the light to penetrate the darkness. The lingering blue hue was magnificent.

Julie and I remained silent, taking in the sights, smells, and sounds outside the VW. The river's babbling could be heard as its swelling water from the melting snow moved along the banks. In the distance, we thought we heard the swish of the wind resulting from its rush over the oak trees that don't drop their leaves until the new leaves begin to bud.

I whispered, "Can you hear that?"

Julie smiled, glancing at me. I met her gaze and quickly turned to look out the sunroof. An awkward feeling grew within me as the silence continued. Sinking lower in her seat, Julie moved toward me to gain a full view of the vast woods illuminated by the moonlight.

"Do you know where the trail leads?" I asked inquisitively.

"Yeah," Julie hesitated.

Silence. Neither Julie nor I felt a need to fill the moment with sound. Nature had provided all the noise I needed between the rushing river and the swishing breeze. Minutes passed...maybe ten, maybe fifteen. Each of us is content with the silence of the moment. The comfort we shared need not be broken with words. Julie leaned back against the seat.

"I could fall asleep right here. Do you like to camp?" Julie asked me.

"Yeah, I think. We haven't done much camping. Why don't we go camping this summer?" I asked, hopefully looking for an excuse to be with Julie.

"Yeah, let's; I know some great places up north."

The silence returned. I was aware of a growing desire to touch Julie. Everything in me was longing for a chance to pull Julie closer. Suddenly, the longing was followed by fear that swept quickly through me. I blushed. The darkness would keep my secret. Julie leaned across my lap to look out the passenger window, leaving a scent drawing my attention back to her. The desire I felt was so painful. Finally, I put my arm around Julie's shoulder as she leaned forward to look out the front window.

"What do you see?" I asked her.

After a moment passed, Julie responded, "I thought I saw someone walking by."

Fear and desire warred within me, leaving me conflicted. As I contemplated the moment, Julie leaned back, allowing her hand to linger on my leg, and her hand touching me felt right. Everything within me wanted more. Visions of kissing her flashed through my mind. I was deep in thought, trying to figure out my desire. Part of me yelled at the other part, telling me I should or shouldn't feel this desire. The ideas penetrated my mind. As usual, the minutes turned to an hour.

"Hey, we should get going," Julie said, calling me back from the unknown.

"Yeah, my folks will be expecting me soon."

As Julie pulled away, we suddenly found ourselves locked in an embrace. Hugs were common upon departure, but this embrace lingered longer than usual. As I went to pull apart, our cheeks lightly brushed. Then I felt her soft lips as I gave way to the desires that were so strong in me. The next moment, we were kissing more deeply and passionately. After surrendering to the moment, we fell again into each other's embrace. The sweet surrender stoked fresh but conflicted emotions inside me.

I finally pulled back. We held each other's gaze as the passion lingered in me. Looking at her, I wondered if she felt what I was feeling.

Julie started the car and headed back to my house. We sat silently as we drove south the short distance to my house. The silence made me wonder if Julie was mad at me. I wasn't sure if what had just happened was okay or not. I dreaded saying goodnight because I wasn't sure what would happen next. When we arrived in the driveway, I feared I would never see Julie again. I was afraid to reach for a hug, fearing I had already upset her. As I moved toward the door, Julie's hand reached for me.

"Hey, I will call tomorrow. Let's get together again tomorrow or Sunday," Julie said—no hint of anger in her voice.

"Yes, sure, I would like that. I have nothing planned, just things I must do around the house tomorrow morning."

I glanced back at Julie and stared momentarily, wishing I could lean in to kiss her good night, but instead, I shut the door and walked to the house.

Part II: A Journey Toward Understanding

"And ye shall know the truth, and the truth shall make you free"
-John 8:32 (KJV).

Chapter Sixteen: I Like Dreaming

"I like dreaming because dreaming can make you mine. I like holding you close, touching your skin, even if it's in my mind"

-(Kenny Nolan, 1977).

"For we wrestle not against flesh and blood, but against principalities, against powers, against the rulers of the darkness of this world, against spiritual wickedness in high places"

-Ephesians 6:12 KJV.

As I got ready for bed, I couldn't help but replay the night in my mind. I could still feel her soft lips and the thrill I felt when we kissed. I also felt the confusion and fear about what happened. I simultaneously loved the kiss and was confused by it. What would our following conversation be like? Would we talk about it? Would she be angry with me? Was she as confused as I was? Did she enjoy the kiss as much as I did?

As I tried to sleep, I kept thinking about the night and

rehearsing what I might say the next time we talked. Before I knew it, I was awakened by my mom telling me the telephone was for me. It was Julie. My stomach flipped. I didn't expect her to call me this early and this soon. This couldn't be good, or could it?

"Hello."

"Hey, sorry to call you so early, but our family is going to the apple orchard today for cross-country skiing. Do you want to go?"

She was talking to me. No hint of anger. This is good.

"Sure, I would like to go. What time?"

"I will pick you up in an hour. See you then".

"Ok, see you in an hour."

I told my mom I was going skiing with Julie and her family. I quickly showered and got dressed. I wondered if Julie was picking me up alone or if she would be with her whole family. I should have asked. I put my skis in the garage and saw Julie alone pulling up in her VW Bug. I was relieved. Maybe now I would know how Julie was doing after the kiss. The drive time to the orchard should give us some time to talk.

"Hello, glad you are ready. I know I am early."

"That's ok. Come in and say hello."

My mom saw Julie at work every day, but she seemed to like it when my friends came in and said hello. We chatted briefly, and I gave her an approximate time when I would be home. I was delighted at the thought of spending the day with Julie. I figured that meant she was not angry with me. We'd have some time to talk in case we needed to.

We loaded up the skis and headed to the orchard. We had gotten several inches of spring snow that night. The wet, heavy snowfall would make the trails slick and well-packed. We were both experienced cross-country skiers. So, too, were her dad and stepmom. Spring snow meant the conditions would be tricky, fast, and icy in the shaded areas sprinkled throughout the orchard. The slippery conditions did not deter Julie and me, and we loved the challenge of spring skiing. The orchard provided a mix of trails; some were flatter than others, some were easy, and some for the more experienced skiers. We both had skied at the orchard many times, but this was our first time skiing together. We loved the orchard because several trails wrapped around the main store and restaurant, and we could stop and warm up with hot cider and donuts and then head out for more skiing and burn off the calories. It was a great place on the city's outskirts to ski.

As we pulled up in the parking area, Jim and Julie's stepmom were already there. They hadn't been waiting long. We chatted as we strapped on the skis. Before long, we were moving in rhythm along the trail. Jim led, Jane followed, and Julie was next while I brought up the rear. It was a beautiful, sunny, crisp day with a hint of spring. The touch of spring signaled that we would only have a few days left to ski. This may be the last ski trip for this season. I was sure that motivated us to spend the day on the trails.

After hours on the trail and a brief stop in the orchard house for hot chocolate and donuts, we headed to the parking lot. Jim and Jane asked us about our plans. We said we would head to their house for a few hours and then planned to go to a movie. We loaded the skis and drove to Julie's house. Upon entering the house, we headed to her bedroom in the basement. Jim and Jane had set up a room for Julie in their basement so she had a place to stay and study while going to school in Grand Rapids. It was temporary but still afforded her privacy and a comfortable space to study or read. Julie generally sat at her desk, and I was on the bed while we talked and listened to music.

Today, our conversation turned to faith and religion. I shared with her about my church and how I learned about this faith in Jesus. She asked many questions. She, like me earlier in my life, occasionally attended mass at a Catholic church. We compared our experiences. We found much agreement about what we liked about the Catholic church. We loved midnight mass on Christmas Eve, the Good Friday services, and the Stations of the Cross. I shared with her that I loved the teaching of the Bible at the church I was attending now, and that was a practice missing from the Catholic mass. I explained that the priest of the church I attended as a kid would talk from a book of published homilies on Sundays. The speeches were like stories with a lesson, but I couldn't tell if those stories were from the Bible. At the same time, the pastor at the church I was attending talked directly from the Bible chapter by chapter or verse by verse, comparing things to other passages and chapters in the Bible. I explained that I learned so much more at this church. I also explained that several groups met on Sunday night and Wednesday to study the Bible, and I enjoyed learning with my peers.

We talked extensively, pulled out a Bible, and looked topics up. I loved having Julie to talk to. She felt like an older sister, a friend, and a confidant all rolled into one. This is something I have missed in my life. Perhaps this was Jesus' way of talking to me? This newly found faith was still so new, and there was so much I did not know or understand. The conversation lagged for a minute. Julie moved out of her desk, slipped onto the bed, reached for my hand, and held it for a minute. I looked up and into her eyes. At that moment, I was so conflicted.

Next, I leaned in to kiss her. She didn't pull back or hesitate. We kissed tenderly, longingly, but briefly. We both pulled back. We were speechless, as usual. Julie looked down and said, "Time to head to the movie." The next moment, we were heading to the car. We drove in silence to the movie theater.

We got our tickets and entered the theater. It was a Saturday afternoon, so the theater was better attended than other matinees during the week. We selected our seats in the back row. As the movie began, Julie placed her coat over her lap. "I'm cold, aren't you?" she asked. I looked over but didn't say anything.

I reached under the coat for her hand. "You are cold," I remarked. I began to pull my hand away, but Julie held tight. We sat watching the movie, holding hands. I was sure the entire world saw and knew. I kept telling myself that no one in the dark theater could see or suspect we were holding hands. I felt guilty, and yet it felt great. These feelings warred within me for as long as we held hands. Holding hands was becoming more common, but it occurred most often when we were riding in her car; I knew no one would see or suspect, so I didn't feel these conflicting feelings of guilt and excitement during those times. I just wanted to feel "normal," but I didn't even know what that was. What felt normal was when we were alone, holding hands or kissing. It just felt right to me. As these thoughts swirled, the movie played on. Soon, the movie was over, and I couldn't tell you anything about the film. I had spent the whole time figuring out all these thoughts and feelings.

As usual, we headed to Fables, one of our favorite restaurants. Fables was a cafeteria-style restaurant where you would walk through a line and pick up the food you wanted after you ordered your main entrée, typically a hamburger. The food was excellent and inexpensive. Generally, we could get a booth in the dining room's further outskirts and hang out for a while. People would come and go while we talked about every subject. Today, we grabbed our usual sodas and snacks and headed to what was soon becoming "our booth." I can't imagine a day when we went there and someone else was occupying "our booth."

As we got settled, we unwrapped our burgers and fries. We dug in. The last time we talked was before the movie. Julie finally broke the silence. "Hey, are you ok? You aren't mad at me, are you?"

"No! No way am I mad at you. Why?" I replied."

"I, I don't know. You seem quiet."

"Yeah. I guess I am." I paused and remained silent.

Finally, I asked, "Julie, are you ok with everything?"

She paused for a minute, weighing her words carefully. "Yes, yes, I am." After a long pause, Julie continued, "What do you mean by everything?"

I was trying to figure out how to answer that. Or did I want to answer that? I was so afraid of losing this new best friend. I feared losing the closeness of the relationship. I didn't know what holding hands and kissing meant, but I did think it meant we were best friends, and I didn't want that to end. So, with all the courage I could muster, I finally answered.

"You know, this closeness, our time together. Holding hands and all." There, now, it was out in the open. Somehow speaking, it made it even more real. There was no turning back now. My heart sank. Suddenly, I could not talk or swallow the bite of hamburger I just took.

"Yes!" Julie paused. "Are you?"

"Julie, this is all so new to me. As you know, I am an only child. I don't have many people to talk to and hang with; you are my friend. My closest friend. I love spending time with you, and I just...." I couldn't finish. I don't know whether the wave of hot that flashed over me was an embarrassment, fear, desire, or all at once. Here I was, spilling my guts to someone and being more honest than I had ever been with myself or anyone about my feelings. Was that all right?

Julie reached over and touched my hand. "It's ok. I love spending time with you, too. I enjoy spending time with you and enjoy all the things we do. Just be you".

We finished eating and turned to other conversations. We started planning a trip up north to see her mom, brothers, and sisters. I knew I would see Therese too and was looking forward to that. Therese and I exchanged letters weekly. We had a lot in common. I just wished she lived closer so I could see her each week, too. However, even if I couldn't see Therese as much as we'd like, I could still see Julie, and I did love this new friendship I had with her. Now, I knew she did, too.

Before we knew it, we were heading to my house. We were always careful to make sure I was home when my mom expected me. I never wanted to disappoint her or be late because I was afraid she wouldn't let me have the expanding freedom I was experiencing by spending time with Julie. As we started down the road, Julie grabbed my hand. "We are ok, Renay. I like this too." Then she squeezed my hand measuredly.

I leaned over and hugged her, or at least what I could while she was driving. She had finally said what I needed or at least wanted to hear. She was okay with all this. As we rounded the corner to turn onto my street, Julie paused as if waiting for a car before she turned left. She looked at me, leaned over, and kissed me quickly. "Thanks for today."

We pulled into my driveway, and she put the car in park. I wanted to lean over, hug, and kiss her, but for now, I would remain content with the assurance of today. I looked at her and said, "I will call you tomorrow night after church. I hope you get your homework done."

"Talk to you tomorrow," Julie replied.

I got out of the car and headed to the house.

Chapter Seventeen:
The Beginning or the End?

"There is no fear in love; but perfect love cast out fear"
-I John 4:18 KJV.

As my junior year of high school ended, I attended prom and a spring fling at church with Bill. Bill ran cross-country, worked with me on the yearbook, and was a senior about to graduate. I knew him from attending church. We dated a couple of times, going to see *Greese* at the theater. I liked him but didn't feel the same about Bill as Julie. I also dated David from the baseball team. We got to know each other because the baseball and softball teams traveled together for away games. We would sit by each other and talk about our games. We also attended church together. I also enjoyed the times Dave and I spent together, but I looked forward to spending time with Julie.

I didn't feel the same sadness I had in previous years as the school year ended. In the past, summer marked the end of seeing my friends regularly because I lived so far away from them. Now, I would still see some of them at church. I also had Julie and knew I would have someone I could spend time with regularly. Julie had talked about going home for the summer rather than staying in Grand Rapids, but she changed her mind. I was relieved.

We generally talked during the week but then spent time together on Saturday. I played on the church softball team on Tuesday nights, and sometimes Julie would come and watch. Additionally, we got together on both Friday and Saturday. It was quickly becoming clear that we were best friends, or at least that is what my mom labeled it. She seemed okay with it and began including Julie in more family-related events. My mom would invite Julie to our lake cottage as the weather got warmer.

Julie enjoyed going to the late house with us. I discovered that Julie enjoyed fishing and swimming as much as I did. While Julie wasn't as much of an athlete as I was, she never minded when I told her I needed to run to get in better shape for fall basketball. While I was out running, she and my mom would talk, typically about work. I think Julie provided my mom with some comfort, too. Julie was a bit more girly than I was, and perhaps my mom found her interesting because they shared some things in common. The cottage had two bedrooms on the ground floor. At night, Julie would sleep in one of the rooms designed to be the main bedroom, and I would sleep in the small room on the other side of the ground floor that had quickly become mine.

In late June, we headed up north to Julie's childhood home. We left on a Friday night after Julie and I finished our hour shift at work. We both worked at the collection agency part-time. What started as a one-time offer by the collection agency to me to help them get caught up on their filing turned into an offer to work during the summer months as well. I appreciated having the work because I knew I was planning on attending college and saving up money to pay for college and buy a car if I decided not to live in the dorms wherever I chose to attend. We didn't see each other at work as I worked the reception area downstairs, and Julie was upstairs. We headed north, and the drive seemed long. It gave us plenty of time to talk. Julie explained to me what to expect. I was much less nervous because I had already met Julie's brother and sisters. Therese and I had corresponded a lot, so I felt like I knew her family. I was a little nervous to meet Julie's mom, and I did remember what felt like chaos when we entered the house upon arrival, given all the children around.

Initially, we pulled into her driveway. We entered the house and were immediately greeted by the gang. I was struck by how excited the young kids were to see their older sister, Julie. I remember thinking how cool these siblings seemed to like each other and get along well. Some of my cousins didn't always like each other and get along, so I often wondered what my experience would have been like had I had brothers and sisters. Therese was still at the high school boys' basketball game when we arrived and would be home soon. I met Julie's very welcoming mom. Her brothers and sisters were happy to see us both, and they remembered me from their visit to Grand Rapids over Christmas. I felt at home. We talked for a while with the family. Therese finally came home, and the greetings began again. Soon, it was time to consider going to bed. We headed to Julie's car to get our bags.

"Follow me, Renay. You will be staying with me in my old room tonight. It's Therese's room now, but we will be in there this weekend,"

"Ok," I responded. I was focused on getting our stuff and getting to bed, and my feelings of tiredness as today had been a long day.

We got our stuff, entered the house, and headed upstairs. We started unpacking, and Julie showed me where to change. We changed and crawled into bed. Julie turned the light off, and we talked a bit more. As Julie said good night, I hugged her. We held one another for a moment. I was not sure what to expect next. Suddenly, I felt her smooth, soft lips on mine. I relaxed. The moment felt so good. As quickly as the moment occurred, it was over. We both laid back and drifted off to sleep.

Saturday was a full day. We all spent time together doing things around the house. We played games, fixed the lawn mower, mowed the lawn, and helped with small tasks around the house. We went bowling late in the afternoon. Afterward, we came home to a great dinner. Then, we headed to church. Julie explained that the family attended Saturday night mass. I looked forward to seeing if Julie's church was like my previous experiences at my family's Catholic church.

Mass was familiar to me because I had attended the Catholic church occasionally as a kid. After mass, we decided to head to McDonald's for dessert. We took two cars because there were too many of us for just one car. I rode with Therese this time so we could have some time together, and the kids rode with Julie. It was great to spend time with her. Theresa and I compared notes about how our basketball and softball seasons turned out. Theresa's softball and volleyball teams each won their district tournaments. I was impressed. We talked about getting ready for basketball in the fall and what we each thought would be like to be seniors in our last year of high school. After dessert, Theresa picked up a friend who would stay at the house tonight. The kids went with Therese, and Julie explained she would show me around their small town before heading home to watch a movie when everyone met back up.

We parted ways. Julie showed me the house they grew up in before moving to the outskirts of town. She showed me their high school and some important places where she grew up. Next, she took me to the park by the river. We parked and got out. We started walking along the river as Julie explained how they would canoe or ride innertubes down the river during summer. The stories she would tell were so funny. I reached for her hand, and we walked hand in hand, talking. Our closeness was becoming comfortable and familiar when we were alone. We paused as she showed me her chosen spot beside the river, under a tree, to sit and read as a kid. We turned and faced each other, and our eyes met. I began to pull her close. She slipped her arms around my neck, and we began to kiss. Our kisses became more profound and longer. We paused and embraced. We both were relaxed and content to be in the moment a little longer. Julie whispered in my ear. "We should get back home; they will be expecting us."

We pulled apart with my hands on Julie's waist and her arms on my neck. The moon was full, so I could see her smile. We held each other's gaze.

"Sure, we should go," I said.

Inwardly, I was not ready to go. As I started to step back, Julie pulled me to her and kissed me longingly. Everything within me came alive. With each passing moment, it became harder to stop.

"We need to go, Julie," I insisted.

"Yes. Yes, we do", said Julie breathlessly. "We can pick up from here later tonight."

We began walking toward the car. I slipped my arm around Julie. Silence embraced us as we walked. I had never felt closer to Julie or anyone else than in that moment. No words were needed.

We arrived home and entered the house to the smell of popcorn. We were hassled for being the last to arrive. We talked about where we had been and then settled into the living room to watch the movie. Julie grabbed a chair. I sat next to Therese and Jodi. The time passed quickly. Before long, we were all heading to bed.

Julie and I quickly got ready for bed. We settled in bed beneath the covers and turned off the light. We could hear the rest of the family scurrying off to various rooms in the house. A longing was building in me. I wanted to hold Julie and kiss her. I wasn't sure what, if anything, I should do, but the feeling was growing intense. As time passed, the urge was becoming so intense that it hurt. I rolled over and snuggled up close to Julie. I whispered, "Do you think everyone is asleep?"

A long pause ensued. Julie leaned over, and I awaited her verbal response. Instead, I felt her lips searching for mine, and in a second, we were kissing deeply. I felt Julie's hands exploring my side. As she slid her hand up and down my side, she found the end of my shirt, untucked it, and slid her hands up to my breasts. I moaned. Julie kissed me and then began to kiss my neck. My body surrendered to her. I felt so relaxed but no longer in control of my thoughts or feelings. I was responding, and everything Julie was doing aroused in me a greater desire. The deeper she kissed me, the more I wanted; she slipped her hands down my waistband. Suddenly, I was saying, "Don't stop, please don't stop."

I wanted every barrier between us removed. Suddenly, I felt her lips on my stomach. My legs shuttered. I was burning inside. Suddenly, I felt her in me. I moaned. We began to move in rhythm. As she kissed my stomach, I could feel her pulling at my skin and pushing harder. She slipped her left arm around my neck and deeply kissed me again. She had me, and soon, the rhythm brought me to surrender. Julie laid back and pulled me into her. We fell asleep in each other's embrace.

The morning sun woke me as it cascaded through the window. I rolled over and saw Julie still asleep. I slid up behind her and put my arm over her side. She rolled over on her back and faced me.

"Good morning. Did you sleep well?" Julie asked.

"I sure did," I replied playfully.

We talked about how we had visited Mackinaw Island as kids and biked around the island with our families. We expressed how we both wished we could take the week and travel further north to see the island and many of the beautiful areas that we both had visited as little kids. It was cool that we each wanted to experience the things we enjoyed, but this time, to enjoy them together. It was fantastic to plan to spend time together and even go places together in the future. These conversations gave me a feeling of permanence and security. We both knew we had to go home today as work awaited tomorrow. We kissed briefly and got ready to face the family.

The day passed quickly, and we got on the road heading home. After an hour, I reached over to Julie and began to place my hand on her stomach. My hand began to search for the end of her shirt.

"What are you looking for?" Julie asked curiously.

"I am not looking; I am taking." Just then, I brushed her bra.

"You are making this hard, you know," Julie said teasingly.

I continued to pull at her shirt and slide my hand under her bra.

"Do you want me to crash? I can't concentrate while you do that".

"Sorry, but I just can't keep my hands off you."

As we continued to drive toward home, the sun started setting in the western sky. The beauty of the evening, the hum of the car, and my mind cause my longing to grow. I wanted to re-live last night, and I had yet to learn when or if we would share another night like that.

"Do we have to go home?" I asked. "I want you."

"I want you, too."

Soon, Julie was pulling off the road. She shut the car off. We were far enough off the road in the parking lot of a closed gas station that the vehicle couldn't be seen from the road. We were soon kissing deeply and actively exploring each other's bodies. We passed the next half hour in this way.

Finally, we started the car and began down the road; the last thirty minutes to home passed too quickly.

Chapter Eighteen: Summer Love

"Summer loving had me a blast; Summer loving happened so fast, I met a girl crazy for me"

-Grease, Summer Nights.

Julie and I spent any free time together we could. Our fears were realized as very few opportunities allowed us to explore the intimate moments we discovered one night in Northern Michigan. It only served to deepen our relationship. As the calendar turned to August, I began training and practicing for my senior year of basketball. My parents were spending weekends at the cottage. Dad kept identifying projects and finishing them as money and time allowed. There were upgrades to the sewer, system fixing crumbling steps, building a retaining wall to level the parking area, rebuilding sections of the dock weakened by years of sun and water, and countless others. I would join in whenever I was at the lake house with them while Dad was working on a project. Each project taught me how to use different tools, better understand safety, or how geometry is factored into decisions. They had a week off in August, but I could only join them on Friday afternoon because I had morning practices and worked in the afternoon. I only had two more weeks to work and wanted to earn all I could. I was saving for college. The more I helped my dad, the more my mom would remind me that I was acting more like a boy than a girl, and if I kept that up, I would never find a man who would marry me. I would laugh her comments off but filed them away in my mind.

On Saturday, I called Julie and talked on the phone as usual. We had family plans that day, so we weren't spending time together. I told her my parents would leave for the lake Sunday afternoon after Dad returned home from work. I explained that they would be gone all week and asked her if she wanted to spend the week with me at my house. I continued to explain to Julie my mom hoped she would stay with me because she worried I would not wake up at night if there were a storm or a fire. I was a sound sleeper, and everyone knew it. Julie teasingly responded, "Sure, I will stay and ensure you stay awake all night."

My stomach leaped. Her teasing made me want to go right through the phone and take her. We hadn't had time to be alone since late June, and my longing was building. Julie's teasing was like a green light. Her teasing told me she felt the same way, and her words confirmed her desire. We finalized our plans for her arrival and the week ahead and hung up.

I told my parents that Julie had agreed to stay the week. They were relieved. They had no idea how relieved I was, too. I needed to release this growing desire. Sunday morning dawned. I went to church and enjoyed the church service. It was always great to see my friends. As usual, I stayed and talked less after the service because I wanted to go home. I explained that my family had plans and I had to go.

Once home from church, I helped Mom get packed for the lake. While she packed clothes for her and Dad, she wanted me to fill the cooler. She told me what to look for in the freezer and refrigerator and to make sure I packed ice around everyone once I t was in the cooler. On weekends, I would accompany my parents to the lake house; I would often be asked to pack the cooler, so I was familiar with this task. The difference this time was the contents were supposed to be for a week rather than 2 or 3 days. I found packing the cooler for the week to be a much more challenging task. As we worked, she kept reviewing the ground rules for the week. She was leaving me her car. She reminded me of the rules for using the vehicle. I had my fill of rules when Dad arrived home. As he changed, I helped pack the car. They reviewed the rules for the house and car again. I wondered if all kids had parents like this or if my parents were more cautious than others. Dad handed me some money and told me to call them if I needed anything. They told me they would check in occasionally to see how things were going, but they preferred I call them because they knew I was busy and didn't always remember my schedule. Then they left.

As soon as they pulled out of the driveway, I called Julie. "Hey girl, they just left. Come on over anytime.".

"It's about time. I have been packed since last night. I am on my way".

It seemed like forever before Julie pulled in and came to the door. As she stepped into the house, I stepped forward and pulled her close. As I leaned in to kiss her, I pulled the door shut. We kissed deeply. There was no rush. Each kiss lingered longer and longer. Once our hunger was momentarily satisfied, we moved apart. My hands were on Julie's waist, her arms on my shoulders. We looked into each other's eyes.

"I have missed you, and thank you," I said.

"I have missed you too, Renay. I thought about this every night since...." Julie's words trailed off.

I pulled her into an embrace. I whispered into her ear. "Me, too, Julie. Tonight, I will show you all my dreams since our night together at your mom's house".

We parted and grabbed Julie's stuff out of the car. It was a warm August day, and we had decided to head to Grand Haven to see the Musical Fountains. On Sunday night, the fountains located across from the boat channel in Grand Haven were used to present a light show using musical hymns. The Fountains provided a show every night, and each night utilized a different genre of music. Sunday nights' genre always included classic hymns. A grassy knoll on the side of the canal across from the Fountains is excellent for sitting to watch the light show. After Julie put her clothes away in the front bedroom, we grabbed a couple of blankets. I grabbed my camera and headed to Grand Haven to watch the sunset and the light show.

Grand Haven was about an hour's drive from my house. We reached Grand Haven and found a parking spot. We had time to explore the shops and walk along the pier. Whenever I saw a guy and a girl walking hand in hand, I wanted to hold Julie's hand. We never held hands in public. Our closeness was shared in private. My fears of someone finding out about how I felt about Julie were always in the back of my mind. Julie and I never spoke about my anxiety. But our actions communicated that we both shared the unspoken fear. Our ability to think of each other's thoughts made this relationship comfortable.

We picked our spot on the grassy area across from the fountains. We waited for darkness to descend. At about ten o'clock, the Fountains lit up, and the music began. Julie asked me if I was cold. I said no, but she said she was and pulled the second blanket over our laps. She then reached under the blanket and grabbed my hand.

We sat holding hands as the show continued. I wish I had thought of it first, but Julie did. Her hand-holding idea was another way I knew we both shared the same desire for this closeness.

After the show, we drove the hour back home. I drove because I knew this side of the state very well. Unlike the VW bug of Julie's, my mother's front seat was continuous, so Julie could sit next to me comfortably as we drove. I put my arm around her. As we went home, we talked about the evening. It was our first time together to watch the Musical Fountains this summer, but this was not our first trip to Grand Haven. We talked about the music and identified our favorite songs. We talked about the pictures we took and how we looked forward to getting them developed.

Before we knew it, we were pulling into the driveway at my house. We entered and locked the doors. I showed Julie the front bedroom where we would be sleeping. My bed was a twin bed, which would be less comfortable for the two of us. My family had always used the front room as a guest room because the room and the bed were bigger. I don't remember ever discussing whether we would sleep together. Sleeping together was an unspoken conclusion. We each got ready for bed and crawled in under the covers. I turned off the lights. As I rolled over to face Julie, I felt her hands around my neck and pulling me close.

"I have waited for tonight since we returned from visiting my mom back home."

"Me, too, Julie."

A brief silence was interrupted when her lips brushed mine, and I rolled Julie over on her back and began to kiss her deeply. As we kissed, I began to remove her clothes. The sight of Julie sent a rocket of warmth through my body. I had to slow down and take in her beauty and the moment. I felt her tugging at my shirt. I stripped off the shirt, and we both fell into deep kissing with a frantic exploration of every inch of our shirtless bodies.

I slowly moved from Julie's lips to her breasts. I lingered around her breasts until I heard her moan with delight. My hands began to explore her. I removed her underwear and touched her as I looked for a way to enter her. As I slid into her, she lurched back and moaned. We began to move in rhythm as before, but I was in control this time. The wetness I felt was new to me. Her smell was intoxicating. Suddenly, it all seemed natural. Everything we did that night brought us both pleasure.

Exhausted, I fell onto my back and drew Julie into my side. I rested my head against hers. Our breathing was in rhythm and slowed by the exhaustion of bringing one another great pleasure.

"I don't ever want this to end," I said.

"Me, either, Renay. I love you so much."

As silence enveloped the room, I felt the love Julie had just expressed. Morning came too soon. Each day of the week ended with passionate nights. I would not let myself think about it often, but I was already dreading the end of the week when my parents would come home. I could not imagine being able to stay apart from Julie again after this week. I began to dream of the day after graduating high school when we might live together.

Chapter Nineteen: Marching to Graduation

"To everything there is a season, and a time to every purpose under heaven"

-Ecclesiastes 3:1 KJV.

As usual, summer gave way to fall. Julie was finishing her last year at the community college, and I was finishing my last year of high school. Julie attended classes two days a week. She had found another job and was no longer working at the collection agency where my mom worked. She had become part of our family, so my mom still enjoyed seeing her when she came over. As a high school senior, I had earned most of the credits I needed to graduate, so I had first and second hours free during the fall semester. Rather than picking up electives, I decided to have study hall first and second hour. My parents filled out a form for the school that allowed me to show up at the start of the third hour. With basketball, the extra sleep would be helpful.

The semester started, and the fall was well underway. I was getting up and foraging for breakfast when I heard a knock on the door. My parents had left for work, so I was puzzled. I looked through the curtains and saw Julie's car. I ran to the door and opened it. Julie entered.

"Are you okay?" I asked.

"No," Julie said. My heart stopped.

"I need to see you. I...," Julie then reached for me and kissed me. She whispered in my ear, "I want you."

We stumbled toward the bedroom. I hadn't dressed for school yet. Julie was dressed for work. That didn't seem to stop us from undressing each other. We fell into bed and began to compete to see who would submit to the other's touch first. There was nothing selfish about our lovemaking. Soon, Julie surrendered, and I slowly brought her to a peak and then sweet release. Her moan often got me to the point of release, but I would wait to give that moment to Julie.

After we were each satisfied, we began the conversation that would have naturally been the prelude to our lovemaking had the urgency not been there.

"It is good to see you. Do you have the day off?" I asked.

"No, I work at ten; I just wanted to see you wearing something other than your basketball uniform. Of course, wearing nothing is fine, too."

After a pleasant conversation, we dressed and readied for our work and school obligations. We left together. As I drove to school, I imagined this morning playing out repeatedly every day after we got an apartment together after finishing school.

This basketball season was very different than the previous two. We were picked to finish in the middle of the conference. Only two of us had played the last year, and another senior had joined the team. Only seven girls comprised the team. My class was not the most athletic; only four juniors joined the three seniors.

Depth and experience needed to be improved on this team. I was being counted on to score more, yet the team needed me to rebound. The team was shorter than the previous two teams. Consequently, we felt we had an advantage if we played a more up-tempo offense not to allow our opponents to set up their defense and use their advantage against us. I worked harder than in previous summers to get in shape because I knew we would run more.

Julie came to most of my games. After the games, we would grab a bite to eat, talk about our day, and go our separate ways. When I got home, my parents would want to know how the game went. I would sit with them for a while and recount the game. Most of the outcomes went against us, but when we did lose, the games were close. We even had a couple of games where we only had four players on the court because three of us had fouled out. If we were winning when a third person fouled out, the game inevitably changed, and we lost. Despite our inexperience and the challenges of only having seven girls, we never believed we would lose and never gave up. Being the most experienced senior, my teammates elected me captain. I was honored because I had been on teams when the players didn't select seniors but those they thought could represent them the best.

As captain, I felt a sense of responsibility to encourage each of my teammates. I remembered all the times I felt like an outsider on the previous teams, and as a result, I made sure I sat with a different player on each ride home from our away games. Little did I realize how well I would get to know the juniors on the team. As a result, I would stay in touch with them and even come to a few of their games during their senior year. I committed I would be a good teammate. This lesson carried over into other competitive situations I played in during the future. It has also carried over into my leadership principles throughout my career.

Throughout the season, I would talk to my coach and the JV coach about whether they thought I could play basketball at the college level. I told them I was applying to Grand Rapids Baptist College, a small Christian liberal arts college. I explained they had a basketball team, and I knew a couple of the girls from church. I knew our best player from the previous year had gone to Grand Rapids Community College and had made the team there. Both coaches encouraged me to consider playing. My coach wrote to the coach at Grand Rapids Baptist College and shared his observations about me and my possible interest in playing if I were accepted. As a result, she and one of her players came to one of my games and watched us. It happened to be later in the season and a game we won. I had played well, and because we were a small team, I could show my versatility in playing various roles except for being a point guard, as I was not a good ball handler. After the game, I talked with the coach and her player and was encouraged about trying out for the team if I was accepted to the college.

After basketball season, I took the winter off from playing sports. That allowed Julie and I to go to her home up north and watch Therese play volleyball. Her team was in first place, and we would cheer them on. I also spent time taking pictures as I loved photographing sports. I would have loved to become a sports photographer, but I knew I had a slim chance to pursue that career. So, I figured I would enjoy it as a hobby. During our visits up north, I got to know Therese better. I asked her if she was considering going to college. She told me she planned to enter the air force after high school. She was the only girl I knew who thought entering a service branch. Her choice intrigued me. I wasn't even sure I realized that, as a female, I could serve in the middle of a war zone after high school. My father and many of his brothers did, and I greatly respected veterans. I have often wondered if I would have chosen to serve had I realized entering a service branch had been an option for me after high school. My grandmother, aunts, and mom were very proper, mannered women with narrow ideas about women's societal roles and marriage. I was already pushing them outside their comfort zone by even talking about going to college. I can only imagine what they would have said about me had I told them I wanted to enlist in a military service branch.

Julie and I spent every minute together we could. The winter months included many opportunities to go skiing. Several snow days gave us even more time together. Whenever Grand Rapids received a lot of lake effect snow and the winds would blow vigorously, schools around the area would shut down. In the mornings, when we might have a snow day, I would turn on the WOOD radio. Dave Stryke would be the morning announcer, and I would listen to him call off the names of the schools that were closing. What was so cool to me was that Dave Stryke's son was in my class. After the school district names were announced, Dave would announce the local colleges that would delay their opening or close altogether. Closures would include the community college because the students commuted rather than lived there. However, by noon on those days, the snowplows would have the roads cleared enough for safe travel. Around noon, Julie would call and ask if I wanted to go skiing. I would agree; she would pick me up, and we would go skiing for the afternoon.

Julie and I each had the same two weeks off for Christmas break. We each spend Christmas Day in Grand Rapids with our families. We planned to visit her mother up north during the second week of Christmas break and to be home on New Year's Eve to spend New Year's Day with our families. My parents and I spent Christmas Eve at my grandparents' house. After opening presents, three of us went to Christmas Mass. I enjoyed Christmas

Mass. The church was fully decorated with decorations and several Christmas trees. The priest narrated the story of Christmas. Father LaSarge was a great storyteller, and I love how he told the story of Mary and Joseph and Christ's birth. After mass, Aunt Silvia, my cousin Deb, and I returned to my grandparents' house. By then, the men had consumed too much alcohol, and I was thrust into the role of bartender. They had to tell me what liquor to mix with various sodas and juices and how much to pour into a glass topped with ice. I didn't drink, but I did try them to know what they tasted like. I believed the Bible taught that any consumption of alcohol was wrong. That was one reason I didn't drink like some classmates. The other reason was I thought alcohol would hinder my athletic performance. The drinking age was 18, so it wasn't against the law. However, the drinking age changed to 21 shortly before graduating high school.

 I went home with Julie the day after Christmas and spent the rest of that week with her family. Our lovemaking became less urgent and more tender. Our time together became more predictable. We often talked about finishing school and what might come next. I got to know her brothers and sister better during the week. We would plan one event each day to take the kids so that Julie's mom could have some time. One day, we went sliding. Another afternoon, we went to the ice rink made by the city in the park. We took the kids bowling and to a movie. The week went very fast, and soon Julie and I packed up our things, put them in the car, and began the commute back to Grand Rapids. We were both looking forward to the spring semester because we were nearing the completion of a significant educational goal.

 I received an acceptance letter from Grand Rapids Baptist College early in January. My parents were happy for me and glad I would stay close to home to attend college. I talked about attending

Michigan State or Ohio State University and how my friends were going to central or western Michigan universities. They feared I would get lost at a big school. My father talked to me about his time at Michigan State College and how he dropped out after two weeks of classes because attending classes with over a hundred students in the class was unmotivating for him. He believed I would have an easier time adjusting to college if I went to a smaller college. I was looking forward to going to Grand Rapids Baptist College and continuing to play basketball and softball while working on my degree to become a teacher.

My senior year felt more like play than school. Because I had enough credits to graduate at the end of the fall semester, I was only taking three courses, enough to be eligible to play softball in the spring. I took a history class because I loved history. I took an art class because I like learning about painting, drawing, and different ways to create art. I also enjoyed reading, so I took an English literature class. I also assumed that class because I like Ms. Poga, who taught the course. She was our yearbook advisor, and I wanted to spend more time with her because she was one of my favorite teachers. When I wasn't in class, I hung around the school. The yearbook staff had a dedicated office in the high school building, so I often used it to do my work on the yearbook. I usually proofread the layout sheets that other yearbook staff members submitted to me for review.

Even though I only had three classes during my senior year, I still spent most of my days at the high school. There were plenty of tasks that needed to be completed. As a senior class leadership team member, I helped plan the February Snow King and Queen dance. I was also a teacher's assistant for Ms. Poga and helped her grade tests or prepare bulletin boards for the next month in her classroom. Ms. Poga knew I wanted to be a teacher. Consequently, she allowed me to be her teaching assistant to gain some practical experience doing tasks other than teaching that would be expected of me as a teacher. Having the opportunity to be her teaching assistant reinforced my desire. I wasn't sure of the subject and was undecided on history, English, or art. I did, however, know I wanted to teach older students.

I continued attending the church with my friends, and my faith and knowledge of the Bible deepened. I was very interested in the Book of Revelation. I would go to the school library and check out books about "end times prophecy." I would also go to the town library to find books on prophecy. I found that understanding the Book of Revelation was complex. However, I wanted to know the end of the story and felt I could understand the entire Bible better if I could understand the Book of Revelation. Occasionally, I would ask Julie if she wanted to attend church with me. Periodically, she would. We talked about faith and God often. We shared our dreams, prayers, and fears.

Soon, it was June, and graduation was a week away. Julie and I had planned a graduation trip to celebrate my graduation from high school and her graduation from the community college. We wanted to travel for a week and a half, spending a few days at my parents' cottage just north of Grand Rapids and then exploring Michigan's northern lower peninsula. Next, we would spend some time with Julie's family up north on our way to Mackinaw Island. Then, we would spend a long weekend visiting Mackinaw City and Mackinaw Island. Our first dream of seeing our favorite places together would come true.

On graduation night, Julie sat with my parents. After the ceremony, Julie went with me to a couple of parties for my friends who had also graduated. This was the first time that many of my school friends met Julie. We planned on leaving for Hess Lake the following day, so she stayed the night at our house. Julie slept in the front room, and I slept in my room. I didn't sleep all night. I wanted to sneak into the front room and be with Julie. I feared my parents would discover us, so I lay awake, reminding myself that Julie and I had the next ten days together.

Saturday morning dawned, and we said goodbye to my parents. Of course, we were given a set of rules and reminders before we left, but the number and length of the rules were getting smaller. This time, it had more to do with lighting the water heater at the cottage than where I could go and when I had to be home. Julie and I drove the short hour to the lake. We were looking forward to the weekend there. We arrived at the cottage and unpacked. We headed to the boat after changing into our suits. We cruised the lake and swam at a popular swimming area where a sandbar made the swimming very appealing. The day was relaxing. We had so much in common that we didn't have to talk about what to do because we enjoyed so many of the same activities.

We docked the boat and set out to make dinner. I grilled hamburgers while Julie prepared a salad. We ate dinner and then spent the evening sitting on the dock fishing and waiting for the sunset. The day was perfect. We watched TV until we started to fall asleep. We naturally slipped into our routine of making love. Julie immediately took control. I lay back as Julie began to explore my body. As she lingered near my waste, she suddenly slipped lower. I felt a rush of pleasure. As she returned to my lips, I surrendered to her.

The following day, we headed to her house further north. Each family was glad we had planned our travels this way, so we had to check in each day to ensure our parents knew we were okay. Society wasn't considered unsafe at this time. However, unexpected things could happen, from car accidents to blowing a tire or getting lost.

While we both were annoyed by some of the requests, we were both gaining a better understanding of why our parents were worried. We were sure they were all calling each other to report that we had arrived safely. At Julie's house, we visited with her family. That night, we slept in the same bed where we first made love. The moment was not lost on us. That night, we had talked about Mackinaw Island, and tonight, we were talking about our excitement to go there finally. Exhausted from the night before, we fell asleep in each other's arms. The following day, we awoke. We kissed deeply, showered separately, and readied to drive north. After saying goodbye to Julie's mom, we headed further north. We found our hotel in Mackinaw City, checked in, and went to the store for snacks. We had dinner and returned to the hotel.

We watched TV and fell asleep. Sometime in the middle of the night, Julie woke me up. She thought she heard something; it was the people in the room next to us. They were a bit loud, but finally, they quieted down. I was holding Julie and loved falling asleep with her in my arms. I felt safe; I felt loved. I reached over to kiss her good night. She rose and pushed me down. She straddled my waist and lifted off my shirt. As she massaged my breasts, she leaned in to kiss me. I wanted more, and my lingering kisses told her so. She began to search my body and slowly entered me. She began to massage me while kissing me deeply. She began to slip down to my breasts and lingered there until my nipples were hard. I began to feel I was slipping out of control. Julie stayed with me until I came and then pulled me into her.

"I can't get enough of you," she said.

I was breathless and couldn't talk. "I love you," I said as out of breath as if I had just run a marathon. "I never want to lose you. I want to be with you forever." My words startled me. Julie kissed me deeply and held me close.

"I love you, too," she responded.

We slept in relatively late. I am sure it is because we were awakened during the night. We explored Mackinaw City and saved Mackinaw Island for the next day. We awoke early the next day, took the boat to the island, and investigated every inch of the beautiful land mass frozen in time. The island was amazing. I loved sharing the day with Julie and dreamed about many more days like this.

Before we knew it, we were headed home to Grand Rapids. We had just spent a fantastic week and a half together. The drive back home was long but always exciting when we were together. Monday morning dawned, and I was back working at the collection agency, trying to save money for college.

My uncle helped me buy a car for college. He worked at a Chevrolet dealership and kept an eye out for a good, reliable, used car that I could afford. I decided to save money by living at home rather than in the dorms. Since I would be driving back and forth to school and the fact that both of my parents worked, I needed a car. The college required first-time students to live on campus unless they lived with their parents. I had my parents sign the letter stating I would live with them. Given my shyness when using the locker room in high school, I didn't think I could live with three other roommates.

Julie had graduated from the community college and was working full-time. She began talking about moving out of her father's house and into an apartment. We talked about getting an apartment together, but I could not do that because I wanted to go to school and couldn't afford an apartment and college. Julie began to explore getting her apartment with a couple of her other friends.

The Sunday evening before I started college classes on Monday, I drove to the college and parked by the gym overlooking the pond. I sat in the parking lot and prayed to Jesus about my first day. I was excited but very nervous. The college was near Julie's house, so I left the campus and drove by to see if she was home. She was still at her church, so I waited for her to get home to have dinner with her and ask her about college and what I might expect that first day. I picked her up and went to our favorite place, Fables. We talked as usual. Before long, I went to drop her off before heading home. We kissed good night. The next day, I would begin my college life.

Chapter Twenty: Baptism

"Know ye not, that so many of us as were baptized in Jesus Christ were baptized into his death?"

-Romans 6:3 KJV.

Monday morning, I headed to my 8 o'clock class. The college opened a whole new world for me. The class I loved the most was the Old Testament Survey. I recall enjoying all my classes. In general, I like learning. I was attending Grand Rapids Baptist College, and the behavioral requirements were stricter than the high school. First, there was a dress code. Girls had to wear dresses daily until the first of November when the weather generally turned cold and snowy. We could not attend movies. We could not drink. We also could not dance. I'm not sure if I realized that these rules were a bit strict at the time because these were not normal activities of mine anyway. While I had attended a few movies with Julie, I figured we could find other things to do. Indeed, I had never been afraid of "discipline" because I had played sports in high school and had bought into the coach's rules about not drinking and smoking.

During the first semester, I took general education courses toward a degree in secondary education as I prepared to be a teacher. I'm unsure if I had decided to major in English or history, but I decided I liked college courses better than high school ones. I took classes in the morning and then worked in the afternoon. I lived at home because I could not afford to live in the dorms. The college usually required all first-year students to live on campus, but they did waive the residency requirement for me because I did live at home. While living at home helped me afford college, it had a downside. I missed much of the typical college life of the traditional freshman. Despite my lack of time on campus, I still met several people through my classes. Consequently, I often returned to the campus in the evening to meet up with my friends or study in the library.

As time progressed, Julie moved out of her father's house. She moved into an apartment with three roommates. She also began dating some guy. We still saw each other often, but those times seemed to come with some internal conflict for me. I was jealous of Julie's new life and felt the pull of new friends. Gradually, we parted ways as we moved on, spending more time with others.

Several people I met at the college attended Alpine Baptist Church near my house. I attended a Bible church since my sophomore year in high school and couldn't have told you the difference between Baptist and Bible churches. I felt the pull to go to Alpine Baptist Church because my new friends were there.

My second-semester courses were just as interesting as the fall classes. I took a class in theology and the New Testament Survey. I was beginning to understand the difference between Baptist and Bible churches. By spring, I was attending Alpine Baptist Church each Sunday. I particularly enjoyed the Old and New Testament Survey courses because they were much like history. I found early in my college career that I had a passion for history.

While attending Alpine Baptist Church, I met Faith. Baptist College required us to perform community or church service, so I worked at AWANA every Wednesday night at Alpine Baptist Church. It was through helping in AWANA that I met Faith, who was an AWANA leader. I would help with game time that my former high school softball coach led. Faith worked with the middle school kids during AWANA. After game time, I would help Faith as she worked with the middle school kids. I wanted to be a middle school teacher, so it seemed natural to work with this group. Group time during AWANA involved studying the Bible. During this time, Faith would tell a short Bible story and work with the kids on memorizing Bible verses. I would work with the kids on memorizing the verses as well. Little did I realize that while helping the kids learn the verses, I was memorizing them, too. I enjoyed this work and looked forward to it each Wednesday night.

Over time, Faith and I became good friends. She would stay after the Wednesday night AWANA and catch for me while I practiced my pitching. I was planning to try out for the college softball team. These pitching sessions allowed us plenty of time to talk and get to know each other. We shared our faith and interests in professional sports. She had attended Baptist College previously to relate to my stories of classes and professors. I felt like I had a new best friend with none of the "guilt" that I was experiencing during the later months of my friendship with Julie. While I enjoyed the intimate relationship I shared with Julie, I gradually developed more profound guilt because the church I attended would periodically share a sermon that led me to believe homosexuality was wrong. I certainly hadn't come to think I was a homosexual, but I wondered whether my longing for a female best friend led me to want to engage in a homosexual relationship with

Julie. I didn't believe Julie was gay. All this wasn't very clear to me, and in time, I concluded that my feelings for Julie were just a passing phase.

School and studying were challenging for me. I felt I had to work harder than most students. Despite feeling like I put in a lot of time reading and studying, I enjoyed learning. Through my theology and Bible studies, I was coming to feel guilty about my past intimate relationship with Julie. I often wondered if "Satan" was leading me astray by becoming physically involved with Julie. Because of the internal conflict I experienced, and our new friends and other pulls on our time, we spent less and less time together. Somehow, I took the growing distance between us as God "cleansing" me of my sin by removing the temptation from my life. I came to see our physical relationship as a fad. I was glad to have a new best friend in Faith where none of those feelings were present. At least, none of those feelings were present for me.

I tried out for the college basketball team. After a couple of weeks, I realized I couldn't afford to attend college without working. Also, during the two weeks of tryouts, I continued working because I didn't want to quit my job if I didn't make the team. Consequently, between classes, basketball, and work, I struggle to find the time to get all of my reading and homework done. I didn't receive any financial aid, and what I earned in the summer covered most, but not all, of my tuition. I agonized over my decision to continue playing basketball in college or forgo the opportunity to continue working and focus on my studies and perhaps playing softball. I shared my situation with our basketball coach. She listened intently but offered no opinions or observations. I felt she was very indifferent about my remaining on the team. That was all I needed to make my decision. While I believed, and still think, it was the best decision then, I always wondered whether I would have made the team and made a difference if I could stay with it and not have to work. Fortunately, after college, I would have plenty of opportunities to enjoy playing basketball. However, those opportunities made me wonder whether I was talented enough to play at the college level. Eventually, I decided to forgo playing college softball as well. This decision, however, I would revisit in the future.

My first year of college was over, and I was fortunate that I was able to continue working at the collection agency full-time in the summers. The summer work helped me save money for tuition and pay for my car insurance. I would work during the day and then hang out with Faith and our friends in the evenings and weekends. During the summer, I played on the church softball team. This allowed me to keep my softball skills honed even though I had decided not to go out for the softball team at Baptist College. I continued to spend the weekends at the lake house with my parents. Faith would accompany periodically as well.

The more I learned about my faith in Jesus and the Baptist theology, the more I became convinced that I needed to be publicly baptized in obedience to God. My mom was surprised when I shared that I considered being baptized at church. She reminded me that I had been baptized in the Catholic Church when I was young. I shared with her that my baptism in the Catholic Church was their decision to raise me as a Catholic. I emphasized that I respected their decision, but now I was old enough to decide. She was aware of how I felt about the Catholic Church. She knew I wasn't antagonistic but that my Confirmation classes were less than pleasant, and the priest at that time wasn't very dismissive and unwilling to answer my questions, which were very important to me. She also knew that I had deeply committed to a faith and was happy that I had a conviction, even if it wasn't the one she had hoped I would embrace.

One Sunday morning, I was "baptized" into the faith. Through my theology class, I learned that baptism was an act of obedience and a public proclamation of my faith in Jesus Christ. I made the public step on a Sunday morning and convinced my mom to attend the service. My mother and I had many conversations about the meaning of baptism because she would tell me of my baptism when I was two months old. While my mom was very supportive of my decision, my dad was very indifferent. My grandmother, however, was very much against it. Much to my grandmother's frustration, I left the Catholic Church during my sophomore year in high school. That was something she never let my mother forget. She frequently told my mother she was going to hell because she did not raise me as a good Catholic, so I left the church. I only remember one time talking to my grandmother about my faith and why it was vital for me to attend a church and religion of my choice. She listened but said little. Only later did I learn how she would criticize my mom after talking about how she had failed as a mother.

I would frequently tell my mother about my faith in Jesus and that one's faith brought one into a relationship with God. My mom expressed a big fear of dying and going to hell. I blamed the Catholic Church and my grandmother for her erroneous beliefs about going to hell because I left the church. I agonized over her fear of hell because I wanted her to know that my actions had no bearing on her salvation. I prayed for her frequently that she would come to understand what faith in Jesus was all about and learn that she would be "saved by faith, not by works." However, she never seemed to grasp the ideas we would discuss. She was interested in finding the same peace she saw in me because she would willingly ask me questions about my faith and church. I didn't push these conversations on my mom. Generally, she would bring up the topic of faith and my interest in attending church. I would then use the opportunity to share the Gospel of Jesus Christ with her.

The Sunday morning of my baptism dawned. The time came for the baptism. Several people, in addition to me, were baptized. We each had an opportunity to briefly share our "salvation story" before being dunked in the water pool. I briefly shared the night beside my bed when I prayed for Jesus to come into my life. I briefly shared that I had put God through all these tests to prove he was real. I shared that I had grown in my faith since then, and now I wanted to proclaim my faith publicly. Then, I was baptized. My mom waited for me after the service while I changed out of my wet clothes into something dry. While she waited, Faith kept her company. When I found them both in the crowd, she was glad to see me and told me how proud she was of me. I was surprised. I wasn't sure what to expect. As we drove home, we talked about the service and baptism. She told me she was glad I found a faith and a church that worked for me. She did explain that she didn't want to attend church with me regularly. I was disappointed but not surprised.

Chapter Twenty-One: How to Find Peace

"To give light to them that sit in darkness and the shadow of death, to guide our feet into the way of peace"

-Luke 1:79 KJV.

During my sophomore year in college, I continued volunteering on Wednesday nights in the AWANA program. This was my second year volunteering in AWANA, and I was asked to lead a group like Faith. The number of middle school students attending AWANA had increased, so there were enough students for two groups. I felt proud to be asked and looked forward to the opportunity; it would help me as I was studying to be a teacher. I had always wanted to be a teacher since I proudly declared such to my kindergarten teacher outside a Meijer grocery store one day when my mom and I saw her leaving the store as we entered. I was five at the time. I always knew I wanted to teach. Women during the early 1980s didn't seem to have opportunities for a career. I recall being told that women could be nurses, secretaries, or teachers. At least I chose a female profession.

My helper was a Baptist College student like I had been the

previous year. Her name was Deb. She began attending our church each Sunday beginning in August, just after the college semester had started. She lived in the college dorms and came to the church on the church bus that ran to the college each Sunday and Wednesday. In time, Deb, Faith, and I became good friends. Deb would go out with us on Wednesday nights for dinner after AWANA. Then Faith or I would drive Deb back to the college.

The more I got to know Deb, the more I felt drawn to her. I wanted to spend more time with her and get to know her. I liked her a lot. She had played basketball in high school, and as we talked, we realized that we had played against each other during a district final. She lived in a city near my parents' cottage at Hess Lake. She had no car while living on campus, so she spent the weekends around campus. Consequently, she began to hang out on Sundays with Faith and I to pass the time.

Soon, I started having feelings for Deb as I had for Julie. I became bewildered. I thought my time with Julie was just a phase that had passed. I often prayed and asked God to take away my feelings toward Deb. I would imagine myself kissing her and holding her. I would then feel overwhelming guilt feelings. I would pray more. Soon, I would begin to memorize Bible verses that I would quote back to myself when I found my mind wondering and "lusting" after Deb. I had come to label these feelings and fantasies "sin." I believed Satan was trying to help me "backslide" in my faith journey. I was taught to stay close to God to resist sin. To fight the "temptation" I felt, I prayed, studied, and memorized Bible verses. All this energy and effort was exhausting.

As the end of the fall semester neared, Deb shared with me that she would be transferring to Calvin College to complete her nursing program. Calvin College was five miles south of Baptist College, so she would still be in town. She also told me she would not be volunteering to help in AWANA. I was sad. I was also worried that I would never see her again. Granted, Calvin College was only five miles south of the Baptist College, but I wouldn't begin taking courses there until next fall. Baptist College had a joint teacher education program with Calvin College, so I would be taking my teaching classes at Calvin. I had been considering transferring to Calvin like many friends did because we all learned it was easier to get our education classes if we transferred.

Despite being sad at Deb's news, I prayed to God, thanking him for removing the temptation from me. I saw this as an answer to prayer. I was bothered that I kept wrestling with feelings toward girls. While it was confusing, I considered it Satan's way of testing my faith. Through my Bible studies, I learned that the Apostle Paul had a "thorn in the flesh." The Apostle Paul wrote, "And lest I should be exalted above measure through the abundance of the revelations, there was given to me a thorn in the flesh, the messenger of Satan to buffet me, lest I should be exalted above measure" (2 Corinthians 2:7, KJV). While scripture does not say what the thorn in the flesh was, Paul chose to remain close to God. I took my feelings toward Deb and my previous physical relationship with Julie as fads and a thorn in the flesh. All I needed to do was stay close to God, and in time, I would grow enough in my faith that I would not experience these temptations.

I decided to transfer to Calvin College a semester earlier during Christmas break. I spent a day at Calvin registering for courses and touring the campus. In talking with the advisor, she mentioned that I could finish my degree program in four years if I transferred during the spring rather than waiting until the fall semester. The advisor explained that Calvin offered more courses in my major each semester than Baptist College and that I could take five rather than four each semester. I found four classes more manageable and was willing to take five each semester to finish my degree in four years. After meeting with my advisor, I went to the admission office, completed an application, and transferred there.

The spring semester was beautiful because I started taking education courses immediately, which I found extremely interesting. Additionally, I had completed most of my general education courses to begin taking upper-level history courses, which counted toward my social studies major. I enjoyed being at Calvin College. One day, I saw a notice calling anyone interested in trying out for the women's softball to make an appointment with Coach Walters. So, I made an appointment and met her. I asked about playing softball and what that required. She explained the requirements, asked about my academic standing and grades, and invited me to the tryouts. After a week-long tryout, I made the team.

Playing softball at Calvin was terrific. I met so many great friends. I was a pitcher and was third in line behind two All-Americans. I still had plenty of opportunities to play because I could hit. At the same time, I pitched during our non-conference games and continued to play during conference play because I could hit. I often hit fourth or fifth as the designated hitter. We had a great year and made it to the NAIA final four, where we lost in the opening game and finished fourth. Several of my teammates were studying to be teachers, too.

Consequently, I was able to see my teammates during classes as well. I felt more at home at Calvin than I did at Baptist College. I wondered why I hadn't known about Calvin College in high school. I figured I would have decided to attend there rather than Baptist College. I concluded that because I attended a Bible church, I knew of both religious colleges, Grand Rapids Baptist College and Grand Rapids School of the Bible and Music, where Brenda had attended.

Only those two Baptist colleges offered me an opportunity to become a teacher, so I chose that college.

The season and semester ended, and I was back working for my fourth straight summer at the collection agency. I was a regular there now. In my first few weeks of the summer, when I could work full-time, I got them caught up with filing and typing collection letters, only to leave for college and return to get them caught up again. This summer, a few new collectors were working at the agency. One of the collectors had recently relocated from Colorado to Grand Rapids. He was funny and had an outgoing personality. At night my mom would frequently talk about work and call him gay-boy periodically. The way she said it and talked about him seemed very judgmental, something I didn't see in my mom very often. She never told me to stay away from him or led me to believe he was a bad person; just how she talked about him made me wonder what it was about him that she didn't like.

Working full day allowed me to have a lunch hour. The office staff staggered their hour lunches always to have someone answering the phones and receiving people who might walk in. I found that I enjoyed our brief lunch hour because I was being treated like a regular employee and got to know each of the other employees. Several collectors were trying to set me up with friends on dates. Finally, one mentioned that her best friend had just begun working for a lawyer in town and thought I should meet this guy. Finally, after endless teasing, I consented to go to lunch with her and her friend and this guy they wanted me to meet. After a couple of weeks, I was told I would go to lunch the following Monday and meet someone who had just started a law practice after passing the bar. They explained they asked him to meet me because I was considering attending law school, and they thought he might help me better understand what to think about. They weren't wrong, but I sense they somewhat embellished the story.

Monday came, and we met for lunch. I was introduced to Dan. Dan had just passed the bar exam the previous summer and was about to celebrate his first anniversary of starting his law practice. The premise of having lunch was that I wanted to learn more about what was involved in law school because I was thinking about attending one. It was true that I was thinking about law school, but that is not why they told me I was coming to lunch. The girls hoped Dan and I would hit it off and perhaps date. While nervous, meeting Dan for the first time was easier than expected. Attending college had been good for me. My painful shyness as a young child had given way to a mild shyness. I was becoming more confident in social settings and becoming comfortable meeting people.

Lunch came and went. I spent Monday afternoon fielding endless questions about how lunch went and what I thought of Dan. The rest of the week was routine, except people asked me daily if I had heard from Dan since Monday. I hadn't heard from Dan and didn't give it much thought. However, when the following Monday dawned, and I hadn't heard from Dan, I wondered if I would ever hear from him again. I was interested in seeing him again because I felt we had much in common and found him interesting to talk with. So, I invented a reason and called him at his law office. I explained that a friend and I had planned to go to the Detroit Tigers game this Friday, but now she couldn't. I explained that I was calling to see if he wanted to go in her place. I was pleasantly surprised when he said sure. We planned to meet on Friday. Now, I had to buy the tickets. I guess I had never considered that I might be unable to purchase tickets, a fact my mother pointed out later when I told her the story. Thankfully, tickets were available on a Will Call basis. We had a good laugh and just waited for Friday to come. I wondered if he ever suspected because if my friend and I had been planning to go, wouldn't we have had the tickets in hand already?

Come Friday, Dan picked me up at 4:00 pm at the collection agency since I always rode to work with my mom to save gas. We drove to Detroit for the 7:00 pm game with the Orioles. Indeed, I thought it was a risky date because it was a two-and-a-half-hour drive to the game, a three-hour game, and then a two-and-a-half-hour drive back. It would have been a long night had we discovered our first positive impression at lunch didn't carry over into our first actual date. However, I found that Dan was straightforward to talk with. We had much in common, from our love of the Detroit Tigers to history, politics, and running. After completing my teaching degree, I was also interested in attending law school as a backup plan because I was worried I might not find a teaching job. So, we did talk more about what it was like to go to law school and prepare for the bar exam. I asked about the importance of attending law school in a state where one might want to practice. We discussed the difference between being a generalist and specializing in a type of law. I even asked if it was realistic to plan to work during law school or whether the demands of studying would be too much to consider working. The night went smoothly, and he was dropping me off at home before I knew it.

As usual, my mother was waiting up when I arrived at home. I sat on the living room couch to talk with her about the night. She had met Dan several times previously as he had done legal work for the collection agency. She was glad to see that I was dating. She knew I had dated a few guys in high school and one guy my first year in college, but she, like my grandmother, didn't think I would ever get married. She felt I was far more independent and seeking to get too much college education that no man would ever want to marry me. After discussing the night, the game, and my impressions of Dan, I politely excused myself and headed for my bedroom. I fell into bed with little thought of the night.

Dan and I continued to date throughout the summer and fall. When I returned to Calvin for the fall semester, I began preparing for another spring softball season. Our softball coach provided each of us with a training plan that included conditioning, weight training, and suggested softball drills. We could go to the gym and spend some time in the batting cage, hitting off a pitching machine. Being a pitcher, most of my drills focused on getting better at pitching. Faith continued to be my catcher during the fall and winter after AWANA and sometimes on Sunday nights after the service as I prepared to make the team for a second year. In addition to attending classes, I would work about 20 hours a week and save every penny to afford to play softball, which would require me not to work. The owner of the collection agency was very supportive and allowed me to take time off during softball season and then return in the summer and work full-time. I didn't realize it then, but he was very flexible with my time, allowing me to be in school, play softball, and count on a job. To play softball, I had to take out student loans for the spring semester to cover my tuition, buy books, and have enough money to commute from home to school and back. My parents helped by allowing me to live at home and ensuring I had the type of food I could pack for the day so I didn't have to spend any money. They also paid my car insurance for the first six months of the year, which was a big help. I was so busy that I didn't spend money on movies or other activities.

I would talk to Dan about my faith in Jesus on our dates. He was a practicing Catholic, trying to understand the difference between my church and the Catholic Church like my mother. Eventually, I explained that I was not sure I could continue to see him because I believed that if two people were going to marry one day, they had to be of the same faith, so there was no conflict when raising children into one religion. I used my parents as an example. My mother was Catholic, and my dad was Methodist. I was raised in neither faith until my parents divorced. By then, I had left the church and made my own decision.

Dan agreed to attend Bible study with me on Wednesday if I attended church on Saturday night with him. I agreed. Before long and after several meetings with his priest, Dan determined he'd instead participate and attend church with me. Finally, one night, on a date, he explained that he had prayed and asked Jesus to come into his heart. I was thrilled. I was so excited that he had come to believe in Jesus and wanted to adopt my church.

As Christmas approached, I agonized over what to give him for a present. Finally, I settled on a Bible. I went to Zondervan Christian Book Store and carefully picked out a Bible. I had it engraved with his name. I was so proud of the gift. I was excited that he was interested in learning more about his new faith in Christ. On Sundays and Wednesdays, when he attended church with me, we would share my Bible so he could look at the verses and passages Pastor Owens referenced. I remember doing the same thing with Brenda when I first attended church. I also remember being so excited when I saved up enough money to buy my Bible and begin reading it each night. Like other books, I would highlight verses that spoke to me or make notations on the blank pages to remember an essential idea I heard from the pastor. Even today, after replacing several of my Bibles with new Bibles, I continue to highlight important verses. I believe this is what is meant by the Bible being the living Word of God. As time passes, the same verses take on new meanings based on the context of the moment.

Dan and I planned to attend a Christmas show in downtown Grand Rapids the weekend before Christmas. After the show, we had plans for dinner at my favorite restaurant, Charlie's Crab. The Christmas show featured Andy Williams and the old Christmas classics. I loved the traditional Christmas music. It had been part of our family celebrations for as long as I could remember. After the show, we went to Charlie's Crab for dinner. As we waited for our dinner, I pulled out his Christmas gift and asked him to open it. He was thrilled with his Bible. We discussed how the Bible was organized and how to use the concordance in the back. He was truly touched.

After dinner, he reached into his pocket and pulled out a little box. As he handed it to me, he asked me to marry him. I was stunned. I didn't see this coming. I didn't know what to say, so I said yes. I expressed "yes" outwardly but felt nothing on the inside. I spent the next thirty minutes trying to fake happiness and confidence. I don't remember what we talked about after he gave me the ring, asked me to marry him, and I said yes.

On the one hand, I was happy someone loved me this much to ask me to marry him, but on the other hand, I had no idea if I wanted to make any lifetime decisions. When the waiter brought the dessert and coffee, I couldn't consume them quickly enough. I just wanted to leave, go home, and pray for wisdom. I was a bit freaked out.

Dan dropped me off at home. I entered the house and was relieved that my mom wasn't waiting for me. I couldn't remember the last time that had happened. I was worried she was sick but remembered they had to get up early on Saturday. I quietly headed to bed, avoiding the conversation with my mom that I knew we needed to have. She always asked me about my day or night. I always enjoyed sharing my activities and friends with her, but I wasn't ready to have this conversation. I walked into my room, shut the door lightly, and turned on the light. I pulled the little box out of my pocket, took the ring off my finger, and put it back in the box. I was happy that I didn't have to explain to my parents, at least then, that Dan had asked me to marry him and that I didn't know if that was what I wanted.

I lay in bed, not knowing what to think, so I prayed. I asked God for guidance and direction. I don't know when I finally fell asleep. I had spent the entire time trying to decide if I should give back the ring or not. I tried to figure out if I was in love or not. I wanted to talk myself into getting married. I tried to talk myself out of getting married. I tried to figure out why I didn't know what was right or what I wanted in life. I knew my family expected me to marry, but I wasn't sure about myself. Little did I realize that this was just the first of many sleepless nights pondering whether I should get married. I remembered my grandmother's words about the only hope a girl had was to find a kind guy who would provide for her. I thought about how fussy my mom was about my friends and how I doubted she would find any man I was interested in acceptable. I was aware she liked Dan. Even my aunts, Sally and Sylvia, liked Dan. I also knew I didn't feel the same way toward Dan as I did toward Julie. I had loved Julie, so I concluded that I likely didn't love Dan. However, I did enjoy his company. The one person whose thoughts I didn't know was my dad.

Chapter Twenty-Two: To Do or Not to Do, That Is the Question

"My confusion is continually before me, and the shame of my face hath covered me"

-Psalms 44:15 KJV.

"For where envying and strife is, there is confusion and every evil work"

-James 3:16 KJV.

I never heard my parents leave the house Saturday morning. They were heading to the lake for the weekend. When I awoke, it was nearing noon. As I went to the kitchen for breakfast, I was relieved I had the day to myself. I needed to think and figure out what I wanted concerning marriage and my relationship with Dan. I needed the time to think. As I ate, I decided to call Faith and meet her for dinner. I wanted to talk with her. My parents would be home Sunday, and I knew I needed to be settled on what I would do and say before they got home. They knew I had gone out with

Dan, and I was going to give him his present, and they would likely ask me if he had given me a gift. I wasn't the type who would lie, and I knew my parents understood me enough that if I had tried to be less than forthcoming, they would see right through me. I knew Faith would help me talk through the situation.

I met her at Fables for dinner. We ordered our usual burgers, fries, and a soda. I didn't feel like eating and shared with her about Dan's proposal; it was clear that she wasn't eating either. As we talked, she raised red flag after red flag. They were the same I had raised the night before. She fed into my fears, too. Dan was 14 years older than me; we had only dated for six months; I still had two years of college left; I was only 20; and he was a new Christian. My anxiety grew. On one hand, that was reassuring because I felt like I was thinking clearly.

Faith was surprised that he had asked me to marry him so soon. She asked me if I had seen it coming. I told her no. She asked about my reply. I said yes because I didn't know what to say and didn't want to hurt him. I continued by explaining that Dan and I had just started discussing what we wanted in our futures. I told her I had even told Dan I wasn't sure if I would find a teaching job and that I was contemplating going to law school and likely wouldn't have time for a serious relationship. He took these conversations to be hypothetical. I didn't think anything I said to him signaled that I was ready to settle down, let alone settle down with him. I continued discussing whether we wanted children and, if so, how many. I explained that neither of us was sure we wanted children. We discussed where we wanted to live, places to visit, and things to do. I don't remember ever thinking I had talked about a lot, specifically with him, because I was still figuring out what I wanted out of life. I knew I wanted to teach. I knew I wanted to travel. I knew that I might want to get involved in politics one day. I shared that I might wish to have two children one day because being an only child was no fun. I couldn't recall ever saying that I wanted that to include him. I enjoyed being with him. He was a great friend. I saw him like a brother. I loved being able to talk with him and share things with him. Some days, I thought I felt more for Faith than Dan.

Wait! Dare I say that? These were the thoughts swirling in my mind as Faith was talking. Finally, I realized she was asking me a question.

"Do you love him?" Faith asked.

I looked at her, and just as it seemed she would ask again, I finally said, "I don't know."

She looked relieved. I started to cry from frustration. I didn't see that coming, either. I wasn't an emotional person. She reached for my hand and just held it for a minute. Eventually, I composed myself, and we finished dinner, or at least what we would eat of the food we ordered. We left Fables and headed to my house to watch television and hang out.

It was nice having the house to myself. Faith and I headed to the basement to play a vigorous game of Ping-Pong. She was the one person who could give me a competitive game. Most of our games were won by one point and after repeated ties. Before we knew it, it was getting late. We headed upstairs, grabbed a soda, and sat on the couch. I turned on the eleven o'clock news. We replayed the Ping-Pong games while sipping soda. At this point, we were each trying to outdo the other with trash-talking; I loved the athletic camaraderie. During one of the pauses in our conversation, Faith looked at me and asked, "How are you doing now?"

The question did not fit the context. "I'm good," I responded.

"You are happy. I want you to be happy," Faith continued. I just looked at her.

She continued, "I am worried you won't be happy if you marry Dan." She caught me off guard with this statement.

"Why do you think I won't be happy," I asked. A long pause ensued. Faith was weighing her words.

"Because he is not your type," she said. She leaned over to kiss me. I pulled back.

"Whoa! I can't go there", I said.

She was stunned and embarrassed. "I love you, Renay, and I can't stand to see you get hurt."

"I love you too, Faith. I'm not going to get hurt. I just am confused right now. I'm just not ready to get married. I just don't know what I want right now, that's all".

"Whatever you decide, please take your time. You have a lot to figure out. You need to figure yourself out first. There is no reason to hurry to get married".

We finished our soda, and Faith said she had to leave. I walked her to the front door, and she paused. She reached out and hugged me. She held me for what seemed like a long moment. She then looked at me and said, "I love you, friend." She quickly kissed my cheek and let herself out.

I watched her walk to her car. After she drove away, I shut and locked the door. I was in for another sleepless night. Sunday dawned, and I was off to church. As usual, I met Faith there. Dan wasn't attending church with me today because he spent time with this family. I had skipped Sunday school, and that had worried her. We sat together during the sermon, and I explained to her that I hadn't slept well that night, so I skipped Sunday school. After the sermon, we talked briefly while we sat in her car. I asked her to pray for me while I wrestled with this decision. Then I headed home.

I was pulling into the driveway when my parents pulled in from their weekend at the cottage. I was glad to see them and helped them unload the car. I then sat in the living room and told them about my date on Friday. After describing the Christmas show in more detail than anyone wanted to know, along with the meal we had at Charlie's Crab, I finally told how Dan reacted to my gift of the Bible. My mom couldn't wait any longer and immediately asked what Dan had gotten me for Christmas. I told her he had asked me to marry him and show her the ring he gave me as I pulled it out of my pocket and opened the box. Her immediate reaction was very positive. She was so glad to hear that we were getting married. She didn't even ask me if I had said yes. She just assumed I had said yes. My father, on the other hand, was taciturn and reserved. I explained to them both that I had reservations and that while I had said yes to Dan, I had doubts. My mom began to tell me why Dan was a great man, the type of man that would be good to me. He was hard-working, kind, stable, mature, and loving. My father remained quiet. Finally, he asked if we had picked a date for the wedding. I explained that we had not chosen a date yet. Everything inside me was telling me to run.

Nothing about the conversation with my parents was reassuring for me. My mom had made good points about Dan as a provider and a good man, just the type of man a woman could want. Dan was a great guy. So, if Dan was such a great guy, why did I have such cold feet? Did I have cold feet because I didn't believe that the only reason to get married was to have a man take care of me and have children? I was raised to be independent and had never given much thought to needing a man to care for me. I didn't even consider having anyone take care of me, for that matter. My dad was not as enthusiastic and even antagonistic toward me marrying Dan. What did my dad see that I didn't see? Neither of my parents mentioned the age difference during our conversations. Only five years separated them. My dad never sought me out to talk about what he thought. Looking back now, I often wonder if my father couldn't speak to me about his thoughts because he knew the divorce still hurt me. My mom's reaction was so positive that it was off-putting and prevented me from talking to her about my feelings.

Dan came over later that Sunday afternoon, and we went to church together in the evening. When he arrived, my mom quickly greeted him at the door. She gave him a big hug and congratulated him. She was very excited about the idea that Dan and I would get married. Her reaction didn't make the situation any easier for me. I was glad to see him. We didn't hang around long and then went off to church. Folks at church noticed the ring, and it was not long until several observant friends congratulated us. I found myself having to share our news. I started to tell myself that I just had a good case of nerves and soon I would be okay with all this. I realized that the more people learned about Dan's proposal, the harder it was for me to walk away. I had considered not wearing the ring, but I wasn't sure what I would tell Dan. This entire situation was more significant than me, and I was unprepared to navigate the situation. Looking back, it was clear that every decision I made dug a deeper hole from which I couldn't crawl out.

As the Christmas holiday came and went, my family embraced the news of our engagement. We hadn't set a date yet, and I'm not sure I had ever really considered what time of year I wanted to get married. I wasn't the type of little girl who dreamed about my wedding or being married. Getting married was something that just seemed like a natural and normal thing that people did, but I didn't give it much thought until now. While several of my friends had often spoken about when they would get married, such views were far from my mind. I remember my grandmother's reaction most clearly. As a young girl, she often told me that she didn't think she would live to see me get married. I figured it was because I hadn't been dating much, and she was teasing me about being too busy for guys. She congratulated me and said she was happy for me and looking forward to the wedding. She then said, "I'm glad you proved me wrong and that I would get to see you get married." This conversation would haunt me as the day of the wedding approached.

I was glad when the Christmas break ended and the school reopened. I was looking forward to beginning the workouts for softball. When classes started, I was delighted several teammates were in some of my classes. That was great fun because I would have friends I could talk to between classes. I was surprised to learn that two teammates had also engaged during Christmas. Brenda and Sharon were so excited about their engagement I certainly enjoyed the excitement they shared—somehow, having two other teammates who were also getting married, normalized marriage. Our other teammates would tease the three of us and play songs to celebrate our love for our fiancé. Somehow, all this bantering made getting married feel like a good thing, the right thing.

Dan and I set our wedding date for August 6th. We began planning the wedding. My mom and her sister, Sally, enjoyed countless weekend afternoons talking with me as we planned the event. We went to shops to find a suitable dress, met with a florist, and picked out invitations. I knew a band I wanted to play, so I contacted them. We made sure to get a good start on the plans because I would begin full-team softball practices early in February, and by the first week of March, we would start our season. At that point, my weekends generally consisted of traveling to games and, when I was home, studying for my classes and attending church. I was only a junior in college, but I needed to stay on track to complete the necessary courses for my degree to be ready to student-teach in the spring term of my senior year. With my student-teaching being scheduled for the spring of my senior year, I wanted to enjoy this year of softball competition as it may be my last. I was unsure if I could play softball my senior year because of my student-teaching.

Dan enjoyed being involved in planning the details of the wedding. We secured the reception hall and the band. We struggled with how to accommodate our very different friends and family. My mom's Polish Catholic family would be expecting a band and a bar at the reception, meaning that, at a minimum, they expected beer and wine. So, too, would Dan's family. Our friends and church family would not approve of a band and any drinking but would come for dinner if drinks weren't served. While such activities were not forbidden at Calvin College, like Baptist College previously, many of my softball family were split on such matters. I never knew planning a wedding would be stressful and involve so much drama.

Rarely did I give the engagement a second thought after the initial weeks of doubts. I was caught up with all the planning for the wedding. I figured that my early doubts were nothing more than nerves. During softball practices, the team often teased Brenda, Sharon, and me about our engagements. When our teammates were serious, they would ask us about the details of our wedding, and they all seemed to enjoy hearing about those plans. We were all planning for a summer or fall wedding. All our teammates were planning on attending each of our weddings. Between practices, I would teach my teammates to dance to the polka. My mother's family was very good at dancing it, and the band we had chosen would be more than happy to ensure they played plenty of those. My teammates were all looking forward to the reception.

Faith continued to be one of my consistent sounding boards.

We were close friends, but she continued to doubt my engagement. I listened attentively and would leave our conversations questioning myself. Often, I attributed her doubts to fear or jealousy. I could not help but think of the moments when our closeness reminded me of my relationship with Julie. I wondered if she wished we were more than friends. My doubts and questions about Faith kept me from seeing what she saw when we talked. She was more in tune with my doubts about getting married than I was. However, it was easy for me to dismiss her doubts because I felt she wanted more from me than being a friend. Therefore, I felt like she was trying to get Dan and me to break up.

As college softball season gained momentum, I spent less time with Dan and Faith. Between practice, games, and studying, I kept plenty busy. In March, the softball team would travel to Florida for spring training. The weather in Michigan in early March was unpredictable. Consequently, much of our non-conference season began in Florida. We would drive 21 hours straight in two vans. The players and coaches took turns driving. We would stop for gas and fast food, but the goal was to get to Lakeland, Florida. I had two aunts and uncles who lived in our church camp. They would visit our cabins several times and come to our games to cheer us on. It was fantastic having a couple of relatives come and watch. They watched more of my games over two spring break trips to Florida than my parents or Dan did. During spring break, our team would spend a day at Disney World. We also watched the Detroit Tigers play an exhibition game, once in Lakeland and once in another city nearby.

Dan prepared income taxes during the spring like he did throughout our marriage. I was playing college softball and didn't realize how much time he spent working during the spring. I often wonder if I had known how much he worked during the spring if it would have set off an alarm bell in my head. The times I spent with Dan during the spring were few but fun after both taxes and softball season.

We asked Pastor Owens to marry us, and he required us to attend marriage counseling for several weeks. We began meeting him on Sunday nights after church as part of our marriage preparation. Those conversations solidified that Dan was a great Christian and I was doing the right thing. I remember getting a book from Pastor Owens about God's design for marriage. While I don't know much about the book, I remember the chapter about God's plan for sex in marriage. I do remember thinking that sex was important in marriage, and it was something I was looking forward to. However, I was becoming aware that I wasn't sure if I wanted to be a mother. I kept wondering if I would parent like my mom did. I found she was worried about everything and, as a result, was very restrictive and even made me worry about things. I didn't want to be a parent like my mom, but I understood I overthought and worried about many things. Nothing during those sessions caused me to worry or question getting married. As spring progressed and the wedding plans came along, I had fewer doubts about my decision to marry Dan.

The spring semester at Calvin and softball season ended all too soon. We won our conference and our district tournament. We finished second at our regional tournament, so the season ended sooner than we wanted. It was great. I decided to take a summer class to ease my class load in the fall as I prepared for my student-teaching in the spring semester. My summer class began on the first of June. My friend, Cheryl from softball, was also taking the course. Summer classes were fun, and the tone of the class was a bit more casual. The workload seemed heavy as we had to accomplish the same amount of work in half the time. The course met Monday through Thursday from 8 to noon. After the class, several of us would go to lunch to talk about educational psychology. After lunch, one day, one of my coursemates walked me to my car.

Jim was friendly, and I enjoyed talking with him during lunch. As we stopped by my car, he asked me what I was doing this weekend. I was caught a bit off guard, and then I suddenly realized he was asking me out. I explained that I would enjoy seeing him but that I was engaged. He persisted and said half-jokingly and half-seriously, "Until you are married, I have a chance." He was very understanding when I turned him down. I didn't think much more about the moment. As I lay in bed that night, I began to think about Jim's question. I was flattered that he asked me out. I wondered about him and what it would be like to date him. These thoughts brought a whole new set of doubts to mind. What if I was hurrying into this marriage thing? I quickly dismissed the ideas and fell asleep.

After class, I worked at the collection agency from 1:00 to 5:00 pm. While I only worked four hours daily, the money was being put away for my tuition in the fall. This was the first summer since my high school senior year that I wasn't working full-time at the collection agency. The girls at the collection agency were all teasing me about the wedding. My mom had already invited all of them. I had come to enjoy working with them. Afternoons at work flew by.

Dan and I frequently spent weekends together in the months leading up to the wedding. We enjoyed times at the beach and the lake visiting my parents. We spent time talking about either buying a house or renting an apartment. He would come to watch me play softball during the week as I played on Tuesday nights with several of my teammates from college. The more we talked about our future, the more doubts began to creep back into my mind. In June, my maternal grandmother was diagnosed with leukemia and died later in the month. Unfortunately, her belief that she wouldn't live to see me get married came true.

One Saturday in early July, I was up early. I had just finished a good run and was sitting at the kitchen table winding down before a shower. My mom entered the kitchen, poured coffee, and sat at the table with me. I began to share with her my doubts about getting married. I asked her if she had cold feet before she married my dad for the first time. She shared that she didn't but was sure many people occasionally have a second thought or two. While she extolled Dan's virtues, she did hear my doubts this time. Finally, after a good talk, she said, "Honey, if you have concerns, you might want to share them with Dan."

She had a point. I hadn't ever shared with Dan that I was having second thoughts. My mom suggested I shouldn't continue forward if I weren't ready. While many of our plans had been made and dresses ordered, things could be postponed or canceled. With that said, I headed to the shower. As the water poured over me, I felt a relief I hadn't felt in a while. I concluded that I had to talk to Dan about my doubts.

Later that afternoon, Dan picked me up. We had planned a day in Grand Haven, one of my favorite locations in West Michigan. I contemplated bringing up my concerns and decided to wait until we were in Grand Haven. We parked in downtown Grand Haven and walked up the main street hand in hand. The main street was lined with many different shops and eateries. I had become familiar with the city as it was one of my favorite places to bring Julie. We selected a restaurant for lunch and sat down. We ordered and began to chat about the Tigers and other topics that had become common when we were together.

"Dan, what if we get a divorce after being married for ten

years?" Indeed, this question came out of the blue. I could see that he was a bit puzzled. He told me that just because my parents had gotten a divorce didn't mean we would. After several futile attempts to bring up the topic, I finally spilled my guts.

"Dan, I'm having doubts about getting married."

There, I said it. I felt relieved. It was almost like putting the truth on the table and somehow lifting a burden off my shoulders.

"What?" Dan said. He looked at me for a moment. "When did this start?"

I explained that I had wrestled with these feelings since our engagement. As I shared my journey, he got increasingly agitated. We had never fought or disagreed, so I was still determining what to expect. Our lunch came somewhere between my doubts about the engagement and coming to terms with being married. It also sat untouched as I continued to explain the last several months of doubts.

"You need to make a decision, Renay," Dan said. "You must decide whether you are getting married if you have these doubts." The gauntlet had been dropped. The ball was now in my court. We finished lunch and headed home much earlier than originally planned. Dan dropped me off at the door. He didn't come in and was rather cold and withdrawn on the drive home. What else could I have expected?

"Call me when you have decided," he said as I closed the door.

He then drove off. I wanted to celebrate and dance. I wanted to cry. I wanted to crawl into bed and sleep. I strolled into the house. My mom was in the kitchen, surprised to see me home soon. She wasn't expecting me for a few more hours. She asked if everything was ok. I explained that Dan wasn't feeling well, so we came home early. I headed to my bedroom to change. Next, I called Faith. We agreed to meet at Fables for a talk.

My mom never asked me if I had shared my doubts with Dan. I wonder if she had already figured out that was why I was home earlier than initially planned. She was highly intuitive sometimes.

As I headed out, my mom asked where I was going and how I could have made plans so quickly after just getting home. She again asked if everything was okay. I told her everything was fine and I was meeting Faith for dinner since I was home early. I told her that I didn't expect to be late. I left the house, got in my car, and drove to Fables. I sensed a relief I hadn't experienced in months as I drove toward the restaurant. By the time I arrived at Fables, I was sure I was okay, but looking forward to reassurance from Faith. I expected that once I had expressed my doubts to Dan, I would never really have to face the situation again. Perhaps I was hoping that he would bail on the marriage. I'm unsure, but I wanted a way out and sought someone to give me that off-ramp.

Faith and I grabbed a soda and headed for our booth. Oddly enough, it was the booth Julie and I often took during our visits to Fables. I carefully explained to her about the past several months and my conversation with Dan earlier. She listened attentively, and I could see her compassion and care. By the time I reached the part when Dan said I should call him when I had figured everything out, she had tears in her eyes. She explained her concerns for me and how she was glad I took this time to consider the decision. She explained what she had observed over the past several months. She explained how she could see my conflict from time to time. She also mentioned that she noticed that I would run from my feelings by planning the wedding or keeping busy with school and softball.

I found myself agreeing with her. I also found myself explaining to her that I was worried about how I would tell my bride's mates and others. I also worried about the money people had paid. I explained how I felt like a failure—hours passed while we talked. I poured my heart out to her in a way I had never done before. I felt like I had let her into my deepest thoughts and fears. Finally, we agreed to go for a drive as we were worried that the restaurant owners would kick us out. We got into Faith's car and headed for an overlook near downtown. We continued to talk as we drove.

When we got to the overlook, it was dark. The lights of the city were shining bright. I wish I had brought my camera. The park was a popular spot for people to come and look over the city. Several cars were parked along the curb. We sat and continued to talk. As we did, Faith reached for my hand and held it while I began to share my fears about telling people that the wedding was off. As I thought through my next steps, including telling Dan I didn't want to see him again, I began to cry. Faith reached over and held me. The safety and comfort I felt then allowed the tears to flow. They were tears of relief and sadness. They were tears of regret and fear. At that moment, I felt every emotion I could imagine.

Finally, there was nothing left in my heart or head. My tears had left me limp. As she held me, she sensed my wrestling give way to abandon. I gave up struggling. She leaned in and began to kiss me. I didn't resist. I longed to be loved in that moment when I felt like a failure and alone. The intimacy was sweet and tender. She continued to hold me for a while. We sat in silence. There was nothing left to say. I never remember Dan holding me like that. I never remember him tenderly kissing me. Kissing him felt awkward and forced, not natural and sweet. Whenever I tried to speak to him about my feelings, he just turned to logic. It felt dismissive and judgmental. Our age difference made it look more parental than rationale. I think I knew what I wanted and found it with at least two women, but I figured it was prohibited and not likely to be found with any man.

We drove in silence back to my car parked at Fables. Faith continued to hold my hand. I didn't want to leave that night, but as I exited the car, I thanked her for being there for me. She assured me that she would be there anytime I needed. I got in my car and drove home.

Chapter Twenty-Three:
I Do

"For this cause shall a man leave his father and mother and be joined unto his wife, and they two shall be one flesh"

-Ephesians 5:31 KJV.

The next day was Sunday. I skipped church. I wasn't ready to share the news that the wedding was off. I was in avoidance mode. My parents planned to go to my grandparents on Sunday afternoon for a cookout. I decided to go with them. I didn't consider that everyone there would be asking me about the wedding. I think I was expecting my mom to tell everyone the news. Again, I was looking for an off-ramp and to be bailed out. I didn't want to face the consequences of the mess I had made. Typically, I didn't shy away from taking responsibility, but I knew I couldn't explain to people why I wanted an off-ramp with this situation. I couldn't imagine that anyone in my life would think my being attracted to other women was a good reason to cancel a wedding to someone so amazing. I could imagine my family saying that once I got married, I would realize that sex with a man was terrific. Yet, I had never heard my aunts or mom speak positively of sex. I had my doubts.

I rode with my parents to my grandparents' house; I concluded, what better place to try out an idea than one's family? After all, I would have to face the music, eventually own up to the mess I had made, and tell people about my decision to cancel the wedding. I was determined in my heart that I didn't need to share the entire reason why, but only the element about having severe doubts. I figured I wasn't ready to make such a big, life-long commitment. After arriving and allowing for some time for everyone to visit, I saw that my Aunt Sally was alone in the kitchen. I approached her. I braced myself and told her I was canceling the wedding. Her reaction surprised me.

"Well, if you are having second thoughts, then you best not move forward," she said.

We discussed my doubts a bit; she was more supportive than I expected. Now, if the others would only react the same way. My grandparents were surprised. Grandma asked me if I thought I could find someone better. I was trying to understand what that meant. My Aunt Sylvia was horrified. The topic was quickly dropped. I felt humiliated and ashamed.

I spent the afternoon acting as if I was happy and enjoying myself when I wanted to be anywhere other than here. As the afternoon progressed, I felt excommunicated. I wondered if lepers were mistreated like this. My mom tried to smooth over the family's reaction as we drove home. She reminded me of how badly they treated my father after the divorce and how they welcomed him back into the family once they were remarried. She tried to explain that my grandmother and Aunt Sylvia were "old fashioned" and were reacting to their own experiences. The more she talked, the more shame I felt for putting my family through this.

I got home and went for a run. While running, I mulled over the family's reaction. Once home, I showered and got in my car. I wasn't sure where I was going, but I was making sure to leave home before I got into another conversation about the wedding. After an hour of driving aimlessly, I decided to head to Faith's house. I was hoping to catch her before she left for church. I pulled up and knocked on the door. I talked to her parents briefly and headed to her bedroom. She was ready for church.

"How are you doing? I missed you this morning in church."

At that moment, her parents called back and said they were leaving for church and would see us there. I then began to cry. I systematically recounted my horrible experience telling my family that the wedding was off. She listened carefully, holding my hand, and reassuring me that I was doing right. By the time I made it through the description of my day, I had stopped crying. Despite all the reassurance Faith offered me, I began to second-guess myself for calling off the wedding. I just wanted someone to resolve it for me. After a while, I returned to my car and headed home. I was happy it was Sunday night, and I could resume my regular weekly activities. Getting back into my routine could put all this behind me.

As the week progressed, I received no calls or communication from Dan. I didn't expect any, but I was missing talking to him. My initial thought was that I wouldn't miss as much in time. I wasn't planning on ever calling him back. My mom, who was initially supportive, seemed distant. Other than Faith and my family, I hadn't shared my decision not to get married with anyone else. My mom started to push me to let my bridesmaids know so we could cancel the dress orders. The pressure was getting a bit much. So, why was it so hard to let people know the wedding was off when I was feeling so relieved that it was off? I felt like the only person in the world who understood me was Faith.

I spent every evening with Faith. She was the only person supporting me and not pressuring me to call the reception hall, band, or florist. I knew I had to do everything, but I wanted someone to do it. I just wanted the pressure to be over. Each time we got together, I wanted her to hold me. I longed for her touch. It brought comfort. It was reassuring. It felt right. I would then go home and feel guilty.

Finally, Dan called. "Well, have you decided?" he asked.

"Can we get together and talk?" I asked.

"Sure. When?"

"How about dinner this Friday night?" I suggested.

"Ok, I will meet you at Vitales around 6. Will that work?"

"Sure, see you there," I said, then hung up.

I bought myself five days to figure all this out. I knew what was right. However, I didn't want to face the consequences of canceling the wedding. It was to be the longest five days of my life to date. I felt alone. I didn't talk to Faith because I knew where she stood. She wanted me to call it off and be done with him. However, given our growing physical relationship, I was suspicious of her motive. I couldn't talk to my mom because she was cold and distant, and I was afraid I had let her down or hurt her somehow. My mom and I were never good at communicating, so I speculated rather than talk to her. I couldn't help but think she said she was supportive and okay with my decision, but I could tell she wasn't ok with my choices. My father had never really said how he felt one way or the other since the first day I told him I was engaged. Even though I had forgiven my father for the divorce and our relationship had improved, it had not improved enough for me to talk to him like I once had.

Consequently, I never spoke to him about my feelings, and he never told me what he thought. Aunt Sally seemed to understand, but I wasn't taking any chances after last Sunday and how the rest of the family had treated me. It was just me all alone to wrestle with this decision. At that moment, I began to pray.

Prayer has been comforting to me since I discovered prayer as a high school student. I'm not sure I ever believed God spoke to me, but I did talk to God. I used prayer time to pour out my heart and soul. I felt like God knew me best. I spent much of the week reading the Bible and studying about marriage and family. I longed to have a family and permanence in my life. I longed to be loved and be close to someone. I recalled the times I felt close and loved. The times I reflected on when I thought about what I wanted in a relationship were when I was with Julie and Faith. Something I believed was wrong and sinful. Somewhere and at some point, I concluded that God had brought Dan into my life to provide me with the very thing I had prayed for: someone to care for, love me, and share life with. After all, I did enjoy being with him. He had become a best friend. I enjoyed his kisses. I enjoyed it when he held me. Perhaps if I let go and step out on faith, I would find what I wanted so badly. Finally, I resigned myself to go forward with the marriage as scheduled.

I shared with my mom and dad what I had concluded the following day. My mom was delighted. My father was quiet. Later that night, I shared my decision with Dan at Vitalies restaurant, an Italian restaurant close to his law office. I told him I wanted to get married and asked him to forgive me for having doubts and fears. He was excited and happy. By the next day, when he picked me up for a date, it was as if nothing had ever happened. When I told my grandparents that weekend, my grandmother squealed with delight and commented that I would be well cared for and should be very happy.

August 6th arrived. My wedding day finally came. As usual, I was up early and went out for a run. On my way to church, I grabbed my customary Raspberry Danish and coffee from McDonald's. I brought enough for the wedding party. As we dressed in the church, none of the bridesmaids knew about my earlier doubts or that I had paused the wedding while I sorted out my feelings. Deb, Cheryl, and Cindy were all very happy for me. I was glad to be sharing this day with my three friends. Faith had refused to be a bridesmaid, as she said from the first day that she believed I was making a mistake. While I understood her decision, I was sad she didn't share the day with me as a bridesmaid. She did attend the wedding.

People began to arrive at the church. I remained in the back of the church and was ready when the song that was my cue to approach the closed door to the church's main sanctuary started. I slowly walked to the entry door, accompanied by my dad. As we waited for the door to open, he told me he loved me, was proud of me, and was glad Dan and I would be together. I had no doubts that day that getting married to Dan was the right thing to do. When the wedding song began and the door opened, I walked down the aisle to the man who wanted to spend the rest of his life with me. My bridesmaids and 250 other friends and family were there, and all eyes were on me.

The ten o'clock morning wedding lasted 45 minutes. Pastor Gordon was then off to serve in the National Guard training he completed every August. The reception was later in the afternoon. In between, my parents hosted a cookout for my father's family, who had come to Grand Rapids from Northern Michigan for the wedding. They would be staying for the reception and decided to use the opportunity to get together and share each other's company.

Some friends who came to the wedding from different areas around Michigan also joined us at the house. The cookout was a nice, relaxed transition between the formal ceremony and the reception. Dan and I had the opportunity to spend time with my aunts and uncles from out of town. Many had not met Dan before that day. Besides a beautiful meal, we played some outdoor games and told stories. He and I could take a brief nap, knowing we would have a late night. Soon, we were getting ready for the evening reception just five miles from our house.

The reception was a celebratory and fun event. The reception hall was only a few miles north of our house. Dan and I, his parents, and my parents arrived at the reception hall early for a photo session. The photo shoot finished in time for us to greet all our guests as they arrived. This time, it was my turn to meet many of Dan's aunts and uncles for the first time. I enjoyed his parents and did enjoy getting to meet his family. Unlike me, as an only child, Dan had a younger sister. She was delightful, and so was her husband. Dan's aunts and uncles seemed much like my own family, and they certainly knew how to have a good time.

After dinner, the band cued up the customary first dance. As someone who didn't like dancing in gym class, I did enjoy dancing. I spent the summer practicing the slow dance with my father and grandfather. I didn't want to step on Dan's feet too often, and I also wanted to look like I knew what I was doing in front of so many people on his side of the family that I hadn't met before. After dancing with Dan briefly, he went to get his mother, and I went to get my father, and we finished the dance with our parents. I spent the following several dances partnered with the groomsmen and other men from our families. Who knew dancing this much could be great exercise?

This series of planning dances and songs ended with a series of traditions. First, the singles ladies gathered in an area of the reception hall, where they waited for me to throw my bouquet. Just before throwing the bouquet, I was subjected to a series of teasing comments by my softball colleagues about ensuring I didn't overthrow the group, resulting in an error. I was reminded that I wasn't throwing the bouquet from the outfield. Indeed, it was all fun. Next, Dan was required to take a garter off my leg and throw it to the single guys in the room. The band struck up appropriate music while Dan figured out how to lift an elaborate dress, find the garter, and remove it from my leg. Indeed, his groomsmen made several teasing comments. The last tradition involved Dan and I cutting the cake. We had both agreed to be nice to each other when asked to feed each other a piece of cake. I wasn't as nice as I promised. After these traditions, the band began to play again while the cake was distributed among our guests.

Soon, I was dancing the polka with members of my softball team from Calvin College. Since many of my teammates were unfamiliar with the Polish dance, I began teaching it to each girl I danced with. Eventually, the entire team was engaged in dancing the polka. Several of our church family came for dinner but left when the dancing began. Faith had come for dinner and said goodbye before she left. I could tell she was happy for me but worried. I tried to reassure her, but now was not the time for that conversation. Just before midnight, we danced one last dance and headed out for our honeymoon. The months of doubt were behind. I had committed, and I knew how seriously I took an obligation. There was no turning back.

Chapter Twenty-Four: The Married Life

"You will know the truth, and the truth will make you free"

-John 8:32 KJV.

For our honeymoon, Dan and I had planned a two-week trip to the West to see some of the national parks. We had identified some general places to visit, but we planned only a few days of our two-week trip to allow us time to relax or see something we had discovered. Our first destination was a small rental cabin overlooking southern Lake Michigan near South Haven. We arrived very late that Saturday night or what turned out to be very early Sunday morning. I didn't know our plans for our honeymoon's first few days, as Dan said he wanted to surprise me. When we arrived, we were exhausted and barely able to bring our luggage into the cabin. We fell into bed asleep before our heads even hit the pillow.

We spent a few days at the cabin enjoying the walking trails, waterfront, and sunsets. We talked about the next couple of weeks and mapped out some potential sites on our way to the Grand

Canyon, the main national park we wanted to visit. During these conversations, we decided that because we both loved baseball so much, we wanted to see as many of the major league parks as we possibly could during our lifetime. Consequently, our first destination became St. Louis. This would allow us to see the Arch and take in a baseball game at Busch Stadium.

From there, we could visit Kansas City and take in a Royals game at Kaufman Stadium. We had already attended a Detroit Tigers game at Tiger Stadium and a Milwaukee Brewers game at Country Stadium in Milwaukee while we were dating, so we counted those two stadiums toward our goal. While we would not attend any other baseball games for the next week and a half, we did talk about how we might accomplish this new goal while driving between destinations.

After the Royals game, we took I-29 to I-90 West to the Black Hills and Badlands National Park. We visited Mount Rushmore, Custer State Park, and Wall Drug in South Dakota. Additionally, we visited Yellowstone National Park and Pike's Peak on our way to the Grand Canyon. We spent a few days at the Grand Canyon and then headed to New Orleans as our last stop before returning to Michigan. While in New Orleans, we heard about a hurricane forming in the Gulf of Mexico. So, we cut our time in New Orleans shorter than planned. What became Hurricane Alicia didn't come on shore in New Orleans but in Texas. However, we were already heading north and out of the effects when it arrived.

In Michigan, we returned to life in a mobile home we had purchased just before getting married. We decided to buy a mobile home rather than rent to establish our credit. I had gotten a coaching job at the local high school coaching the junior varsity girls basketball team and was beginning practices the day after we returned from our honeymoon. Classes at Calvin started a week later. I wasn't working other than coaching, so I enjoyed the opportunity to be just a student during the semester for the first time since I started college. I planned on student-teaching in the spring semester and playing softball at Calvin for my senior year.

As the fall semester progressed, Dan continued to build his law practice. I turned the mobile home into a comfortable home. I also decided to forgo playing softball for my senior season and concentrate on my student-teaching. Teaching jobs were scarce in 1984, so I wanted to do a great job, hoping to get a position. I was student-teaching at Baptist High School; I was already coaching their junior varsity girls' basketball team.

As January began, so did my student-teaching assignment at Grand Rapids Baptist High School. My love for teaching was reinforced by my previous opportunities to teach at church and in practicums before an entire semester of student-teaching. I was assigned to an experienced teacher who taught middle school civics and American history. Since I had coached the girls' junior varsity team in the fall at the Baptist High School, I could speak with him and ask if he would be my mentor for the spring semester. When he agreed, I completed my application for student-teaching, listing him as my mentor teacher. While Calvin didn't guarantee any assignments, even if we could get a teacher to agree to take us as student-teachers, in this situation, they did approve my request.

In February, the softball coach at Baptist High School approached me about being his assistant coach during the spring. I was excited to gain some additional coaching experience. It was an excellent opportunity as I was already missing my teammates at Calvin and wondering whether I had made the right decision to forego my senior year of college softball. A couple of the girls who played for me during the fall on the junior varsity also played on the softball team. Additionally, I knew some of the girls from varsity basketball since our teams traveled together. When practice started, I could work with the pitcher on their technique, given my experience with pitching in high school and college.

The spring semester gave me a real sense of what it would be like to be a full-time teacher and coach, which was my hope as I began looking for teaching jobs after graduation. While very few public school teaching jobs were available within driving distance of Grand Rapids, I was becoming aware of the extensive Christian school network in the area. Until now, I wasn't unaware of how many Christian schools existed in Grand Rapids. As I became aware of openings for high school or middle school social studies teachers, I prepared an application and sent it off, hoping to get a call for an interview. I also began talking with Dan about what I might consider doing if I couldn't find a teaching job. We talked about obtaining a job and continuing the job hunt or the possibility of going to law school, which was another interest I had while completing my undergraduate degree. He seemed a little excited about the option, but he was rooting for me to get a teaching job because he knew that was my priority.

I graduated from Calvin College in May and continued looking for a job. Many of my friends had already gotten a job at various Christian schools in town. Most were in science areas, and I was so happy for them. Within weeks of graduating, I learned that the Baptist High School, where I was teaching, had a middle school social studies opening at their elementary campus in Hudsonville, eighteen miles from where we lived. The opening occurred because the Baptist elementary school was breaking away from the founding organizing and wanted to add a junior high school in the fall and needed teachers. So, I applied. I also obtained recommendations from my supervising teacher, the varsity girls' basketball and softball coaches, and the high school principal, who could all speak of my teaching and coaching abilities and my integrity as a Christian teacher.

I received word in early June that I had been hired. I believed everything was falling into place because I had obeyed God and His will by marrying Dan. I thought I had forsaken the temptations I faced with Faith, and now I was in God's will, which is why everything was falling into place so perfectly. When Dan came home from work that day, I excitedly shared the news with him. I don't think he even stepped more than two feet into the house when I told him my good news. He was excited for me and suggested we celebrate when the weekend arrived by going out to dinner with my parents. Next, I called my parents and told them I had a teaching job for the fall. We then planned to go for dinner on Saturday night to celebrate.

Dan and I continued attending Alpine Baptist Church, where we married. We joined a new Sunday school group for young married couples and continued to participate in the mid-week Bible study as well. I played softball for the church team on Tuesday nights, playing shortstop, and Faith was the first baseman. Faith and I remained friends after my wedding, but I didn't spend as much time with her as before. Nothing about her concerns about my decision to get married caused us to drift apart. I felt the pull to get home and spend time with Dan, so I wasn't spending as much time with any of my friends. She began to hang around with a lady named Stephanie. I was glad to see that Faith had found another friend to hang out with, filling some of the void my new light must have left in her life.

As August began, I prepared for my first year of teaching by going to work each day at the school. I returned to coaching at the Baptist High School in Grand Rapids for my second year. I had a full plate but was enjoying getting my career started. My first fall teaching middle school history and English was excellent. My seventh-grade class was civics, the same class I taught during my student-teaching. I used some of the lessons and the unit I had designed during student-teaching. My eighth-grade class was American history. This class was new, and I needed to work hard on creating each week's unit and lesson plans. Friends and mentors warned me that my first year of teaching would require much time to develop lessons with interactive activities and assessments. They encouraged me by sharing that each year after the first year would be easier concerning lesson design and planning. That was some of the best advice I received as I prepared for my first year of teaching.

In addition to teaching civics and American history, I taught seventh and eighth-grade English. The English classes consisted of grammar and literature. I also introduced spelling words to the class each week, but I didn't hold any spelling bees in class, given my dislike for them when I was in school. I also taught elementary physical education for two hours each day so that each teacher could get a break for at least one hour per week. Teaching physical education was a completely new experience for me. I enjoyed meeting and working with some of the elementary kids. I certainly learned a great deal about human development by teaching elementary and early adolescents. It was an incredible experience I would never have had if I had taught in a larger school.

As the Christmas break approached, Dan asked me if I wanted to do anything for the holiday. He mentioned that he would like to take the week between Christmas and New Year to rest for the tax preparation season beginning in mid-January. After considering several ideas, Dan and I decided to go to Florida for Christmas break. We knew we would need to drive rather than fly to Florida, but we enjoyed driving to our destination because we felt we could see different things along the way. Florida might be a good destination at this time of year because we both liked the warm weather more than the snow. Also, Dan had never visited Disney World before and thought he might like it based on my description from the spring training sessions I spent in Florida while playing college softball. I was excited to visit Disney World during the holidays, often wondering how festive it might be, all decorated for Christmas.

We both informed our families that we would travel before Christmas so we would not spend Christmas with them. While disappointed, they were glad we could get away given all the work we have each been engaged with as we started our careers and life as a couple. We left for Lakeland, Florida, the Saturday morning after my fall term ended. We drove all day and night, arrived in Lakeland on Sunday, and checked into the hotel we had reserved for the week. The week went very fast. We visited Disney World, Epcot Center, Bush Gardens, and the Kennedy Space Center. Unfortunately, the weather wasn't warm enough to enjoy the beach as much as we originally planned or swim in the ocean anytime during our week in Florida. However, the one day we spent at Daytona Beach was warm enough to sit by the water and enjoy time reading while listening to the waves. While I wished the week would never end, I was excited to return home and begin my second-semester teaching. I enjoyed the moments when Dan was away from work and relaxed. I appreciated his sense of humor and adventure. These times allowed me to talk to him about American history, as he had previously earned a degree in history. His perspectives often led me to read more about an event and incorporate some ideas and concepts into my teaching. I saw this as a way for him to share in my career, and I valued his interest in my thoughts and opinions.

As January began, Dan started to spend more and more time

away from the house as more and more clients made appointments to have him prepare their tax returns. With each passing day approaching April 15th, the number of clients he saw grew. Despite working every night and the entire day on Saturday, he could only take Sunday mornings off and attend church with me. After church, he would come home and have lunch before returning to the office to finish some of the tax returns that were started the prior week. He constantly reminded me that most of his yearly income was made during the year's first quarter, and he had to take the work while it was available. I understood his need to be away, but I was lonely on Friday nights and Saturdays when he worked. While I used my time on Saturday to get ready for the next week at school, I still missed him.

I was again asked to coach softball at the Baptist High School in Grand Rapids in the spring. I was an assistant coach for the varsity team. The school hadn't yet started a junior varsity team. Indoor practice would begin in February, and I was glad to be coaching again after basketball season had ended. Coaching for me was another way to teach. The competitive sports setting gave me a different perspective on whether my teaching/coaching was successful. Unlike the classroom setting, where often the formative and summative assessment of student learning occurred well after the teaching, in basketball and softball, the teaching and game preparation could be assessed the following day. I was thankful for the opportunity to coach softball because tax season didn't seem as lonely between teaching and coaching softball. When April 15 finally arrived, Dan's work on tax returns ended, but he now needed to get caught up in his law practice. By the time he was caught up, coaching softball was done.

As my first year of teaching and coaching was nearing the end, I began talking with Dan about the need to continue education classes to keep my teaching certification. I also told Dan that the school I taught at provided a raise in pay if I were to get my master's degree. Dan was supportive of my decision to begin a master's degree. I investigated the college options to complete my degree in the Grand Rapids area. Our local college, Grand Valley State University, had an education program with many summer offerings to accommodate the teaching year. Also, Michigan State University and Western Michigan University had programs in the downtown area for teachers wishing to complete a master's degree with similar summer offerings. Each university offered degrees with slightly different focuses, so I had choices about where to focus on strengthening my skills. I decided to begin a master's degree at Michigan State University and start classes during the summer. Once we knew my summer schedule, Dan and I planned an early July trip to Washington, D.C., as we both had always wanted to visit the place and were looking forward to being there for the first time together.

Early in the academic year, the school's board decided that now that they had broken away from their founding organization and added a junior high, it was time to add a high school as well. This would mean they would add another grade each year over the next four years until they graduate the first class, currently the eighth-grade class. Only two of us, Tim and I, taught in the middle school now. As the school would begin adding high school grades, they would also need to add more teachers, an English and science teacher, after this school year. I was excited because I looked forward to teaching various social studies and history classes rather than splitting my time between social studies, English, and physical education. Tim seemed to share my excitement. I felt very blessed to have a good colleague in Tim. I valued his wisdom and insight into our students. Because there were only two of us, it was easy to quickly meet after school and share observations should we see one of the students struggling. These insights helped each of us better support the students in each of the subject areas.

Within days of the school year ending, I began graduate classes at Michigan State University in their Grand Rapids location. My advisor and I developed a plan allowing me to complete all my courses in town or take classes in East Lansing during the subsequent summers should I wish to finish my degree more quickly. That summer, I also prepared to teach 9th-grade world history, given the school board's decision to add the 9th grade beginning in the fall of 1985. I enjoyed my graduate courses even more than my undergraduate courses at Calvin. In some ways, the classes seemed easier because the work directly applied to my teaching job. Throughout the summer, I continued to read American history and world history books as my schedule allowed, ensuring that I continued expanding my knowledge of the disciplines I taught.

When my first graduate course was over, I had a ten-day break before the start of the second summer term. That was when Dan and I decided to visit Washington, D.C. On our way to D.C., we planned to spend a night in Philadelphia first to visit Veterans Stadium and watch the Phillies play. This continued our commitment to see all the major league stadiums in our lifetime. Even if my beloved Detroit Tigers weren't playing, I thoroughly enjoyed the game. On July 2nd, the Phillies beat the New York Mets 6-5. Tim, my teaching partner at the high school, was a huge New York Mets fan. I had to root for the Mets because of him. However, the Phillies won the game in the bottom of the ninth with two outs. Bob Dernier led off the inning with a single. He advanced to second base on a sacrifice bunt by Pete Rose, a player I enjoyed watching when he played for the Cincinnati Reds. The Mets pitcher, Jesse Orosco, intentionally walked Mike Schmidt. Bo

Diaz was batting for the Phillies when Bob Denier stole third when the Mets tried to pick off Mike Schmidt on first base only to commit an error that allowed Dernier to score to end the game. The end of the game was exhilarating. Dan and I were so excited by the ending despite the team we were rooting for losing.

The following day, we visited the Constitutional Hall in Philadelphia and learned more about the drafting of the U.S. Constitution. Later in the afternoon, we left Philadelphia, drove to Washington D.C., and checked into our hotel, where we would spend the next five days. While in D.C., we visited Mount Vernon, home of George Washington, Monticello, Thomas Jefferson's house, the Smithsonian Natural History Museum, and the Smithsonian Air and Space Museum. We walked the Mall and visited all the monuments. We also visited the U.S. Capitol and White House while we were there. I was still an avid photographer and brought a lot of slide film to use the photos I took in my history and civics classes when teaching. I loved combining my love of history and photography into lessons for students. The week flew by, and as we left, I reminded Dan that now that I was teaching world history, we might want to consider visiting some historical sites worldwide.

The school year began after Labor Day weekend. As a teacher, I felt more confident about teaching and good about starting my graduate degree. This year, I wasn't feeling like every night, I had to work three or four hours to prepare for classes the next day because I had taught many of my classes the previous year. I was modifying existing lessons rather than creating them from scratch. This significantly lowered the amount of time each night I spent on work. The only new course for me was 9th-grade world history. I worked each Saturday preparing for the world history class for the week to ensure that I could work a little less on weeknights, giving me more time to spend with Dan when he was home.

My second year of teaching was uneventful beyond the excitement around planning to add 10th grade beginning in the fall of 1986. As my second year of teaching ended, I decided to double up on my coursework during the summer to get my continuing education license before the State of Michigan changed from a permanent certificate to a certificate that needed to be renewed every five years. That meant spending four days a week an hour away in East Lansing. We hadn't planned for a summer vacation, so doubling up on my courses would help me complete my master's degree earlier than I originally planned. Because I knew I would be teaching 10th-grade geography in the fall, I asked for the teacher's edition of the book to use over the summer to begin planning my lessons. I was starting to understand how to design better teaching units and lessons in my graduate courses, so I thought I could lessen the amount of curriculum work during my school year if I could get lessons developed in the summer. If those lessons could also satisfy some of the assignments in my courses, I felt I was using my time as efficiently as possible.

In June, Dan's secretary took another job, and he was about to place an ad for another secretary. Over dinner, he asked me what I would think if he hired my mother as his secretary. I thought it was a great idea. She had been a legal secretary at the collection agency for eight years and would be familiar with the legal terminology. Dan thought she would be a good fit, too. I was fortunate that Dan was well-liked, fit in with my family, and liked my parents. The next night, we took my parents out for dinner and pitched the idea to them about my mom coming to work for Dan. My parents seemed excited and promised to let us know by the end of the week. Come Friday, she agreed to join Dan at the law office. That same day, she gave her two-week notice at the collection agency where she had worked since my parents divorced and where I worked late in high school and the first couple of years I attended college. By the first of July, my mom was working for Dan. While at first, I wondered whether working every day for Dan might mean I would see my parents less on weekends or that Dan might not want to see my parents on weekends because he saw my mom all week, I soon found out it didn't impact the amount of time we spent with my parents at all. Neither my mom nor Dan talked about work when we got together as a family. This was a powerful revelation and lesson for me. It was valuable to see how people could separate their work and family lives when they worked at the same location.

In August, the school where I worked had a welcome picnic for all the teachers to introduce the new teachers, including the third and fourth teachers at the junior and high school levels, to those of us who had been teaching at the school previously. Dan went with me to the picnic. Once there, Mr. Brinkerhoff introduced Karen, who was hired to teach middle and high school science. Tim would now teach Bible and math. He was happy to hand off science, just like I was happy to hand off English. Mr. Brinkerhoff also introduced us to Joy, who was hired to teach English and Spanish. Joy was why I no longer needed to teach English, allowing me to pick up teaching middle and high school physical education courses. Dan and I also met the new teachers hired to teach in the elementary school. The school was growing, so a couple of the early elementary grades had now become large enough to be split into two classrooms. I was excited to see the growth.

In addition to adding another grade, the school began a junior varsity girls' basketball team. I was asked to coach. I informed the Baptist high school that I would no longer be able to coach their junior varsity team in the fall as I would be coaching where I worked. I thanked them for giving me my first chance at coaching and allowing me to develop my coaching skills. I knew it was more likely than not that my new junior high team would face them later in the season. What was good about the opportunity to coach where I was teaching was that I no longer had to drive 30 minutes to Grand Rapids each day to coach. Now, I could do it after school, where I taught. This significantly reduced my time on the road after school, giving me more time to work on lessons or grading papers. Having some extra time to myself helped me begin to reengage with my hobbies, like drawing and bicycle riding, which I didn't have time for in the first couple of years of teaching. The school also began planning to build a new wing of the high school. All the changes allowed me to dive further into my career. Being able to coach and teach at the same school had been my dream, and now I could live that dream.

That spring, Dan and I began to talk about buying a house. The mobile home was an excellent start for us. It had allowed us to establish credit, but now it was time to consider a house. We talked about what we wanted and needed in a house and where we should live, given that our jobs were 30 miles apart. Every neighborhood Dan identified I vetoed. He wanted us to get a house close to his law office. I wanted to get a house between his law office and where I taught in Hudsonville. While Dan was looking at different options in Grand Rapids, I would drive around the areas between Hudsonville and Grand Rapids, looking at homes. On weekends, we each shared with the other what options we found and then scheduled a time to walk through the house. Each house we visited, we walked away, agreeing that the house wasn't for us. Finally, I found a ranch home for sale in Hudsonville, close to my job but over 25 miles from Dan's law office. That weekend, I took Dan out to look at it. The realtor met us there. We toured the home and fell in love with it. It was a one-story ranch with an unfinished basement on twenty acres. We negotiated to buy the house and five acres of land. The buyer took our offer, and we arranged to move into the home in early August.

We were excited about the house. It fits the characteristics we had discussed before we started looking for homes. Because the house was outside the greater Grand Rapids area, we could purchase it at a lower price than our budget. Dan and I were happy that we didn't have to max out our budget to buy the house and saved the remaining money, if we needed, to upgrade any infrastructure. While I knew Dan and I weren't sure what location to consider for our first house, I didn't know that Dan was not as enthusiastic about the Hudsonville area as I was because it meant he had a thirty-mile commute to work. He never mentioned it when we looked at the house. I learned he disliked the commute later in the year when he complained about his already long day becoming an hour longer.

The 1987 fall school year began after Labor Day. I started working a week before Labor Day as I coached the girls' basketball team. We were now considered a varsity team, as I had two 11th-grade players and eight 9th- and 10th-grade players. However, we were very inexperienced and would be playing teams comprised mostly of juniors and seniors. I was expecting the year to be long and the wins few. Therefore, I kept my focus on fundamentals. I worked to improve individual and team skills, knowing that the experience the younger players would get would be invaluable for the following year when I would return two seniors and eight juniors and sophomores.

The science teacher, Karen, volunteered to keep the score at our games. Our season was better than expected, winning about half of our games. I got acquainted with Karen because she accompanied us to away games. She drove, which was a relief to me. That allowed me to think through my pre-game talk and review our strategy. We played games every Tuesday and Thursday and practiced on Monday, Wednesday, and Friday. Because of the routine, the season was over quickly, and I was looking forward to some time for myself after school. Once practice was over, I could use the extra two hours after school to get ready for the next day, allowing me to get home earlier and, upon arriving, use that time to enjoy my hobbies or get caught up on watching movies.

Like the girls' basketball program, the school started the boys' varsity basketball team in the winter. Karen volunteered to keep score for the boys. Their coach was single, and we all figured she was trying to get to know him. She had dated Tim a few times the year before. She was single, and all the students tried fixing her with the single men on staff. I love junior high students' optimism. They see love as perfect and want to ensure every teacher is dating or married. I can't remember if Karen ever dated the coach, but it was all the talk among the middle and high school girls for a few weeks.

Karen encouraged me to attend a few of the boys' home games. Their games began in November and were scheduled for Tuesday and Friday nights. I would go to their Friday night games because I knew I didn't need to get up early the next day for work. I enjoyed watching them play. Between attending a few of the boys' games and the Thanksgiving and Christmas holidays, it was January, and Dan was slipping into his tax routine. It seemed like I would never see him beginning every mid-January until a few weeks after April 15th. Every year, he got busier and busier as he gained more and more clients. He was good at writing taxes and seemed to like preparing them. Now that we lived thirty miles from his work, he was getting home later. That meant I had more time to myself. I filled my time by getting more and more involved at school. I went to more of the boys' basketball games. The school also began a girls' volleyball team. Karen and Joy were asked to coach the girls' volleyball team. In a small Christian school, we all wore many hats, so it was not unusual for each of us to coach or be an advisor to one of the student clubs. Many of the girls who played volleyball also played basketball for me. When the girls began playing their games, I also went to the game to support them.

We began hanging out on Friday nights when Karen wasn't coaching or working the boys' basketball games. Dan already worked on Saturday, so I was free once I finished any schoolwork I wanted to complete or projects around the house. This year, Dan added a new element to his long tax season and stayed at the office overnight when his tax schedule became full. His office had an apartment above the law office. It was vacant this tax season, so it was a perfect location for him to go upstairs and sleep after finishing work. At first, Dan would stay over on Friday night. He said he would get a few hours' sleep after calling in late on Fridays. He explained that this would allow him to get an early start on Saturdays so he could still attend church with me on Sundays. In February, Dan was still coming home on Saturday night and then going with me to church on Sunday. As the first of March neared, Dan began staying at the office on both Friday and Saturday nights, and I wouldn't see him come home until very late on Sunday night. I hadn't seen this before and decided to ask him if he was seeing many more clients than in previous tax seasons. He told me he needed to stay over because he couldn't afford to give up an extra hour on Friday and Saturday. After all, we lived so far away from his law office. I think the extra hour each day for travel didn't justify the additional time staying overnight and working all day on Sunday. Something was different, and I couldn't figure out what had changed.

Since I knew Dan wasn't coming home on Friday nights, I was more willing to do something with Karen. On some Friday nights,

Karen and I would shop in Grand Rapids. Eventually, we began hanging out together on Saturday. This started because I would go to school some Saturday mornings to change seating arrangements or bulletin boards for the next week or new units. Often, Karen was there when I arrived. Eventually, we would both go together on these mornings. With each other's help, the projects seemed to be completed more quickly. I know I appreciated the help, and I was sure she did. After getting our work done at school, we may stop for a quick lunch or go cross-country skiing if the weather permits.

Karen had been a home economics teacher before working at the same school where I worked. Consequently, she loved to sew and was into arts and crafts. Some of the Saturdays, we spent time on these types of projects. She showed me how to cross-stitch. I came to love cross-stitching. I could do it while watching television or sitting in the sun on a warm summer day. During tax season, Karen and I often hung out at my house on Saturday nights and watched movies while cross-stitching.

As Dan was spending all his time at the office, Karen and I continued to spend time together on Friday nights and all day Saturday. Dan was even starting to get home later and later during the weeknights. I noticed and was beginning to resent it. Before moving to Hudsonville, Dan would be home by 10:00 pm during the week. Because when we lived in our mobile home, we were only 15 minutes from his law office, which likely meant he would have left the law office around 9:45 pm. This year, he was arriving home around midnight. We no longer had time to talk briefly to get caught up on each other's days or information. Consequently, the conversation was almost non-existent except for a quick note here or a brief hello if I was up when he arrived home.

The commute from his law office to our home in Hudsonville was about 30 minutes, so he worked until 11:30 pm. The additional hours during the week, coupled with the extra hours on weekends, should mean he was seeing way more clients than in the past several years. I wasn't sure I was buying that story. I would know based on the amount of money he earned this year. Sometimes, when I talked to my mom, I would ask her if she thought Dan was seeing more clients this year than in previous years. She would receive telephone calls from clients and schedule their appointments. She would say Dan took more appointments this year on Saturday and later into the evening than in previous years. I knew my mom wouldn't be covering up any affairs or nefarious behavior, so her observations about his schedule generally quieted my suspicious mind. After talking with my mom, I told myself that I had no reason to think Dan was lying to me or there was more to his work than a growing clientele.

One Friday night, Karen and I had planned to go to Kalamazoo for a concert. Kalamazoo was about an hour and a half south of Hudsonville, so we knew we would get home late. Because of the late night, Karen suggested she spend the night at my house rather than going home after dropping me off. I agreed, and we planned accordingly. As expected, we got back to my house around 1:30 am. We changed and went to bed. She slept with me as our spare room lacked a bed because we used it as an office. We only had a two-bedroom ranch but planned on finishing the basement soon to add a third bedroom. I offered her to pull out the couch, which I used on weekends sometimes to watch movies, but I doubted it would be comfortable for a complete night of sleep.

I was sure we would fall asleep quickly as the night had been long after a long workday. We chatted for a while before Karen fell asleep. I couldn't fall asleep. I wanted so badly to have Karen hold me. I flashed back to times with Julie and wished for that now. The guilt welled up in me. I hadn't felt this way in several years. I thought those feelings were long gone. I was puzzled and bewildered that they had returned. Soon, the intense feelings gave way to sleep. In the morning, I quickly got up and made coffee. Soon, Karen was up and joined me in the living room. We planned our day. I called to check on Dan and gave him a description of my plans. He informed me that he was spending another night at the office. I wasn't happy, but what was I to do? I knew this was his busy time and that he needed the revenue from preparing taxes to ensure a stable income. I appreciated his hard work and brushed off that I was annoyed that he was never home.

Karen and I headed out to a few fabric stores. She promised to show me how to make shorts today. We picked out some fabric and then went to her apartment. It was a two-bedroom apartment. One bedroom was set up as a sewing room. We spent the day making clothes. She had been a home economics teacher for many years. I'm sure she had taught students who were much better than I was at understanding patterns. She was patient, but I am sure I tried what patience she had. By the end of the afternoon, I had cut out fabric for two pairs of shorts for the summer. We broke for lunch and decided to go to a local restaurant that we both enjoyed. After lunch, we returned to her apartment to finish sewing for the day.

She showed me how to use the sewing machine, and before long, I had finished my first pair of shorts. We agreed to leave the second pair for next weekend. At that point, I planned to head home and clean the house. Karen said she needed to finish a couple of additional projects she was working on for others. I went to get my coat. I didn't want to go but didn't know how to explain to Dan that I hadn't cleaned the house. I was feeling torn and wanted to stay. I also knew we had spent much time together, and Karen probably wanted some time to herself, too.

As I went to leave, I reached to hug Karen. We hugged, and she held me for a moment. I held on as well. We parted, and I told her how much fun I had and how I looked forward to next weekend. I hugged her again, and this time, she kissed my cheek. I pulled back and then reached in to kiss her. We kissed. The kiss didn't last long, and I quickly left. As I drove the three miles home, I was in heaven. I had wanted to kiss her so badly.

We spent many weekends together after that day until tax season ended. We found ways to spend more time together during the weekdays by attending the boys' basketball games. The boys' basketball team was on the road one Friday, so we decided to shop in Kalamazoo rather than our customary trip to Grand Rapids. Karen had attended Western Michigan University in Kalamazoo and was familiar with the city and mall. It gave us another destination to travel to while spending time together. We left for the Kalamazoo Mall after school was over that Friday. The mall was enormous, and we took our time wandering through it. As the 9:00 pm closing time neared, we left the mall and returned to Karen's car.

On the ride back to my house, I reached over and held Karen's hand as she drove. I felt sad and needed to be held, but keeping her hand was the next best thing. She had a stick-shift car, so I couldn't slip over and sit next to her. Instead, I leaned over the center console and leaned against her shoulder. She put her arm around me. I felt close, and this helped me feel content. We talked on the drive home and pulled into the driveway of my house. We entered the house and unpacked the items we had purchased while shopping. We sat and watched TV a bit and then headed to bed.

As I lay next to Karen, I felt a deep longing inside. I ached. I wanted her so badly. I rolled over on my side and put my arm across her waist. She didn't resist. I relaxed. I moved closer to her. I began to caress her breasts. Next, I leaned over and kissed her cheek softly. She rolled over on her back. I leaned over and kissed her on the mouth. The kisses became more profound and more intense. My hand explored her body. I wanted more. Shortly, we stopped, and I just rested my arm across her waist. We said nothing but good night and fell asleep. In the morning, I awoke and resisted the urge to begin again. I quietly got up and made coffee.

Karen awoke, and we sat with coffee in hand. We did not speak of the night or our intimate moments. We planned our day and set out for our first destination. Before long, the day ended. Dan spent another night at the office, so we spent another night together. Again, we found ourselves making out in bed. As I reached to undress Karen, she stopped me. She went to kiss me to reassure me, but I knew where the line was drawn. This pattern would play itself out many times before April 15th. I hated to see the end of tax time because my intimate time with Karen would be diminished.

The school year ended, and summer came. I was taking my last few classes and expected to graduate with my master's degree. Karen and I continued to spend time together when I wasn't in school or studying. We were inseparable. We found a few moments here and there to share a deep kiss or hold each other while we talked. The guilt was eating me alive. I began to memorize the entire book of Romans in the Bible, thinking that all I needed to do was renew my mind, and I would be freed from this temptation. However, I knew in the past with Julie and Faith that the only way I could stop this temptation was to move away from the friendship. The thought of ending my friendship with Karen killed me. I knew I loved her and loved her like I had loved no one else. I knew I couldn't walk away. I also worried that God might take her from me if we continued to share intimate moments. I was very conflicted.

Finally, we each confronted the topic of our intimacy and our need to stop. She was feeling the same guilt. She was much stronger than I was concerning avoiding times making out. I had been there before and knew the sweet feeling of making love to a woman and having a woman make love to me. I longed for that precious feeling again. However, I would not cross that line with Karen. The more I struggled, the more I memorized scripture. The harder the struggle, the more I shared that struggle with Karen, and the more we avoided moments where I would give in. I saw this as my fault. I believed I had led Julie into a sexual relationship, and now I thought I had led Karen into a gay relationship. I blamed myself.

The more I blamed myself, the more I got angry at Dan. My relationship with Dan was growing distant. Our intimacy was non-existent and had been since our second year of marriage. I wondered if he was seeing another woman. The less we were together, the more I wanted to be with Karen. The more I was with Karen, the more profoundly I desired to make love to her. I spent the summer depressed. I was not the same. I did not have the same energy. I kept busy finishing my degree and bicycling. When I wasn't driving to East Lansing to take classes or study, I would find a day to get on my bicycle and ride the 18 miles to Lake Michigan. After a rest, I would ride back. I would do anything to avoid feeling the pain of longing for a forbidden love. I also felt empty because I lacked the romance and intimacy I needed.

I had always liked to read. Summer was my time to read things other than history materials for teaching. This summer, I spent a great deal of time reading Christian books. I was trying to clean my soul one more time from this temptation. Our Sunday school class was studying a book by Tony Campollo entitled *"Twenty-hot Potatoes."* Each week, I read the chapter that would be the lesson for the coming Sunday. That day, I was lying on the couch and reading, hoping to keep my mind pure. The chapter was on homosexuality. I saw myself coming alive on the pages as I read the chapter. The chapter described the struggle that homosexuals have with natural longings. Finally, someone understood what I was going through!

As I read, I concluded that the struggles I was resisting were natural, but to act on them was a sin. I prayed and acknowledged to God that I struggled with homosexual feelings. I prayed for strength to resist following through on them. The prayer and realization were comforting. I concluded that, as a Christian, I was not at fault for feeling what I felt. However, I was responsible to avoid acting on those feelings. I committed to God that day that I would stay faithful to Dan and avoid times of giving in to my natural feelings and longing for women. Somehow, knowing the truth that I had homosexual feelings gave me relief. I realized that I wasn't going to change those feelings. I was free. There was nothing wrong with me. The chapter led me to believe others felt the way I did. I now knew I couldn't change those feelings but learned that I could decide what to do when I felt those feelings. The truth had set me free.

Part III: A Journey of Faith and Freedom

"How, then, shall they call on him whom they have not believed? And how shall they believe in him of whom they have not heard? And how shall they hear without a preacher?"

-Romans 10:14 KJV.

Chapter Twenty-Five: Now What?

"Therefore to him that knoweth to do good, and doeth it not, to him it is sin"

-James 4:17 KJV.

The realization that other people experienced homosexual feelings and attractions was helpful. What wasn't helpful was the realization that the feelings would never go away. It brought another dilemma. What should I do about being in a marriage when I know that I'm not attracted to Dan and I might never be attracted to Dan? I loved Dan. However, my love for Dan was more like a sister's love for a brother. I wondered whether it was possible to have a successful marriage if I was not romantically in love with Dan. After contemplating this new scenario, I eventually concluded that a marriage could be successful because I knew of others who loved their spouse but were not romantically in love, and their marriage survived.

It never crossed my mind to share these revelations with Dan. There was no reason to upset him or cause a problem when one didn't exist. I was determined to commit myself to my marriage and teaching career. I vowed not to put myself in situations that would tempt me to compromise my marriage by acting on my attraction for women. It seemed reasonable to me that many men and women experienced attraction to other people while they were married. Those people, like me, faced a choice of whether to act on those temptations. In some ways, I thought the temptations I faced were like those of others, but the only difference was that my attraction was to women, not members of the opposite sex. I didn't realize that to accomplish my goal of remaining faithful to Dan, I would become more distant from the people I loved and cared about. I had heard about LGBTQ+ people being "in the closet" and didn't understand the terminology until now. Once I understood and admitted my feelings, I became hypersensitive to keeping them to myself. Little did I know the consequences of keeping part of myself in the closet. The journey ahead would soon reveal those consequences to me.

In the fall of 1987, Dan and I decided to finish the basement of our house. Karen said she would rent the apartment if we finished it. The basement was large enough that half of it could easily be an apartment while the other half served as a workout room for Dan and me. Michigan winters could be snowy, so working out at home was an excellent option on days too cold or too snowy to get outside and safely run. It was time to put the exercise bike and treadmill in the basement and get them out of what was supposed to be the formal dining room. As Dan and I began the renovation in the fall, we enjoyed spending time shopping. Since the realization that I had homosexual feelings and sharing them with Karen, she and I didn't put ourselves in any situations that would cause me to be tempted. We talked about my struggle and my commitment to be faithful to Dan. I felt that if Karen understood my struggle, she could help me avoid being in a situation that would lead me to "sin." I never worried about telling Karen about my attraction to women, nor did I fear she would react adversely and decide to stop being my friend. She was very understanding and empathetic about my attraction to women.

The basement was finished by Christmas of 1987. Karen moved in during Christmas break. It was great to have her close by as tax season neared since I knew that I would not see Dan much as the months marched toward April 15th. I had become close with Karen's family just like she had gotten to know my parents. We also managed to visit each of our families during Christmas break. During the break, I helped Karen move her furniture, clothes, and other items from her apartment into our basement. She spent most of the holiday break putting her things away and organizing. She wanted to be settled into the apartment before classes started in the spring term. Also, she had to vacate her current apartment by December 31st. That meant we had to spend a day cleaning that apartment and return the keys to the landlord. While I helped her during the day to unpack things, she would help me each night with supper. It was common for Dan, Karen, and I to have supper together. After supper, Karen and I would do the dishes. She would retreat to her apartment in the basement. Dan and I would then have time to catch up on each other's day.

If I had any frustration during this time, I knew my relationship with Dan was not what I had hoped it would be. Like many people, I had ideas about what I wanted from my marriage. Society, church, and family all impose upon people ideas about what makes for a successful marriage. My marriage was far from what I had pictured as an ideal relationship. The message about marriage I received from my mom and her family was that women needed a man to care for them. As women didn't have as many opportunities in life, they should be content to find a good man who cared for and provided for them. My dad sent very few messages to me about marriage. However, his affair that caused my parents' divorce, despite them remarrying each other, reinforced the notion that women in marriage were helpless. My church at the time advanced the idea that men were the head of the household and women should be submissive. I took submissive to be meek, weak, and obedient. I, likely, was far from that. The church reinforced the idea that marriage was to ensure the strength of the family unit. A married couple was expected to have children, and children should obey their parents.

On the one hand, I was acting upon these cultural and familial messages by getting married, yet on the other hand, I was bucking the trend because I didn't act like the submissive wife but as independent, strong, and career-focused. I hadn't yet decided what I wanted concerning having children. I was conflicted on this matter. But at this point in our relationship, I was unwilling to consider introducing children into the equation because of all the questions and frustrations I was experiencing.

Romantically and sexually, Dan and I were distant. That distance caused me to feel empty and lonely despite having many people in my life. I concluded that the distance between Dan and me was due to my attraction to other women, which resulted in my inability to provide the closeness Dan might be looking for. I thought about my inability at times to allow myself to be close to Dan, which caused him to distance himself because he wasn't sure how to interpret my distance. Was this my "thorn in the flesh," like the Apostle Paul wrote, *"And lest I should be exalted above measure through the abundance of the revelations, there was given to me a thorn in the flesh, the messenger of Satan to buffet me, lest I should be exalted above measure. (8) For this thing I besought the Lord thrice, that it might depart from me. (9) And he said unto me, "My grace is sufficient for thee: for my strength is made perfect in weakness....*" (II Corinthians 12: 7-9, KJV). Indeed, this thorn did keep me close to God through prayer and Bible memorization.

My worldview included the belief that someone can't have it all, so I believed I should be thankful for what I have. I had a great friend in Dan, and we enjoyed doing many things together; that was certainly something to be grateful for. I interpreted Paul's story about his thorn in the flesh to be a message to me that people have their own "thorn in the flesh," which is something to be thankful for because, in that struggle, God's grace will be sufficient. Paul normalized struggles and provided hope through God's grace. I am naturally optimistic, so I approached my relationship with Dan optimistically, choosing to look at what I had rather than what I didn't have. I knew of friends and relatives who were in marriages far worse than mine, and that knowledge was a reminder that things could be worse.

On New Year's Day of 1988, Karen and I decided to host a gathering to watch the Michigan State Spartans play in their first Rose Bowl game since 1965. Between getting Karen settled into her apartment and cleaning her old one, we found time to plan a Rose Bowl-watching party. That also meant we needed to secure decorations appropriate to support the Spartans. The party allowed Karen to show her apartment to her parents and sister. We invited my parents as well. I teased my mom and dad because this was the first time since 1966 that Michigan State beat the University of Michigan and Ohio State University. My dad was a huge University of Michigan fan, and my mom remained a loyal Ohio State fan since giving birth to me in Columbus. I often reminded them I had to attend Michigan State University, so I didn't take sides. The watch party was also an opportunity to cheer for the university that would soon be my alma mater. I was expected to graduate in May from Michigan State with my master's degree.

Between excellent food, great conversation, and much teasing, we watched Michigan State defeat the University of Southern California 17-13. Karen's parents got to know my parents during this event, and they stayed in touch regularly as a result. Karen's parents also liked her apartment and were happy that she lived close to us, school, and church. We all considered the Rose Bowl party a big success primarily because of the MSU victory. We all enjoyed a great day and an excellent start to the new year.

The spring semester for me was relatively routine. My focus was completing my last class and master's thesis so I could graduate in May. Part of my thesis involved keeping a journal throughout the fall semester to record my thoughts about lesson planning, observations about students' performances, and decisions I would make while delivering lessons. The journal's purpose was to understand how I think about teaching and learning. My thesis contributed to my mentoring professor's research on teacher decision-making in education. As part of my thesis, I was to use the spring semester to analyze my journal, looking for themes about how I thought about lesson and unit planning, observations about lesson delivery, and the types of decisions I would make in class to change up a lesson, and observations about students during a lesson that gave me indications that they were either understanding and learning the concepts or were needing extra time to learn or a different learning method.

As I was analyzing my journal and writing up my results, I was also learning how to use an Apple computer. This required saving the document on large floppy disks. I remember losing my work on several occasions, once to a power outage and a second time when the floppy disk was "corrupted," and I couldn't retrieve my document. Thankfully, I had hand-written my analysis first, so I would always have a backup copy to return to and start my typed document again. Back then, the computer was a relatively new technology; I was introduced to it early in its evolution. Little did I realize then just how impactful the computer would become for the remainder of my life and career.

In May, I graduated from Michigan State University, but I didn't attend the commencement ceremony because the length, size, and location of Spartan Stadium didn't sound like something I wanted to be part of. I was no less proud of my accomplishment and the university I was now an alumnus of. School ended for the summer in early June. Now that my master's degree was complete and summer was here, I was looking forward to an opportunity for Dan and me to go for another vacation.

After considering several ideas, we settled on traveling to Stratford, Ontario, Canada. Stratford was known for the Stratford Festival, often featuring Shakespeare's plays. The Toronto Blue Jays would host the Detroit Tigers June 24-26 for a three-game series, so we settled on late June for our vacation. This trip would allow Dan and I to visit Exhibition Stadium, home of the Blue Jays, before they moved into their new stadium the following season. We joked about how this development, moving to a new stadium, meant we would eventually have to return to Toronto to see the new stadium.

We left on Thursday, ensuring we could arrive in Toronto in time to check into our hotel on Friday. The Tigers and Blue Jays played on Friday, Saturday, and Sunday, so we decided to get tickets for all three games. This allowed us to see the city of Toronto as well. The Tigers lost two out of three games. There were many players on the 1988 version of the Tigers who had also played on their 1984 championship team. Consequently, I was excited to see them play and was also able to secure many autographs of my favorite players.

After a long weekend in Toronto, we drove to Stratford. We spent three days there and obtained tickets for a different Shakespeare play each day. As a college student, I often found it difficult to read Shakespeare, but I loved to hear him being read. I was even more impressed with seeing a Shakespeare play in person. The venue was intimate, and I felt I was in each scene with the actors and actresses, not just watching the play. After each play, both Dan and I found that we continued to talk about the themes and the quality of the performance.

At the end of the week, we needed to return home. We decided to visit Buffalo, New York, and Niagara Falls on the way home. While we only planned on spending two days in Buffalo, it was a fantastic experience. Visiting the falls and seeing the geography gave me an appreciation for the area and its interconnections to the high school classes I taught. I learned more about geology and geography, which was quickly incorporated into my Geography class. Additionally, the information was also applicable to my American History class. I enjoyed experiencing how traveling was strongly linked to learning and what I was teaching.

Once we returned home, I had the remainder of the summer where I wasn't taking a college class for the first time since graduating from Calvin. Karen and I would spend time together doing crafts, going to the beach in Holland, or just hanging out. Because I had unplanned days, I went bicycling to fill some of the time. I could bicycle a long way while listening to the radio. The emergence of talk radio provided a new listening experience. I spent at least two afternoons during the week jumping on my bike and riding on the farm roads in the region. Before that summer, the primary way I would stay fit was to go running. However, now that I had more time that I could devote to fitness, I turned to bicycling. I kept running as well and periodically considered competing in a biathlon. While this consideration has yet to materialize, bicycling has become a mainstay in my fitness routine.

Karen and I decided to walk the Mackinaw Bridge over Labor Day. This meant visiting my parents at the cottage they had purchased in northern Michigan. Except on Labor Day, walkers were not allowed on the Mackinaw Bridge, which spanned Lake Michigan and Huron between Michigan's upper and lower peninsula. The Mackinaw Bridge Walk tradition became an annual Labor Day event in 1958 when the bridge was dedicated. The walk begins very early on Labor Day. Karen and I got up early and drove 60 miles north from Boyne City to Mackinaw City to participate in the walk. Once in the city, we boarded a bus to the St. Ignas side of the bridge, where we began the five-mile walk south back to Mackinaw City.

Karen and I were surprised by how many people turned out to walk the bridge. Walking the bridge was an entirely different experience than driving across it. I was struck by just how high the bridge was above the water. Also, the bridge had a sway to it. The swaying wasn't something someone would experience when crossing the bridge in a car. The day was sunny but cold, as is typical by the end of August in northern Michigan. After we completed the five-mile walk and received our bridge walk certificate, we spent some time in Mackinaw City visiting the little shops along the waterfront.

We wandered the city and then headed for our car and began the five-hour trip back to Hudsonville. We both had to work the next day as the fall semester began. I was sad summer was over but looking forward to the girls' basketball season because I had a more experienced team. The early practices indicated that we would have a pretty good season. Also, I was the senior class advisor for the inaugural graduating class from the school. I was looking forward to guiding the seniors toward planning graduation and beginning to develop senior traditions that would be handed down to future seniors.

As expected, the fall was busy. The senior class formed a planning committee for graduation. We decided to work with Jostens to select the colors of the graduation robes offered to the students—the committee chose maroon robes for the boys and white robes for the girls. The students designed their graduation announcements and their senior class ring. Additionally, the class planned the order of the ceremony, including the songs and speakers, and picked a location at a church near the school.

I was teaching government to the seniors in the fall semester. They would take an economics class with me in the spring. It was unusual for me to have two new courses to plan since my first year of teaching. I love both subjects and had the time I needed to devote to creating lessons now that my graduate studies were completed. One experience I was able to plan for the seniors was an opportunity to attend a presidential rally in Grand Rapids. George H.W. Bush announced that he would be visiting Grand Rapids to campaign. At his rally, former president Gerald Ford would also be speaking. I arranged for a bus to take the entire senior class to the event. I knew the federal representative from Grand Rapids and was able to arrange VIP passes for my students. Indeed, not all the students or families were Republicans. Consequently, I would later plan an opportunity to take the entire class to a Democratic campaign event. While Democratic candidate Michael Dukakis wasn't present, I thought it was important for students to see the different types of events that candidates would hold.

The 1988 presidential election made teaching government more relevant and fun for seniors. We engaged in a simulation throughout the semester where the students were randomly divided into two political parties. They were to draw numbers out of a hat, and those who received either a number one or a number two were to become a political party for the remainder of the semester. They had to create a name and a party symbol and plan events to emulate the political process. They held a primary election during the semester and a convention where the entire high school attended and heard the acceptance speeches of each candidate. Each political party developed a campaign for the entire high school leading up to a vote on election day. The day after election day, we all knew the outcome of the national election, and I also announced the winner of the high school election. The simulation was a great way to help the students understand the political process.

During Christmas break, I discovered Christian Sports Outreach International. This organization encouraged Christian athletes to use their skills to play sports as a vehicle to share the Gospel of Christ in Europe. I talked to Dan about the opportunity, and he encouraged me to try it. I sent off my application and prayed for it to be accepted. When they invited me to travel with them during the summer, I trained to be in playing shape and began raising funds to support my summer travels.

As part of the commitment to traveling with Christian Sports Outreach International, I had to raise support to offset the cost of traveling, housing, and meals. At a minimum, I needed to raise $4000. That felt like a great deal of money in 1989. I wrote a letter sharing my opportunity with an appeal for funds. I sent these appeal letters to friends and family, asking them for financial help and prayers. I was amazed at the support I received.

When I returned to school as 1989 began, I shared with my principal my plan to participate in a sports-related mission trip in the summer—the principal where I taught committed to helping me raise funds. The school organized a free throw event at the end of the school day near the end of the academic year. At the event, I would share information about the missionary trip, including using sports as a vehicle to share the Gospel of Jesus Christ. Students supported my trip by soliciting pledges for each free throw I made from 100 attempts. My church helped me raise funds, giving me time on a Sunday night to present to the congregation my mission trip and allowing me to appeal for support. Additionally, the church leadership arranged for me to speak at other local churches and youth groups, sharing the opportunity.

I was training for my trip, making presentations about the upcoming ministry at churches and youth groups in the area, and excited to do something to share my faith and the hope I found in Christ. Putting my energy and focus into the upcoming mission trip helped me keep at bay my feelings for Karen and my frustrations about my marriage. This experience taught me that I could manage my emotions and frustration by channeling my energy into productive activities. I used this technique over the next several years to manage my commitment to stay faithful, stay married, and be the best person I could be. On the surface, this worked; however, I failed to understand that while the feelings and frustrations were masked, they were still there, and eventually, they would resurface, but with a harder punch.

The day of the free throw contest arrived. The students made signs, and all grades from kindergarten through high school entered the gym and sat in the bleachers. The gym was packed. Someone turned on the scoreboard and prepared to count attempted free throws. I asked two of my students to be my rebounders so I could just focus on shooting. They were ready and full of affirming cheers. Both were players for me on the girls' basketball team and were so happy to support me by being part of this event.

As the principal introduced the event, the gym fell very silent. That made me more nervous than the raucous cheering. Dr. Brinkerhoff announced it was time for the event to begin. I approached the line, took a deep breath, and sunk the first shot. The students cheered every time I made a basket. I could feel their energy and support. I felt like I was in a rhythm and focused on my shooting form. I made the first twenty shots before I missed. Once I missed, I focused on the next shot, no longer counting the number of attempts in my mind. As I finally faced the last attempt, I instinctively knew I had exceeded my previous personal best number of free throws during all the months of practice. When the final shot fell through the net, the scoreboard counted 84 made free throws out of 100. Tears of joy fell on my face as I quickly thanked God for the focus and ability He provided. The gym went wild. Next, Dr. Brinkerhoff announced the final total raised, well over $4000.00. All the students were excited and congratulated me as they returned to their classrooms to head to their buses to go home. Everyone felt a part of something important to me, and the love I felt was overwhelming.

Now that I had met and exceeded my fundraising goal, I could focus on finishing the school year and training for the July trip. Hints of spring were in the air, making running outside more enjoyable. The school where I taught approached me about starting a girls' softball team. I asked Tim, a fellow teacher of mine, if he would be a co-coach with me. Tim and I had taught together for five years; we were the first teachers hired, so we had always shared a special bond. He agreed to share the coaching duties with me, and we coached the girls through their first season. I was happy to help but didn't want to be the head coach as I concentrated on my upcoming missionary trip, working with the senior class to plan their senior trip to Washington, D.C., and contemplating another change in my life.

No one knew, except Dan, that I contemplated resigning from my teaching position to pursue law school. I quietly took the Law School Admission Test (LSAT) in January and began researching my options. In February, I applied to three law schools that were reasonable options, given that I wanted to stay in Michigan because that is where I planned to practice law with Dan. I received a notice in April that I had been accepted at two law schools. I chose one and was scheduled to begin the following January. Dan was very excited. I shared with my parents the good news, and my dad was very excited. He had always wanted me to be a lawyer. As I explored my law school options, I unconsciously was rebuilding my relationship with my dad. The relationship grew stronger again, and I began to confide in him my concerns about my relationship with Dan. He was very supportive and said he would be there if I left Dan. He shared his concerns about Dan's work habits and how he just wanted me to be happy. For the first time since my parents divorced in 1976, my father and I began to reconnect on a deeper level. It was now 1989. After thirteen years, the wall between us finally started to crumble.

In May, Dan, myself, the principal, and his wife escorted the senior class to Washington, D.C., to visit the sites and meet with our state representatives. Additionally, we were scheduled to meet with Beverly LaHaye, president of Concerned Women for America, a pro-life advocacy group. I enjoyed the writings of her husband, Tim LaHaye, who authored several books on biblical prophecy. We also were to meet with our local state representative and two senators. Dan and I were excited to be traveling with the class. We both knew this would be my last significant time with them.

The most memorable event from the trip was being stuck in the Capitol elevator with ten seniors. Our weight caused something to be triggered, stopping the elevator midway between two floors. I pushed the communication button and notified the voice on the other end that our elevator was stuck. The voice was reassuring and said they would have someone right there quickly. However, one of the girls became highly distraught. She seemed to be having a panic attack. I and two other senior girls sat next to her after getting her to sit on the elevator floor. We all tried to help her realize everything would be okay. When the elevator started to rise again, she seemed to calm down, but she was the first one off the elevator when we stopped at the next floor. Interestingly, we all took the steps more often during the remainder of the trip.

After we returned from the senior trip, I notified the school that I would not be returning in the fall of 1989 because I would be attending law school beginning in January of 1990. Many students were surprised and saddened. June was to be the school's very first high school graduation. I had been the graduating class advisor since their eighth-grade year, so it would be a special occasion for me because I felt close to these students. It was also a bittersweet time, but in my heart, I knew I needed to take the steps necessary to care for myself so I could provide for myself in the future and then leave this trap called marriage. Deep down, I believed that once I became a lawyer, I could support myself, get a divorce, embrace who I was, and search for a more fulfilling relationship. I don't remember much about graduation, as my mind and emotions raged. I remember crying when the senior class presented me with a dozen roses and a card. Likely, I would have been sad even if I hadn't resigned because I had become close to those students as we grew from junior high through 12th grade.

As the school year ended and the summer began, the July date for my mission trip departure was only a month away. I kept training for the opportunity to play basketball in Europe and share the good news of Jesus Christ. Each of us selected for the trip with Christian

Sports Outreach International had to write a couple of different versions of our testimony. One version was to be very short. We had to memorize the brief testimony and be prepared to share it when called upon. The second testimony could be longer and written as we might not be able to remember that one. We could use the extended version if asked to present our testimony formally in situations such as at church or before an assembly.

Each day, I would go for a run. On shorter runs, I would recite my brief testimony to be sure I was ready to *"... answer every man that asketh {me} a reason of the hope that is in {me} with meekness and fear"* (I Peter 3:15 KJV). For the longer testimony, I would read it out loud, practicing looking around the room to look like I was speaking more and reading less. Teaching in front of students daily was one thing, but speaking before a large crowd was another experience I rarely had.

I left in late June to meet up with the one-hundred-plus athletes who would be a part of the summer tour for Christian Sports Outreach International. We met in Newark, New Jersey, and departed for the Netherlands through London. This represented the first time I had traveled outside the United States, except for visiting Canada and Mexico. We arrived at the London Airport after an overnight flight, boarded buses, and headed to Sittard, Holland. We were to stay at the Netherlands National Sports Center in Sittard.

On our first day in Sittard, we practiced in the morning and then attended a football game. Some of the members of our contingent were football players who played against a local team. The afternoon was cold and rainy, but people were in the bleachers cheering for their lads as they played against a team of Americans. While the game was underway, many of us wandered through the bleachers, sharing our short testimony, and handing out literature written in Dutch. During the bus ride to the stadium, the softball coach asked if any woman on the bus had any softball pitching experience. She mentioned the pitcher who was initially scheduled to be on the trip could not come, and the softball team needed someone to throw fastpitch softball. I made my way to the front and explained I had played softball in high school and college and was able to pitch. I asked a few questions about how playing two sports might impact my time and was comforted to know that the softball and basketball games rarely overlap so that I could participate in both. However, the basketball coach wasn't as comfortable with this development. During the trip, particularly on softball game days, I felt the basketball coach held my softball participation against me. The softball coach had adjusted practice times to allow me to prioritize basketball. Playing on both teams was fun and tiring, but it was my best possible experience. I met twice as many people and had little time to consider my relationship frustrations with Dan.

One of our days in the Netherlands took us to the city square near the Royal Palace. Here, we began a full day of street evangelism. After some time, when we worked individually, approaching people to give them literature about the Gospel, we began organizing into one colossal choir. We drew a crowd who fell silent when we started singing. As the centrum began filling with people, we finished our songs, and then our pastor stepped forward and preached the salvation message.

When he began preaching, we again dispersed into the crowd to hand out literature, share our testimony, and pray with anyone who took up our offer to pray for them. I was surprised by how many people spoke and understood English. I was able to share my testimony in English with several people and even had an opportunity to lead a young lady in prayer, where she asked Christ to come into her heart and life. This experience gave new meaning to the verse, *"Where two or three are gathered together in my name, there am I in the midst of them"* (Mathew 18:20 KJV). That day was the first time I began to understand and want to learn more about the ministry of the Holy Spirit. I could feel a spirit among us. I could sense the power and see the ministry of the Holy Spirit that day. I never recalled a sermon about the Holy Spirit in the past, but now I was hungry to understand the ministry of the Holy Spirit.

Not much of our time in the Netherlands involved ministry. We had opportunities to play basketball and engage in sightseeing activities. I enjoyed an afternoon riding the canal boats throughout Amsterdam and the surrounding cities. The architecture was so different from anything I had experienced in the United States, except for a few towns along the East Coast in New England. I met so many amazing men and women during the month-long travel. We represented so many of the states in the United States. It was fun to learn about each person and the various lives they lived.

Besides spending time in the Netherlands, we went to Germany and Austria before returning to the Netherlands and, subsequently, the United States. I was blessed to share my testimony on July 4th at an army base near Frankfurt, Germany. We were celebrating America's birthday on an army base. The time spent on the base was extraordinary. On July 3rd, we began our stay at the army base, where our track team participated in a 24-hour running marathon, competing against several American military marathon teams. Those of us not participating in the other track and field events during the evening stayed at the track and cheered on our friends participating in the marathon. Each team was comprised of four runners. Every hour, one runner circled the track continuously. After the hour, the next team member would take turns running around the track for the next hour. This rotation occurred for each of the four team members over twenty-four hours. Four runners meant each participant would run eight hours within 24 hours. We, spectators, ensured they had water and protein bars during and between their one-hour runs. Between each one-hour rotation, the other three teammates would nap and take care of their legs to return to the track after a three-hour break. I was in awe of these runners' stamina. The marathon winner would be the team that accumulated the most laps within 24 hours. After the twenty-four-hour event, our team won the marathon. As part of the event, we were invited to share songs and testimonies before our pastor preached a sermon about how Jesus Christ paid the ultimate price by dying on the cross as atonement for our sins.

After leaving the army base and before departing for Austria, we had the opportunity to visit Frankfurt, Germany. The original plan was to spend several days in Frankfurt. Games were scheduled for each sports team, including one basketball and one softball game. Something must have changed our plans because when we returned to our hotel room after visiting Colone, Germany, and touring the cathedral, we were informed we would leave early the following day for Austria. Before heading to dinner at the hotel, we were advised to stay in our rooms that night and not leave the hotel.

We boarded our bus early the following day and drove to Austria. We were stopped at the border along the route, where we got off the bus and had to show our passports. Once back on the bus, we crossed into Austria. Our home base in Austria was Kuchl. The town is located just outside Salzburg, Austria, and sits at the base of the Alps. This was my favorite stop on the trip. We woke up early each morning and practiced basketball when we didn't have a game. The afternoons were free and allowed each of us to explore Kuchl. After basketball practice, I would walk over to the softball field and train for another couple of hours. Despite my fatigue, I wouldn't let an afternoon pass without a walk into town. Austrian coffee and pastry were terrific. The mountain views were captivating. I had been to Pike's Peak and the Rocky Mountains in the United States, but the Alps were so much more beautiful. I would sit at the deli, slowly eat my pastry, and stare at the Alps. While there, I would write in the journal I was keeping.

My thoughts were often about the daily devotions our pastor led. He was different from the pastors I had learned from. He shared more about how to have a relationship with God the Father, Jesus the Son, and the Holy Spirit. His words emphasized the relationship more than the legalism and ritualism I was used to in the churches I had attended. Little did I realize then that this foundation would alter my faith over time. As I continued to understand myself better, I found that I was far more interested in learning about God the Father, Jesus, and the Holy Spirit than the church's legalism. I also learned how to listen to the "still small voice" within me and recognize God's leading by learning more about him through reading the Bible.

One day, while in Austria, we were able to visit Salzburg. So many of us wanted to tour the VonTrap family home, the backdrop for filming the Sound of Music. The tour was terrific. Our guide perfectly described each movie clip filmed within the house as we moved from room to room and into the courtyard. We all wanted to watch the movie when we returned to the United States. Because of that tour, The Sound of Music became one of my favorite movies, as much for the location as the history depicted within the storyline.

Our time in Austria ended too soon, and we were off to Rotterdam, Netherlands. This would be our last stop before returning to London, where we would depart for New York and go our separate ways. In Rotterdam, the softball team was able to play the Dutch national team. I surprised myself by pitching two games back-to-back. We won both games. That evening, the basketball team suited up to play a local team from Rotterdam. While I didn't play, I was happy to be with all my teammates and enjoy our remaining time. The next day, we spent time at the beach in Rotterdam. I wanted to visit the Haig, but the court was in session, and visitors weren't allowed. Several of us found another boat tour, enabling us to see more of the area and better understand the canal system throughout the Netherlands. I was fascinated by the canals and thought that if I had ever to leave the United States and live somewhere else, I would want to live in the Netherlands. I also thought about how such a trip like this would have been so helpful for teaching geography in the fall if I were still teaching and not planning on going to law school. In the afternoon, after having gone our separate ways earlier in the day, our entire group met for a picnic and a robust game of touch football. That evening, each team gathered for the final time to share their experiences. I gathered with the basketball team to reflect on our time in Europe and presented mini skits depicting our time together on the trip.

The next day, we packed to leave for London. We spent the morning learning from our pastors and praying for our future ministry and those who received Christ during our time in Europe. I had never experienced such peace and the presence of the Holy Spirit like this before. It was here, during this summer, that I realized that Christianity was a relationship rather than rules and laws. I had studied doctrine and theology while at college. I memorized scripture and tried to apply it to my daily life. But for the first time, I learned what it meant to focus on one's relationship with the Father, Son, and Holy Spirit. Likely, this foundational experience ensured I would remain committed to my faith in Christ when all that legalism and theology taught me was that I was a sinner and dammed to hell because of the innate attractions I couldn't change.

When I returned home in late July, my family, friends, and pastor met me at the airport. Being back home and among the people I loved was great, but that feeling was short-lived. I had to figure out what was next for me now that I had resigned from my teaching job and waiting for the start of law school in January. My short-term goal was to find a job to begin saving money for law school. I applied to the closest sporting goods store, quickly received an interview, and was hired part-time. I enjoyed the change of pace from the long hours of teaching. I would go to the store, punch in, work a shift, and return home without obligations to grade papers or prepare lessons for the next day. I knew it was only a short break because law school would be challenging and require long hours of studying, drafting briefs, and researching case law.

Early in August, I received a telephone call from a local Christian college administrator who had received my name from a mutual friend. Bill, the vice president for academics, explained that he was looking for a part-time instructor to teach history this fall and that he had been given my name by someone who thought I might be interested in picking up a class to teach. This was an excellent opportunity to stay busy and earn money as I waited for January and the start of law school. I met with Bill, and before I left the interview, I was scheduled to teach at 8:00 am American History class on Monday, Wednesday, and Friday. The eight o'clock time worked great with my work schedule at the sporting goods store that didn't open until 10:00 am. As I left the interview with a new opportunity, I couldn't help but think that when one follows "God's will," everything falls into place.

Despite my work schedule being less busy than when I taught full-time at the Baptist high school, Dan worked more each week than before. I was used to this during tax season from January through April, but this was a new development during the non-tax part of the year. I usually didn't work weekends at the sporting goods store and hoped Dan and I would spend some time visiting my parents at the lake or touring some of the areas in Michigan we often discussed. Whenever I suggested something for the weekend, he made excuses, mostly involving him going to the office and working. I resented being home alone and doing things alone. There was a greater distance than I had experienced before.

One night in mid-August, Dan came home from work. I decided at dinner to ask why he was working so much. He looked at me and explained that he did not know if he loved me anymore and had decided to move out. He told me he would live in the apartment above the law office and stay in touch while figuring things out. The following day, he grabbed his suitcase and headed for his car. I watched him drive out of the driveway and sat stunned at the kitchen table.

Now what? I thought. Eventually, Karen came upstairs to see about our plans for the day. I filled her in on the latest pronouncement by Dan. She was stunned. We sat at the kitchen table for hours, dissecting the events and figuring out why neither of us could see this coming.

I immediately feared for my future. My decision to go to law school was based on potentially working as a lawyer with Dan as a husband-and-wife team. That idea now seemed to be in doubt. The Christian community was very judgmental. Likely, finding a job in a Christian school was no longer an option if we were divorced, and finding teaching positions in public schools was still difficult as very few openings were available. I was sure I would be relegated to the side or blamed for the situation because I was not the conventional Christian wife who stayed home with the children. I was not sure I wanted a divorce, but I was also unsure if I could trust Dan again. Maybe this was a blessing in disguise. While I was at a loss for what to do next, going to law school still seemed the best direction.

I decided to take a risk and visit my pastor to seek guidance. As I sat in his office and tried to explain what happened, I was overcome by fear. I was afraid he would somehow blame me and tell me I needed to be more like a "traditional" wife and support my husband. However, much to my surprise, he was very supportive and tried to explain that perhaps Dan was feeling inadequate. The pastor explained that I was a tremendously popular teacher at the high school. I was very well-liked and respected in the community and at church. He then said that Dan saw himself as a family lawyer and perhaps felt threatened by my success. I couldn't help but think Dan had already talked to Pastor Jim and that he knew something I didn't know. I was beginning to think God was punishing me somehow for the secret I harbored in my mind about my attraction to women. However, I couldn't imagine why a forgiving God would punish or test me. After all, I acknowledged my homosexual feelings to God and committed to staying in the marriage. I wondered if this was a test by God to determine whether I was serious about staying committed to the marriage. I knew if this was a test, I was committed and would follow through on my decision to remain married to Dan. I knew my self-discipline and determination; once I made my mind up, I did what I committed myself to do. I learned countless times that these traits, self-discipline, determination, and commitment, helped me succeed as a student, athlete, and teacher. The closet was lonely. I was left with my thoughts because I couldn't share this part of the story with Pastor Jim or Dan. My other support system was my parents, and I hadn't even told them about my secret. At that moment, I wasn't aware that my natural reaction was to think about the situation in a legalistic manner rather than turning to God as my father and seeing my relationship with him as an opportunity to seek guidance and support.

I left that meeting angry at Dan and angry at my pastor. I couldn't help but think Pastor Jim had already spoken with Dan, and he knew more about what was happening with Dan than he was telling me. I felt deceived and potentially lied to. I also couldn't help thinking that all this had occurred while I was in Europe serving the Lord. I couldn't believe God would let this happen. The still, small voice reminded me of Ephesians 6:12, *"For we wrestle not against flesh and blood, but against principalities, against power, against the rulers of the darkness of this world, against spiritual wickedness in high places"* (KJV). As I contemplated that much of life is spiritual warfare, I realized I needed to study the Bible more to understand better how one fights within the spiritual realm. As I learned more, I came to see that while God allows for free will and, thus, a spiritual war, He has also made way for us to win. While reading the Bible, I was reminded, "*Ye are of God, little children, and have overcome them: because greater is he that is in you than he that is in the world"* (I John 4:4 KJV). I trusted that what was unseen required more faith than I had mustered previously. However, the battle strengthened my faith and knowledge of the Bible. As these verses began coming to mind, I started recognizing how God was reaching out to me. I was beginning to recognize the relationship with God and how he spoke to me through his Word. This moment was a catalyst for many more moments when I would begin to turn to the Word of God rather than dwelling upon the legalistic doctrines of the church or the spoken expectations of church leaders.

My friends rallied around me as we tried to keep the situation from becoming public. I tried to be my usual self, but nightly, I would go home and face the reality that things were not as I wanted. I began searching for solutions, knowing I would need to take care of myself if Dan filed for a divorce. This brought severe doubts to my desire to go to law school. I would need a full-time job if Dan decided to divorce. However, finding a teaching job in public schools was a long shot because the need for teachers was minimal. I used to pray for God's leading, but he was sometimes silent. The closet felt deeper, darker, and colder than ever before. I now began to search for an understanding of why there were times in my walk with God when He was silent. In time, I would recognize that this was God's way of telling me to stay the course. I slowly realized the silence was not punishment but the absence of further guidance. Hence, I learned to trust in the dark what God had already revealed in the light. The more I sought to understand God and who He was, the easier it would become to hear his voice and to understand his silence.

I began to question whether I wanted to put the relationship back together. Suppose we were to get back together, whether that was an opportunity for me to buy time until I figured out a better way forward or just a temporary arrangement to allow me to concentrate on going to and graduating from law school. I wasn't sure after Dan's declaration if I could trust him again. Periodically, Dan would call or stop by the house for something. When he did stop by the house, he may stay for dinner or a conversation over a soda or ice cream sundae while living in the apartment above his law office. In those moments, I saw a glimpse of the friendship that had drawn us together previously. Mostly, I felt like I was walking on eggshells, not knowing if I wanted things to work or wanted a way out. On one visit, I approached Dan about seeking couples counseling while we lived apart. I was surprised when he agreed. I took that as a good sign that he, too, might want to explore whether this relationship could work.

Dan agreed to go with me to talk to Pastor Jim and ask him if he could work with us while we figure out things. I think we were both expecting Pastor Jim to be our counselor. Pastor Jim explained that while he was a trained counselor, he believed counseling anyone under his church ministry wouldn't be good. He encouraged us to seek counseling and recommended another pastor in the area, a trained counselor, who would often see members from Pastor Jim's church. Dan agreed to see a counselor during that meeting to discuss our issues. Of course, I was still trying to figure out those issues. During our meeting with Pastor Jim, I gained no greater understanding of why Dan felt he no longer loved me than before the meeting. The session didn't last long as it was clear Pastor Jim was referring us to someone else he knew. We left the office and went our separate ways. Before we parted, Dan said he would call the counselor Pastor Jim recommended to see if he would see us and would let me know what he learned.

While waiting to hear from Dan to see if the recommended person would see us, I prayed daily, seeking guidance. I committed to memorizing the Bible's entire book of Romans to replace my homosexual thoughts and feelings when they would surface with the Word of God. I also thought memorizing scripture could be a way for God to show me the next steps I should consider. I promised God to continue my commitment to my relationship with Dan until I received other guidance from Him. Eventually, Dan called and told me the counselor had agreed to see us. Dan shared with me that our first appointment would be on Saturday.

Dan and I attended counseling every Saturday morning for several months. During those sessions, I never talked about my homosexual thoughts and feelings. I did talk about the lack of romance in our marriage. I talked about how I felt lonely and that Dan wasn't emotionally available. It seemed like this counselor was avoiding the entire subject of sexuality and romance. Dan talked about how my career meant I wasn't ever home, even after he admitted that I was no longer teaching but scheduled to go to law school. The counselor seemed focused on having Dan and me spend meaningful time together and prioritizing each other over work. That was easy for me at this moment because I was only working part-time. Yet, I wondered if Dan would prioritize spending time together in addition to our time in counseling and breakfast afterward or participating in an occasional 5K or 10K event together.

As September progressed, we continued attending counseling together but continued to live apart. I decided to keep making plans to go to law school. I was still sure that I would need to change careers if Dan chose to file for a divorce, and nothing so far from our counseling sessions gave me any indication if Dan had one foot in the relationship or one foot out of the relationship. I was not convinced that Dan was putting his whole heart into counseling or wanted the relationship to work. There were also times when I wasn't sure if I had one foot in the relationship and one foot out of the relationship.

I decided to seek legal counseling just in case Dan filed for a divorce. Dan was a lawyer, and I was worried about being taken advantage of if he finally decided to walk away. I made an appointment with Mr. Roane for a consultation. Karen accompanied me to my meeting. As we met with Mr. Roane, I explained that I had been married for six years, and Dan had left after I returned from a missionary trip in Europe. Eventually, I said Dan was a lawyer. I was worried he would take advantage of me if he initiated a divorce, even though we were in counseling trying to determine whether we wanted to make the relationship work. Mr. Roane stopped me as I was about to continue and stared intently at me for a moment. Then he asked me if my husband was Dan, who had a law practice on Leonard Street. I responded affirmatively. He then said something that startled me. He explained that the rumor on the street was that Dan was having a relationship with another man. He quickly clarified that it was only a rumor and had no idea whether it was true.

I was numb. Mr. Roane said he would happily represent me should Dan and I seek a divorce. I thanked Mr. Roane and promised to call him if I needed his services. Karen and I stopped for lunch and discussed the meeting I had just left and the news we had heard. At first, I wasn't sure if I had heard Mr. Roane correctly. Karen affirmed that I had heard Mr. Roane correctly. Next, I wasn't sure I believed the rumor. We were surprised that the rumor came up because nothing in my conversation would have led Mr. Roane to bring it up in the first place. If the rumor was true, Karen and I agreed that the rumor would explain many things I had experienced the past year and perhaps the past six years.

I prayed for guidance and clarity as I lay in bed that night. The realization that Dan might be gay was a possibility I had never considered. Now, I had no idea what to do or think. I contemplated confronting him with the information, but I had no proof or reason to believe he would tell me the truth. I also thought that if I confronted him, he might turn the table on me and accuse me of being a homosexual. I wasn't sure I wanted to deal with that issue right now. The situation I found myself facing was nothing I was prepared to handle. Ironically, knowing others struggled with homosexuality after making this discovery by reading Tony Campolo's book, *20 Hot Potatoes Christians Are Afraid to Touch*, was comforting. Still, it left me with no answers about navigating the future or my relationship with Dan.

Chapter Twenty-Six: Coexistence

> *"And we know that all things work together for good to them that love God, to them who are the called according to his purpose"*
>
> -Romans 8:28 KJV.

Two things became evident as I reflected on my meeting with Mr. Roane. First, I didn't know Dan like I thought I did. As I replayed specific conversations with Dan and some of his behaviors and reactions during our six-year marriage, I became convinced there was an element of truth to the rumor. Indeed, that would explain the lack of intimacy in our relationship. It would also explain his familiarity with homosexuality, whether it be commentary about his favorite actor, Errol Flynn, or the rumors about other lawyers' sexuality that he would periodically bring up to me. It also reminded me of how angry he got when I had asked friends to help us move to Hudsonville because he felt moving was too personal, and I was so unthoughtful to ask people we barely knew to help. Second, I needed a plan to ensure that no matter what happened, whether we got a divorce or reconciled, I could take care of myself financially now and in the future. If the rumor was true, and I was beginning to believe it was, no matter what level of commitment I made, it would only be a matter of time before one of us decided that we could no longer live in this marriage.

Dan and I continued to see the counselor, who finally suggested that Dan move back into the house to work on the issues that divided us. The counselor only offered us to prioritize spending meaningful time with each other. I couldn't help but think that was a ruse because the issues that divided us never surfaced during counseling. Part of my issue was that my attraction to women got in the way of my relationship with Dan because I wasn't fully prepared to give him my entire self, emotionally and physically. And now I had information that led me to think Dan might be experiencing the same challenge. We both led our counselor to believe that the problem stemmed from each of us working too much. Working too much was partially the problem, but putting out a fire at one end of the house didn't mean the fire at the other end of the house was under control. I was buying time until I could figure out a way forward, which was likely a way out. I had no idea what Dan's strategy was for navigating the relationship.

As Dan moved back home, we worked on spending time together and doing things we enjoyed. We both enjoyed running, so we often ran together in the evenings. We would run in 5K and 10K races on Saturday. We enjoyed watching movies and reading history. We loved politics and current events. We had much in common and didn't lack for things to discuss during meals. We entertained selectively by inviting other couples for dinner or playing cards. The problem was that such commonalities masked the deeper conversations we should have been having. It was clear that we liked each other and doing things together. What was missing for me was deep romantic love and intimacy. While I enjoyed Dan's friendship, I longed for something more profound and fulfilling. I found that I was insatiably sad. I did not express my sadness or desire for love and intimacy because I feared rejection. Somehow, hearing him say he wasn't attracted to me would be more painful than his actions, which indirectly said the same thing.

One day, Dan came home from work sad and depressed. I hadn't ever seen him so down and emotional. In fact, throughout our entire marriage, I wondered if he felt any emotions at all. He would have been a great clone of the original Star Trek character, Dr. Spock. I asked how he was, and he asked me to sit in the living room because he had something to tell me. He explained that he had visited his doctor for his annual check-up and was waiting on test results. He explained that he was worried. I asked him about the tests, and he continued to be vague. I pressed him for more information about the tests, and he finally said that he was tested for high blood sugar. He was worried that his blood sugar counts were too high and that he might have diabetes. His answer seemed odd. His worry seemed too great to be related to a blood sugar test. I wasn't aware that diabetes was present in his family. Also, I hadn't seen any symptoms, which would have led me to believe he might have diabetes.

I was suspicious that he was not telling me the whole truth, but happy that for the first time I could remember, he had shared something deeply personal with me and was willing to share his fear. On the one hand, the depth of the conversation was encouraging. He let down his guard and let me see his feelings and fears. On the other hand, I didn't believe it was about diabetes. Trust continued to erode.

Dan came home three days later, and his somewhat optimistic nature returned. He explained that the test returned negative results, that everything was normal, and that he was fine. He was in a celebratory mood. He had brought home ice cream to celebrate. I asked him why he didn't tell me sooner about his check-up, and he changed the subject. We never spoke about the blood sugar tests and his worry again. However, his behavior, coupled with the information Mr. Roane had shared with me, made me wonder if there was something else he had been tested for other than his blood sugar levels. I knew it was just a matter of time before I discovered or confirmed what I was beginning to conclude: Dan was gay and was involved with other men or having an affair. The realization finally sunk in that we both might be using this marriage to hide who we were or perhaps to practice who we should be. There was no comfort in that thought. If we were both hiding in a marriage, it would never be what God intended and I longed for.

Dan seemed excited about the prospect of my attending law school. We often talked about practicing together and the benefits of my working during law school as his legal clerk. He would advise and give insights about attending law school from his experience. I knew the opportunity to work for Dan would be a good experience, but I wanted to see if we could keep the relationship together while I attended law school. Would working together draw us together or push us apart? I knew I was preparing myself for my next step, becoming more financially independent, which might allow me to escape this empty relationship. However, I couldn't help but think Dan was using me to live a double life. I didn't believe I was living a double life because I had vowed not to act upon my attraction to women while we were married. Yet deep down, I knew I was not being authentic to myself.

I continued to teach at the Christian college and work at the sporting goods store. I didn't even let Karen know I was contemplating a divorce. There would be time for that conversation after I started law school. While my parents knew I was planning to attend law school, they didn't think I was considering it a step toward divorce. Having a plan kept me hopeful. It became a way of life. It seemed that I was always living for a time in the future, and the here and now were nothing more than steps toward the goal. Time would only tell if my plan would come together.

One late fall day, Dan came home with exciting news. He had been asked to be a part-time magistrate for a court. As a part-time magistrate, he would be asked to sign warrants, marry people, and supervise mediation hearings. He was extremely excited because this would provide him with a steady income to smooth out the times when the law practice experienced the average highs and lows of caseloads and revenue streams. Dan and I always worried about the need for a steady income flow from being self-employed in a service job that entirely depended upon people walking into the office. My income was stable and predictable when I worked full-time, offsetting our concerns. Now, I was working part-time, but we knew expenses were coming with attending law school. There were times when the law practice was busier than others. Dan had always talked about wanting to become a judge because he would have a consistent income and working hours. This was a life-long goal for him. I was excited for him because it was clear he was excited about the opportunity to be a magistrate. I asked him how this would impact his work preparing people's income taxes. He said he would continue preparing taxes between January and April around the court schedule.

I was happy that Dan had found something that made him happy. I enjoyed teaching college students and history again, which made me happy, and I wanted him to have that similar fulfillment. The college students were more motivated and engaged than the high school students. They asked good questions, and in turn, those questions motivated me to read more and learn more. Having the opportunity to teach college students rekindled my love for teaching. What I found most enjoyable was the opportunity to prepare lessons that included a greater depth of content, requiring me to study deeper. I liked the complexity of knowledge and the chance to explore that complexity through classroom instruction. However, this enjoyment made me doubt my commitment to law school and being a lawyer.

One day, Bill, the Vice President of Academics at the college, asked me to stop by his office after class. I picked a day I wasn't scheduled to be at the sporting goods store until the evening, so I had time to talk. During our meeting, Bill shared his observations about my class and teaching. He was hearing positive things from the students. After summarizing his remarks, he asked me if I wanted to teach American History and Western Civilization during the spring semester. I told him I would give him an answer later in the week.

That evening, while I worked at the sporting goods store, I couldn't help but think about Bill's offer. I enjoyed teaching. I contemplated my doubts about attending law school and eventually becoming a lawyer. I challenged myself to understand my motive for going to law school. Initially, I thought it was an avenue for spending more time with Dan and sharing everyday work experiences, expanding our conversations and time. However, that was when I was more committed to staying married to Dan. Now, I was questioning my commitment, given that I doubted whether Dan was committed to the marriage and that he was only using the marriage to hide who he was and what he might be doing. I also saw law school and being a lawyer as the best way to provide for myself after a divorce. However, I was now challenging myself about the best way to provide for myself. While being a lawyer may be financially beneficial, would I enjoy it? If I didn't enjoy being a lawyer, would I be happy? I also knew my dad wouldn't like to see me give up law school. I reminded myself that I needed to seek what I loved to do; if I did what I loved, I would be good at it, and likely, if I were good at it, I would also find the career to provide the financial support I needed. As I fell asleep alone in bed that night, I was beginning to rethink my commitment to attending law school.

The next day, I stopped by my parents' house for lunch on my way to work at the sporting goods store. I was scheduled to begin work at 2:00 pm. Over lunch, I explained the offer by the college to teach in the spring. I explained that I had second thoughts about attending law school and felt I was going for the wrong reasons. I explained that my decision to attend law school was more for Dan than me. My parents listened as I poured out my heart. I felt awkward because my mom worked for Dan, and I was unsure how she felt about what I said. I never thought my mom would tell Dan anything I shared, so I didn't hold back my concerns that if we were lawyers, my life would consist of work and work-based conversations. I knew she saw how much Dan worked and how little time he spent with me. Yet she never shared her opinions or observations unless I asked.

My mom weighed in first. She was supportive as usual and expressed her unfailing love. She just wanted me to be happy. She also surprised me when she said she could understand how I might not want to work with Dan because both working with and living with Dan might be even more challenging to our relationship. She explained that she wasn't sure it would benefit any marriage. My father surprised me even more when he said that if I was going to law school for all the wrong reasons, I shouldn't go. He did explain that he didn't want me working retail for the rest of my life, likely because I was also working at the sporting goods store. He had worked retail and wanted a better career for me than that. He also explained that I should follow my heart no matter my decisions. He said I shouldn't worry about whether the relationship would survive or stay in the relationship just because I worried about being able to provide for myself. He committed that he and my mom would help me when or if I needed help. He encouraged me to teach if that is what I enjoyed doing.

After lunch, I headed off to the sporting goods store job. I enjoyed the job and loved sharing my knowledge of skiing and running with customers. I relished having a job with a set start time and a scheduled end time that allowed me to walk away at the end of the shift and not think about working again until my next scheduled shift. As I worked that night, I thought about my discussion with my parents. Their support was terrific. It gave me the strength to talk to Dan about my doubts about attending law school. By the time I punched out to drive home, I had decided to forgo law school and begin a career teaching at the college level. Now, I just needed to let Dan know what I had decided. I also needed to understand what it would take to qualify to teach full-time at a college or university, which likely meant going back to school, just not law school.

I taught my American History class the next day. After class, I found Bill, who was glad to see me. I told him my decision to accept his offer to teach both courses in the spring. He was delighted. He shared the schedule and provided me with the books for the World History course. He asked if I would be interested in working as a recruiter for the college. He said the college wanted to create a full-time job for me, including teaching two classes and working the remainder of the time as a recruiter in the admissions office. He explained that he had talked to the college president and that they would like me to seriously consider taking their offer of a full-time position that involved teaching and recruiting students. I don't know if the outward smile matched the inward excitement, but I hope it did. I was very excited about this opportunity. I told Bill I would likely accept the offer but wanted to see the details before officially taking it. I shared with Bill that because of this first semester of teaching, I had become very interested in pursuing a career working at the college level. I asked him more about what I would have to do to become a full-time faculty member at the college level. He was glad I was thinking about the next steps in furthering my education and provided me with sound advice. I left and headed home. I could not wait to tell Dan about my decision to forgo law school and work full-time at Bible College. I was overjoyed that the college wanted me to be part of their team rather than just having a part-time teaching opportunity, so they offered me a full-time opportunity. I didn't expect anything like that.

That night, when Dan arrived home, I had dinner waiting. I was looking forward to the conversation, bracing for all reactions. Over dinner, I explained to Dan the incredible offer that the college had made me. He asked me why I was entertaining the offer if I were going to attend law school. It was the opening I was looking for. I explained to him that I had decided that I didn't want to attend law school. I continued explaining my decision despite his shocked look. I explained that I felt I had decided to attend law school for all the wrong reasons. I explained that I thought I was doing it for him, our marriage, and my father and not doing it for myself. I explained that I had rekindled my love of teaching through the opportunity to teach history at the college. I added that I would like to explore completing my doctoral degree rather than go to law school so I could continue to pursue teaching at the college or university level.

The silence that ensued was uncomfortable. I knew I had dropped a bomb. However, I was so sure of my decision that I was ready to accept all the fallout that came with it. Dinner ended in silence. Dan helped me with the dishes, and we headed out for a run together. As we ran, he said he was surprised about my decision, but if that was what I wanted, he was glad I discovered that before my first semester in law school. He said little else as we ran our usual four-mile route. Once back at the house, we showered and settled into our evening routine. We never discussed my decision again. I never had second thoughts about it, either.

In the meantime, my teaching load at the Bible college expanded to include the second course for the spring semester, and I began working in the admissions office as a recruiter. Additionally, the Bible College asked me to coach the women's basketball team after their current coach could not continue due to family circumstances. With the new opportunity to coach basketball, the college told me they were putting together a long-term contract to bring me on full-time. Nowhere in my undergraduate preparation for being a teacher did I consider teaching in college a career opportunity. I looked back at this moment and wondered why. Now, I was immersed in several activities at the college and enjoying the new demands required of me.

During the holiday break, I canceled my law school admission and applied to universities to begin a doctorate. In late January, as the usual tax routine began, Dan started to prepare income taxes for his clients, and as each day of the tax calendar passed, Dan began to spend more and more time at the office. The rhythm was well established by now. First, it started with working later during the weekdays. Then it would expand to working Saturday. Then, working Saturday morning turned into working all day Saturday, which eventually included working all day Sunday. When he accepted the magistrate appointment, he promised me he wouldn't have to work as much this tax season because he had a steady income. Apparently, that wasn't true, or if it was confirmed when he accepted the job, he was working for other reasons.

By the end of January, I had been accepted to three universities to begin my doctoral degree. I chose the one university that offered summer classes so I could start in June and attend year-round. I had been researching college-level teaching opportunities and knew I needed my degree to apply for college teaching jobs. As I researched college teaching positions, it was clear that many more were available than public school teaching jobs. This gave me hope that, eventually, I could secure a good position, allowing me more freedom from worrying about Dan's choices or even allowing me to file for a divorce. I saw this opportunity as my way forward and committed to attending the university that would allow me to complete my degree as soon as possible. I told Bill that part of my next two summers would be spent in Detroit working on my doctoral degree. He was very supportive and willing to cut back my time in the admissions office during the summer so I could work on my doctoral degree.

By March, Dan said his workload had become so large that he again stayed nights and weekends at the office. The rumors about his homosexual relationships and the suspicious blood sugar tests fueled my skepticism that his decision to stay at the office was about something other than all the work he said he had. Irrespective of why he decided to stay at the office, I had come to accept and began to enjoy his absence, though I wanted to understand what was behind it. I would randomly call or drive by the office to test my suspicion. Sometimes he would answer, and sometimes he wouldn't. Sometimes, the lights would be on, and sometimes, they wouldn't. Was this just confirmation bias, or were the circumstances such that the rumors were true?

I kept busy with teaching and coaching at the college. Karen was coaching volleyball at the high school where I used to work, so when I could catch her team's game, I would. I began a full schedule of officiating boys' basketball and girls' volleyball. I was trying to save money for my tuition for my doctoral program, and officiating was a great way to earn extra money. It was also a perfect way to keep busy while Dan was away. Little did I realize that all this busyness was my way of filling time and space, so I didn't think as much about my circumstances. Some people turn to drugs or alcohol to cope, but I channeled my energy toward work, justifying my actions as saving for tuition. My working was nothing more than a coping strategy that was no more helpful than turning to drugs, alcohol, food, or other distractions. Eventually, I learned that working to fill the void was like numbing my pain and emptiness with alcohol or drugs.

One Friday night, Karen and I headed out for some shopping and dinner. I finally shared with her my plans to attend a university this summer. She looked a bit surprised. I explained my reasoning and my desire to do what I loved. She was worried that this might be my way of avoiding working on my relationship with Dan, so she encouraged me to work on my marriage despite Dan's work routine. She noticed his work habits. She knew my frustration and desire to have a life partner who wanted to spend time with me and share my passions, hobbies, and dreams. One thing I didn't share with Karen that night was that my long-term plans were to leave Dan. I vowed I would keep that plan to myself. My closet was closing in as I began to keep out the one person I was the closest to. I didn't realize the amount of energy all this was sapping from me and how these secrets robbed me of my joy.

Early in June, Dan came home and shared that he had been asked to become a full-time magistrate at a court in Grand Rapids. As we sat at the dinner table having supper, he explained that he would need to live in the court district to accept this position. This meant we would have to move. I was okay with moving back to Grand Rapids now that I was teaching at a college there. I was happy for him. His life-long dream was to become a judge, and I knew this would be a step closer for him. I hadn't seen him this happy in a while. I told him how proud I was of him and glad his hard work paid off.

As we talked and contemplated moving, a car pulled into the driveway. We didn't recognize the vehicle or the person who got out and came to the door. Dan answered the door and invited the lady into the house. She introduced herself as Hazel. She was a realtor and asked us if we wanted to sell our home. Dan and I both burst out with laughter. Hazel was a bit stunned at this reaction. Then, as she sat at the dinner table sipping the soda we had offered her, she heard the story about how we had been talking about moving to Grand Rapids and selling the house over the past two hours. We all agreed that providence had intervened.

The next day, Karen and I decided to spend the day in Holland and enjoy a beautiful summer day at the beach. I shared with her Dan's good news about being offered a full-time job as a magistrate in a Grand Rapids court. She was genuinely happy for him. I also shared with her our need to move because of the residency requirements for court employees. She knew that meant she would have to move as well. She was sad but understood. She explained that she would talk to her parents about moving back with them if she didn't find somewhere to live in the Hudsonville area. She surprised me by explaining that she was thinking about leaving the Baptist School we taught at, so moving back home was something she was already thinking about. I was surprised she was considering leaving the Baptist School, but I knew she wasn't happy with the administration. She had been exploring opportunities at another Christian school north of Grand Rapids, so moving in with her parents would be closer to that school if she was hired there. Again, it seemed that all the pieces were falling into place. I felt optimistic that God was still in control.

As the summer progressed, Karen notified the administration that she was leaving the Baptist School. While she hadn't heard from the other school yet, she was not worried about her future. She decided to get a job at a fabric store while exploring other teaching opportunities. One night, on our way to play in our church softball game, she announced that she would move back in with her parents. So much had changed in such a short period. I saw all the changes as a positive movement toward a way out of an unfulfilling marriage.

Dan began his magistrate job in May, so he moved in with his parents, who lived in the court district where he worked to comply with the city ordinance requiring a city employee to live there. By June, our house in Hudsonville had sold. We immediately began looking for a home to buy within the court district. We found the perfect home, two miles from Karen's parents and five miles from the courthouse. We made an offer and soon learned it had been accepted and that we would move in after Labor Day weekend. Everything was moving quickly and smoothly. I attributed it to "God's will."

We had to leave our house in Hudsonville by the first of July. We stored our furniture and items in Dan's parent's garage. When July came, I moved in with my parents. Dan's parents didn't have much room, and we didn't want to impose on them any more than we already were with storing our things in their garage. I didn't mind being away from Dan for a month or two. I was working as many hours as I could at the sporting goods store, and Dan was working a lot in the evenings to make sure his law practice continued while he was working two full days at the court plus the part-time magistrate job, he worked before receiving the full-time magistrate job. I didn't teach during the summer at the college, so besides working at the sporting goods store, I umpired softball games as often as possible.

I began teaching again at the college the third week in August, and we moved into our new house on Labor Day weekend. Everything had fallen into place nicely. Dan was the happiest I had seen in years. I was full of optimism about exploring a new type of teaching career at the college level. Besides enjoying the unique challenges of teaching, I even enjoyed working part-time at a sporting goods store while waiting for graduate school to start. Ironically, I looked forward to what the future held but was finally enjoying the here and now for the first time since I could remember.

Chapter Twenty-Seven: The Professor

"Not many of you should become teachers, my fellow believers because you know that we who teach will be judged more strictly"

-James 3:1 NIV.

I enjoyed teaching classes in the spring, coaching, recruiting college students, and working at the sporting goods store. Dan worked full-time and part-time as a magistrate in two courts while continuing his law practice. Anyone could see this situation wasn't good for any marriage, let alone Dan and my relationship. In addition to my responsibilities at the college, I was about to add to the demands by attending graduate school at Wayne State University.

After applying to three different colleges and being accepted, I chose Wayne State University because they offered courses all year round and a full schedule of classes in the summer. The course schedule ensured I could finish promptly and obtain my doctoral degree, a minimum requirement to consider applying for post-secondary teaching positions. As I spoke with graduate advisors throughout the process of making my decision, I discovered that I could teach future teachers at the college level by pursuing one of three different degree options. I might enjoy that opportunity to teach education-related courses as much as teaching history at the college level, and teacher education positions were far more prevalent than history positions. I settled on preparing to train future teachers at the college level as my future goal. Another reason I chose Wayne State was because my degree plan would allow me to study history as part of my program of study. I felt like the university and the program was tailored to my interests and career goals and still allowed me to work at the Bible College during the traditional academic year. I was excited about going back to school.

In May of 1992, I headed to Detroit for my first summer semester. I rented a room on campus and spent the next ten weeks taking a full schedule of education and history courses. I lived on campus Monday through Thursday and came home Thursday night after my evening class. I spent all day Friday studying. Dan and I spent the weekends at home.

When I came home on weekends, Dan and I participated in 5K and 10K running races throughout the area on Saturday mornings. Many of our friends from church also ran 5K and 10K races, so it was nice to see our friends when I was home Periodically, Karen would walk in the 5K or 1 mile event while Dan and I ran the 10K race. After the race, we frequently went to breakfast with Karen and the people we knew at the race. The routine was comfortable and predictable. It also offered me plenty of time to study as I prepared for the next week in Detroit. Sunday after supper, I would get in my car and drive the two-and-a-half hours to my apartment in Detroit to prepare for the week ahead.

Dan and I ran a race close to home at one of the 10K races in late August. Before the race, Dan introduced me to a man he identified as someone who worked as a probation officer with juveniles at the court where he was a magistrate. I didn't catch his name but wished him well in the race. Dan and I took our place at the back of the pack and waited for the gun to signal the start of the race. After the gun went off, the group began to race down the road. It was a hot day for a race, which started later in the morning than most races. I pushed myself hard because I hoped to break my personal best since I knew the route and ran portions of the course during my training. I knew I could pace myself because of this knowledge. As I was reaching the end of my energy, I saw the finish line ahead, pushed hard as I saw the clock, and knew I was within seconds of achieving my goal. I finished before Dan and waited near the finish line to cheer him on. I ran with him the final leg of the last mile. He had a good race and achieved his best but was exhausted. As we walked toward the refreshments, I saw the person he had introduced me to before the race. As Dan walked on, I asked his friend how his race went.

After several brief attempts to interact with this juvenile probation officer, he looked at me in frustration and said, "Why don't you go look after your husband." He oddly emphasized the word husband and walked off. I was stunned. I wasn't sure if he was being sarcastic or rude. I had just met him, and I didn't think I was being impolite to ask how he did. I thought about his interaction for several days, trying to make sense of an odd encounter. I wondered who this person was because, before the race, he seemed rather friendly with Dan but very standoffish toward me. Then, after the race, he was downright mean toward me. I was also surprised by Dan's unwillingness to tell me more about this person when I inquired about him on our ride home. He brushed it off as just some guy he knew from work. I was finally determined to move on but often wondered about the strange interaction during the subsequent week. I couldn't help but wonder if this person knew more about Dan and me than I would have otherwise expected. I asked myself if Dan confided in him or was even involved with him in a relationship other than a work-related co-worker. More and more circumstantial evidence began to solidify my belief that Dan may be gay.

That Sunday, I returned to Detroit for my final week of summer classes. Once classes were over, I moved back home. I was relieved to return home and excited that my first semester of doctoral work was complete. I enjoyed the challenge of graduate studies and looked forward to teaching in the fall. I knew I needed to keep making progress on completing my doctorate, so I scheduled one class in Detroit in the fall and planned on driving the two and half hours one way to class two days a week. The schedule was comfortable and allowed me time to study and prepare for teaching my two classes. I continued to work as a recruiter for the college as well. I was convinced more than ever that being a college professor was what I wanted to do.

Working as a recruiter at the college, I knew that enrollment at the Bible College had been declining for several years. The demand for a Bible College education was less important than in previous years. The college prepared pastors for the ministry and missionary aviation pilots. Others who studied at the college received their associate degree in general education. Because of the declining enrollments and the few program offerings at the Bible College, talk about the Bible College and a larger, local Christian college merging began heating up. Those conversations left many wondering what that would mean for our jobs.

I kept focused on completing my doctoral coursework. I knew that no matter what happened with the merger, I would need to complete my doctoral degree to continue teaching at the college level, whether at the college that absorbed the Bible College or another college. The Bible College merged with the Christian college as the spring semester ended. I was granted an interview to work in the teacher education department as a teacher certification officer at the Christian college that absorbed the Bible College. That job also allowed me to teach two courses each semester. God had been good to me. I knew I had been "in His will" by pursuing a teaching career rather than attending law school. Several of my friends from the Bible College got jobs at the Christian college after the merger as well. We were all looking forward to beginning our new careers in the fall.

I spent a second summer living in Detroit and working on my doctoral courses. I took a full load of classes and knew that by the end of the summer, I would have completed half of the necessary coursework toward my degree. I talked to Dan each night while I was in Detroit. I would come home on Thursday night and spend Friday studying while he was at work. I spent some weekends at my parents' cottage up north and the others at home with Dan. I was continually frustrated by Dan's unwillingness to visit my parents with me up north. Every time we had plans to go, he had an excuse for staying home. Dan was never home during the week between his full-time job and a part-time job as a magistrate at two different courts and his law practice and tax work. I was never home between my travels to Detroit and being away during the summer. The few weekends in the summer when Dan was home, I hoped we could go up north, escape the distractions, and enjoy the lake and each other. However, it became clear that he did not want to spend time with me. We were growing further apart, and I didn't know what to do about it, nor was I sure I wanted to do anything.

The summer term at Wayne State ended, and I returned home and prepared to begin my first year working at the Christian college that absorbed the smaller Bible College. It was nice to see familiar faces at the Christian college as I began employee orientation and also met new employees who, like me, were starting that fall. Immediately after high school, I attended this Christian college in the early 1980s for a couple of years before transferring to Calvin College (now Calvin University) to complete my bachelor's degree. Working with and teaching alongside professors I admired as an undergraduate was an honor. While not all my previous professors were still at the college, several were. To my surprise, I received the respect of the people who used to be my teachers when I was a student. I also found that I was growing confident in my abilities as a college teacher and researcher. I finally felt I had found my calling. I finally felt like I fit in somewhere.

My friend Karen and I continued spending our free time together whenever possible. She had begun to date a man she had met through a dating site on the computer. As her dating relationship continued, it was clear that Karen was planning to marry and move to Nebraska, where her new husband resided. She asked Dan to marry her and Jon. We spent the next few months planning her wedding. I found myself growing more and more distant from her. I felt like I was losing my best friend. Ironically, while one of us was planning on leaving a marriage, the other was planning on entering a marriage. I wanted her to be happy, yet it was hard for me because I was unhappy and had become skeptical about relationships.

In June, Karen and Jon were married in her parents' living room. Dan did a great job of presiding over the ceremony, and it was fun sharing the special day with Karen. She was happy. I was devastated. Shortly after the wedding, Karen moved to Nebraska. I was lonely and missing my best friend. I was finishing my last summer of required coursework at Wayne State and was glad to have the distraction. Dan grew more and more distant.

Dan and I spent less and less time together. There was no talking to him about it either. Any time I brought it up, he would tell me that he had to take the work at the law practice when it was there. He made excuses about not being able to control the court schedule. He even started working on weekends more often. Working weekends during tax season had been typical, but working on weekends the other months of the year was new. I couldn't help but feel like he was running from or hiding something. Periodically, I wondered whether he was working on the weekend or spending it with someone else. I decided it was best not to make waves and go along with the new developments. I was no longer committed to making things work and trying to turn the marriage into what I hoped and dreamt. Now, it was about staying focused on completing my degree and seeking a teaching job outside of a Christian college where being divorced or gay would not be an issue.

By August 1st, I finished my summer coursework and began studying for comprehensive exams in the fall of 1994. Dan came home one night and informed me that his mother had put her house up for sale. Her husband had died the previous summer, and she decided to sell the house because it was too big and challenging for her to take care of independently. Dan explained that she planned to move in with us once her home was sold. I clarified by asking him whether this was temporary while she found somewhere else to live. He countered by telling me she was planning on living with us for the foreseeable future. I was furious. We hadn't talked about this first. I felt like the decision was already made, and I was trapped in a situation I was unsure would work. I almost felt like he was trying to make me miserable and pushing me to leave.

I told Dan that the timing could not have been worse for me. I was preparing for my comprehensive exams and doctoral research proposal. Since it was clear his mother would move in with us, I asked that it wait until at least January because I would have the most stressful part of my doctoral studies behind me. He assured me that her house would not sell that fast and that nothing would likely happen until spring. His answer was disrespectful and condescending.

The three weeks between August 1st and when my teaching assignment began in the fall were lonely. I was missing my best friend, Karen. I was also angry at Dan for his absence, distance, and disruption to our home life. He was never home; when he was, he only ate, read, and watched TV. There was little conversation between the two of us. I tried to keep as busy as possible to cope with my frustration and loneliness. I enjoyed spending my days at the Lake Michigan beach in Holland. I would head out to the beach daily, around ten in the morning. The first thing I would do after finding a suitable parking space was open my trunk and strap on the roller blades and blade on the trails from one state park to another. After a good two-hour workout, I would return to my car, change out of my rollerblades, grab a chair and a cooler, and walk to the beach to enjoy the afternoon. I loved the sun and water. I also wanted the opportunity to read and watch people. By four in the afternoon, I would head home to make dinner. I took solace in nature and water. The beach was a place of peace, strength, and renewal.

One rainy day, while I sulked around the house waiting for the fall semester to start, I received a letter in the mail that caught my attention. It was from Kate. I met Kate when her sister, Deb, was an undergraduate at Calvin College. Her sister was my maid of honor at my wedding. I read the letter with great interest. Kate gave me an update on her life since I last saw her in the late 1980s. She had written about her accomplishments over the past ten years and closed the letter by saying she would love to see me but would be happy to hear from me. She left me her address.

I remember sitting down on the couch and praying to God. I thanked God for the letter and for hearing from Kate. I asked God if this was His way of filling a void in my life left by Karen's marriage and her move to Nebraska. It was exciting to think that God was meeting my needs during this challenging time through reconnecting with Kate. After I prayed, I wrote her a response.

Before long, the fall semester began, and I was busy preparing for my comprehensive exams. Kate and I now corresponded regularly. She was working at a local college as a police officer about 45 minutes away. With Kate and I working at colleges, we had many opportunities to exchange exciting stories that we both could relate to. It was one of many connections we shared.

Dan came home one September night and told me his mother's house had sold, and she would move in with us in the next couple of weeks. So much for his belief that his mother's house wouldn't sell quickly and she wouldn't move in with us until spring. I was already upset that he hadn't discussed this decision with me, and now the timing of her move was very problematic for me. I didn't appreciate this disruption while preparing for exams and my research proposal defense. I felt Dan was being incredibly insensitive. Nothing I could say would deter him from his plans. Despite my anger, I felt determined to make it work because likely it was not his mother's fault that he didn't discuss the decision with me. I was pretty sure I would have agreed to have his mom move in and that selling her house was a good idea, but what bothered me the most was that Dan made a decision that affected me without talking to me first.

Despite the distractions, I completed my comprehensive exams. My research proposal was also accepted, and I began to prepare for my doctoral research, scheduled to start in January 1995. My doctoral work kept me focused on my goal and helped me cope with Dan's distance and our new tenant. In January 1995, Dan began his usual tax schedule. He was never home. That meant I spent more time with his mom than he did. I found I enjoyed spending time with her. Despite being busy teaching and completing my research, I appreciated the opportunity to get to know her better. She also saw how much time Dan spent away from the house during tax time. This helped her become more understanding of my frustration with Dan.

I was also spending more time with Kate after the New Year. We had finally met for dinner in November after corresponding for several months since that surprise letter had arrived in August. With Dan working every weekend, I enjoyed having Kate's company. One Saturday night, we met for dinner and shared memories about our high school and college days. She got quiet. Soon, she told me she wanted to share something important with me. I could tell she was having a difficult time starting the conversation. This was unusual because we usually talked freely and comfortably whenever we were together. I couldn't imagine what she wanted to share that might be so difficult.

Eventually, she told me about her college roommate and how they dated and lived together for many years after college. She explained that through this relationship, she realized she was gay. She shared with me about her journey to understand her sexuality. She shared how she wanted to be honest with me about who she was so that I could choose whether I wanted to be her friend, explicitly being a friend of someone who was gay. After pouring her heart out to me, we both sat quietly.

I didn't know what to say. I knew that I wanted to say something honest and supportive. I looked at Kate, placed my hand on her leg, and looked her in the eye. "Kate, I can't image what this journey has been like for you. I am honored that you chose to share this with me. Who you are does not change the fact that I like and enjoy you as a friend. I hope you believe me because what you shared tonight doesn't change anything but increases my admiration for you".

Kate cried. I put my arm around her as she wept. Finally, when she could catch her breath, she hugged me. Shortly after this intense conversation, she left for home. I sat and contemplated what I had heard. I admired Kate for her strength and courage. I also wondered if I should have shared with her my conclusions about myself to let her know that we had another thing in common. As I sat, I prayed and asked God if I should share my belief that I might be gay with Kate. I prayed for guidance and looked forward to seeing how this friendship would unfold.

Chapter Twenty-Eight: One Moment in Time

"Before I formed thee in the belly, I knew thee, and before thou camest forth out of the womb, I sanctified thee and ordained thee a prophet unto the nations"

- Jeremiah 1:5, KJV.

The winter turned to spring, and I continued to gather data for my research; I had planned to write my dissertation over the summer. Kate and I spent more time together during the spring as I tried to stay away from home since Dan's mom had moved in. I have nothing against her and enjoyed my time with her, but my house no longer seemed like home. First, I wanted Dan's mom to have some privacy and not feel obliged to entertain me while I was home and vice versa. Second, the house didn't feel like a home because I found little love or warmth. Dan was never home, so I felt no desire to be home when he was not present, but his mom was. The house just felt cold and lonely.

I finally decided to tell Kate about my predicament, i.e., my attraction toward women. I was worried that she would take my decision to refrain from acting on my homosexual feelings as being judgmental of her because she had decided to live openly expressing her sexuality. One Saturday night, I began to share my story of how I had cognized my attraction to women. I also told her that, being married to Dan, I wanted to honor my commitment to him, and had it not been the case, I would probably have made different decisions. I cried while narrating my story to her. It was the first time I had publicly expressed my attraction to women. It made my homosexuality more real than it had ever been before. There was no turning back now. I could no longer deny who I was. I stepped out of the closet momentarily, and it felt so good.

I explained to Kate how afraid I was to be "found out." She was very supportive and understanding and explained that she had figured out I was gay before I had. She also said she admired me for staying committed to Dan despite discovering my sexual inclinations. I was stunned at her support. I felt so free for the first time in my life. Finally, someone knew. Finally, someone accepted me after learning that I was gay. I finally had someone to talk with, understand, and support me. I wept uncontrollably. Kate held me as I poured out years of pain through my tears.

At that moment, I impulsively kissed her. She was stunned. However, before we could stop ourselves, we were making out. I felt so free and so honest at that moment. Kate didn't resist. I didn't think about anything but the moment. Finally, we were able to compose ourselves. I looked into her eyes and apologized, but she told me not to. She explained that she participated willingly, too. We promised to maintain our friendship and not anything more. I didn't want to lose Kate's friendship, so I was not going to do anything to jeopardize it.

Lying in bed that night, I wondered if the promise I made to stay in this marriage was something I wanted to keep or should keep or could keep. I knew that for the first time in my life, I felt so honest and free. I also felt so good in her arms, knowing I wanted that. I began to pray for guidance. However, now that I experienced freedom, understanding, and authenticity, I realized that continuing the current path would be far more complex.

In May, the school year ended. I was excited for the summer. This was the first summer since 1992 that I wasn't taking classes or living in Detroit. I looked forward to spending the weekends with my parents in northern Michigan at their cottage. I spent the weekdays writing my dissertation. The end was in sight. The dissertation defense date was October 2nd, my father's birthday.

During the weekends, Dan was nowhere in sight. He no longer wanted to run in races together. His excuse was that he needed to work because his caseload at the law office was heavy, and his ever-increasing work as a magistrate didn't allow him to finish his job during the week. He excused himself from going with me to northern Michigan on weekends, saying he needed to be available to sign warrants as magistrate for the police. However, he didn't stop me and encouraged me to go. When I asked him about a vacation, he reiterated that he needed to stay in the area. My gut feeling was that there was something more to all this, but I couldn't figure it out. It was clear that he was not interested in spending time with me. I was certain he was avoiding me and couldn't help but think he might be spending time with someone else. However, this time, I was no longer blaming myself for the situation or concluding that God was punishing me because I was gay. I began seeing the problem clearly and realized Dan and I, not just me, contributed to the ever-expanding distance between us.

I decided to enjoy summer weekends away in northern Michigan, never giving much thought to what Dan did on weekends while I was visiting my parents. I enjoyed the freedom to spend time with friends. Kate and I didn't see each other much during the summer because her schedule had changed, and she worked weekends. Another friend of mine, Kathy, whom I had met while working at the Bible college, was another person I enjoyed hanging out with. She had gotten a job at the Christian college when the Bible and Christian colleges merged. She had become friends with Dan and me when Dan helped her with her divorce a couple of years earlier.

Kathy and I often visited my parents in northern Michigan during the summer. One day, on our morning walk, I shared with Kathy my conclusion about my sexuality. She listened intently and tried to understand. She was very supportive. She was the second person I came out to and quickly became a sounding board for me because she expressed her continued support. We both began to read avidly about homosexuality. I searched to try to understand my sexuality. I also wanted to figure out what it meant. I read everything I could find, including the Bible, to learn what it says about homosexuality. I was moving further away from the closet, one step at a time. Each step made me realize I wanted to live authentically and find a life partner who shared my sexuality and other interests.

I had to reconcile what I thought I knew about my faith, my relationship with Jesus Christ, and the proclamation by Christians who declared homosexuality a terrible sin. Much of my perceptions about Christian beliefs concerning homosexuality came from the television. The news media continued to show Christians holding signs about God hating homosexuals. I could not comprehend that. My lack of acceptance of this idea was not because I didn't want to believe that God hated homosexuals but because I studied the Bible. I recalled various Bible verses I had memorized. One drove home to me my belief that God loves everyone. The Bible states, *"God so loved the world that he gave his only Son, that whosoever believed in him would not perish but have everlasting life"* (John 3:16 KJV). God's love was so vast that he sacrificed his Son. How could a God who sacrificed his Son because he loved us and wanted a relationship with us be a God who hated homosexuals? It didn't make sense to me.

I was one of those "whosoever believed" in him. I knew in my heart that I had accepted Jesus as my Lord and Savior and that because of my faith in Jesus, God loved me, forgave me, and that in the end, I would spend eternity in heaven with him. I also knew that God knew my innermost thoughts and feelings and that my homosexuality did not surprise him. It might surprise people I come out to, but it did not surprise him. I was puzzled that Christians had labeled homosexuality as the worst sin of all. In the Bible, I don't recall God ever ranking sins. God hated all iniquity because sins were what separated us from him. To address sins, God sent his son, Jesus, to be sacrificed to atone for all sins, allowing us to enter a relationship with him. Through faith in Christ, God made way for us to have an eternal relationship with him, not because of anything we did but because of what his son, Jesus Christ, did. God's grace saved us through faith. God sees his children who've accepted his Son, gay and straight, through the completed work of his son, Jesus Christ.

Consequently, seeing people who proclaimed to be Christians expressing hate didn't make sense to me. If someone identifies with Christ, they should be filled with love, not hate. I also think that, as a Christian, it was not my place to judge people. The Bible showed me that God would judge all people in due time. I felt my responsibility was to share God's love with people.

Before I knew it, the summer was over. I was looking forward to defending my doctoral dissertation on October 2nd, my dad's birthday. Part of preparing for my dissertation defense was ensuring that my thesis manuscript was completed and in the format required by the university. That required a couple of trips to Detroit to work with the graduate school on formatting. The day of my dissertation defense arrived. Dan, our friend Kathy, and my parents accompanied me on my drive to Detroit, a drive I had made many times before when completing my coursework. We arrived at the College of Education and found the room where my dissertation committee awaited me. I introduced them to my parents, Kathy, and husband. My dissertation chair began the event by explaining the defense process and then turned it over to me to make a summary statement about my research.

The entire defense lasted 40 minutes. After my opening statement, committee members asked about the research design and why I chose the method I did. I was asked about my survey development and whether I had measured validity and reliability. I was asked if I had considered surveying the parents of the students who participated in my study. For each question, I spent time explaining the theory around my decisions. Soon, the question-and-answer session began to feel like a professional discussion I had with colleagues at the college where I taught. And I knew that I had successfully defended my research. My dissertation chair stopped the discussion and asked me and my guests to leave the room. Within five minutes, he emerged from the room, walked over to me, and congratulated me on a successful dissertation defense. He also congratulated my parents, friend, and husband, remarking they now had a new doctor in their lives.

The remainder of the fall semester was enjoyable as I awaited my official graduation from Wayne State. I graduated in December with my doctorate. My parents, husband, and friend Kathy also accompanied me to the graduation ceremony in Detroit. It was scheduled for the evening, so we left early to stop for a leisurely lunch before driving to the Cobo Center in downtown Detroit for the event. My husband had purchased my graduation robe as a gift since I would use it again each spring for commencement ceremonies at the college. It was a meaningful gift that I would use many more times over the years after this ceremony. After commencement, we all drove back to Grand Rapids, singing Christmas songs and recounting the day.

I saw this as an essential accomplishment for me, professionally and personally. Now, I could begin looking for a job at other colleges, ones that didn't care if I were divorced or if I were gay. I knew that I needed to get out of the marriage. I knew my depression was because I could not express my sexuality. I also knew I longed for a companion with whom I could share a meaningful relationship and life. I knew Dan was unhappy but would not leave the marriage because he believed that would hurt his future career as a judge. I was sure that I would have to be the person to initiate change.

While I had finally decided to leave the marriage, the actual leaving was not as easy. First, my mom worked for Dan, so I had to figure out how to tell her. I was worried that Dan might fire her if I were to divorce him. I didn't think he would be that calloused, but I didn't want to take the chance. She had been battling breast cancer, and I didn't want her to deal with cancer, my divorce, losing a job, and learning that I was gay all at once. Her working for Dan also felt like a barrier to me because I felt at a loss to talk to either her or Dad about my life and plans. I felt alone but determined not only to seek a divorce but at the right time to file for a divorce. I believed I would know the right time to tell my parents.

Christmas of 1995 was particularly enjoyable for me because, for the first time in a while, I could enjoy the winter break without the haunting thought hanging over me that I needed to be working on my doctoral dissertation. As usual, Dan and I hosted a Christmas celebration for our families. Kathy had become one of our family members and was invited to join in with our celebrations. My parents liked Kathy, and she and my mom had become good friends. I even went cross-country skiing and sledding over winter break, something I hadn't done in years. There was a sense of freedom I was feeling. I did attribute it to the fact that I had finished my degree, but likely, it was also because I had decided that when the time was right, I would take action. Winter break passed quickly, and New Year's Day marked the beginning of a new year, which I was sure would be interesting.

The year began with Dan's mom announcing that she was moving out and getting a townhouse near her sister. Next, Dan started working late nights and long weekends. He justified it because he had picked up more work in the court system and said he needed every minute he could find. I, once again, spent many nights and weekends on my own. Now that my doctoral studies were over, I realized just how little time Dan spent at home. I began seeking opportunities to restart umpiring softball games in the spring. I was able to secure a full schedule of high school girls' softball games and was even able to secure several college tournaments to umpire. I was excited to be able to reengage with an activity I enjoyed.

Since I hadn't umpired in several years, I asked the college softball coach to come to some of their early practices and call balls and strikes in the hitting cage to get used to seeing the softball and strike zone again. This offer led to her offering me an opportunity to accompany the softball team to Florida during spring break and help work with pitchers and catchers so they would be ready for their season. I quickly agreed. Spending time helping the college softball team and returning to umpiring brought me joy. I was even asked to umpire high school district and regional tournaments that spring. That was an accomplishment as often people asked to umpire tournaments were nominated by the coaches of the various teams that saw them umpire their games during the regular season.

To receive this opportunity after spending several years away from the game was very fulfilling.

When the college spring semester ended, I began looking forward to visiting my parents at their lake home in northern Michigan. My time there had been limited the past three summers because I had spent them in Detroit working on my degree. I was excited to have some free time once again. This would be the first summer in a very long time when I wasn't teaching or taking a class. I hoped Dan would go with me a few weekends to visit my parents and enjoy the lake. I went just about every weekend to my parents' house that summer. Sometimes, Kathy would join me. After the first few trips, my parents stopped asking if Dan would accompany me. On one occasion, I remember my mom recounting to Kathy and me a story about how the lawyer renting a space in Dan's law office often remarked to Dan how he wished he had the opportunity to go to a lake in northern Michigan. My mom continued her story by telling us that he told Dan that he didn't deserve me because he took me for granted. Later, during a walk I shared with Kathy, I felt that Dan's tenant summed up the situation accurately.

The summer was also interesting in another way. What should have been one of the most enjoyable times of my life was clouded by depression. There was no outward reason to be depressed. Anyone assessing my life would conclude I had many positive things; I was living the "American Dream." I had a great job. I had a loving family and friends. I had accomplished my educational goals. Despite all the good things, I was depressed. I was very in tune with this depression because I had more downtime than ever before. I would get up each day after Dan left the house for work. I would make coffee, open the paper to scan the headlines, and plan my day. I found that it was getting more and more difficult each morning to plan my day. Nothing seemed to be enjoyable. The things I used to enjoy were no longer fun and no longer distracted me from the hopeless feelings I felt.

One day, I had plans with Kathy to go to the beach. I picked her up at the agreed-upon time. I walked into her living room and half-heartedly said good morning. We loaded up the car and began the hour-long drive to Holland. Our conversation was light. We got caught up on the news, mutual friends we had talked to or seen, and the schedule for the day. Finally, Kathy asked me how I was. I responded with my usual answer. "I'm good today; how are you?"

Kathy didn't let that answer pass. "You don't seem fine. Are you sure you're okay?" Kathy inquired.

"Sure, I'm a bit tired this morning because I read until late last night." I diverted.

My diversion didn't work this time. Kathy began to describe what she had observed over the past several weeks. We were close friends; she knew I trusted her and believed she cared about me. Consequently, I knew that her observations were more accurate than most, and I trusted what she told me. We delved deeply into the conversation as we drove to the beach. As we arrived at the beach, Kathy encouraged me to see a psychologist. I reluctantly agreed, and we went about our plans for the day.

I mulled over Kathy's suggestion several days after our drive to Holland. In between spending time together, Kathy and I spoke on the telephone. Every conversation included a question by Kathy about whether I considered seeing a professional. She expressed her concerns about me with more regularity. It was getting more and more challenging for me to get out of bed; I concluded that if I didn't get help, this depression would win. I finally mustered the courage to call a psychologist and make an appointment.

I was surprised that I could get in to see a psychologist within the week. The day came and I reached the clinic. As I sat waiting, I had second thoughts about whether seeing someone was a good idea. Just then, he called. We spent the first half of the session getting to know each other. The first sessions seemed useless. I wouldn't say I liked small talk, and this felt like small talk. We scheduled several future appointments over the next few weeks, but I wasn't sure what to say. Somehow, I felt like I was supposed to come in with an agenda. I was relieved when he started the session by asking how I would explain my depression. As I began to describe how the depression felt to me, he redirected me and asked me to explain why I thought I might be feeling this depression. I started by explaining my frustration with my marriage. I explained how Dan was distant. I said that he never seemed interested in sex and wondered if something was wrong with me. I explained that I wanted intimacy so badly, longed to be close to someone, and believed this contributed to my depression. I talked about his long working hours and feeling lonely and wanting to spend time with him. My expectations of a married relationship were far different from my daily experience. I even expressed that my problem might be my inaccurate expectations about marriage and relationships.

I was stunned when he asked if I ever suspected my husband of being gay. I wondered how he could draw that conclusion based on what I had shared. I probed his reasoning for asking. He shared with me how and why he asked that question. He found Dan's behavior puzzling. I asked him why he thought Dan might be gay rather than Dan might be having an affair. He responded by explaining that he wasn't ruling out that Dan could be having an affair. Still, because the duration of his behavior had occurred throughout our entire marriage, his behavior had to be explained by more than a short-term affair. He said Dan's behavior was likely linked to his long-term disinterest in sex, possibly because he was androgynous or, more likely, gay. His observations made sense. I contemplated sharing my belief that I was gay, that my sexuality might be the actual cause, and that Dan's behavior was because of me, not him. However, the psychologist's comment made me realize that Dan had also contributed to this situation. He said that in the next session, he wanted to talk about why I tolerated this situation so long and that he wanted me to think about that question in anticipation of our next session.

Our session ended on that note, and we agreed to meet next week. I went home and contemplated the conversation and the question he wanted me to consider. I knew the answer. I had suspected that Dan was gay. However, I had no proof other than several circumstantial incidents. But more important than Dan's sexuality was my sexuality and my need and desire for intimacy and living in a fulfilling relationship. Here, I had blamed my poor relationship with Dan on my sexuality and me alone, never accounting for Dan's part in the relationship. I knew that even if Dan was gay, his sexuality did not matter. What mattered now was what I wanted and needed out of life, out of relationships, out of a marriage, and my responsibility to change the circumstances I tolerated, not by changing Dan or myself, but by doing the right thing for my happiness.

I spent the next week contemplating the idea that Dan might be gay. I talked endlessly with Kathy about Dan possibly being gay and seeking her opinion and observations. I began to remember several situations that focused on the plausibility of the psychologist's hypothesis about Dan. There was Dan's exaggerated concern over a sugar test. Could that have been a concern over an AIDS test? Then Dan told me he wasn't sure he was in love with me anymore upon my return from a mission trip. Had he been seeing someone, perhaps a man, while I was on the mission trip? Then, there was the conversation with Mr. Roane, who implied that Dan was involved with another man. Then, there were countless times he stayed at the office during tax season. Was he working or having an affair during all those hours and weekends, staying at the office? Then there was that runner at a 10K race a few summers back who had acted strangely and condescendingly told me to tend to my husband. Could that person have been Dan's lover? I was becoming confident that Dan might be gay. I began to ask myself whether we might have been homosexuals hiding in a marriage because of our conservative church, family norms, and society's attitudes. If this were true, would this draw us closer if we were honest with each other, or would it be the reason to part ways?

The third session with the psychologist arrived. I shared my observations with him. I explained that I had spent much time considering why I stayed married the previous week. I shared with him that I had decided to put myself first and do the right thing to allow myself to pursue the type of relationship with someone who would meet my needs, bring me happiness, and provide the intimacy I longed for. He explained that he could help and support me as I began to act on that decision. I told him I would take a week and consider whether I wanted to meet with him again to discuss my choice and next steps, but I needed time to weigh my options. What I didn't share with him was that I believed I was gay, too. Somehow, I felt that was irrelevant, or perhaps it was something I still didn't want to share.

At this point, I was clear that whether Dan was gay was not the issue. What had become clear to me was that I needed the freedom to seek the type of relationship I wanted and longed for. I had often questioned my looks because Dan was never interested in me. His attitude toward me made me question my weight, dress, and attractiveness. Knowing that Dan might be gay didn't provide me an excuse to end the marriage, but it allowed me to realize that his lack of interest had nothing to do with me. I was beginning to know

I was ok. The positive outcome of believing that Dan might be gay was that I could let go of some of my hurt and pain because I realized Dan's reactions to me were not about me but about him. It also made me realize that my decisions about staying in the marriage were about me, and I had the power to change that. I decided I needed to do what was best for my health and mental well-being, and I also needed to know whether doing what was best for me was an unforgivable sin.

Based on my Bible study about marriage and divorce, I decided I needed to talk to my pastor to seek answers to several questions, so I made an appointment with him. I attended a massive church with over 10,000 attendees, and seeing the senior pastor was almost impossible. I picked up the phone, called his office, and, much to my surprise, the senior pastor agreed to see me on short notice. He no longer regularly performed counseling as the church had professional counselors on staff who were available for churchgoers to see. However, some of those counselors were on vacation, so he was willing to fill in for more urgent appointments.

When the day for the appointment arrived, I sat down with my pastor and asked him for guidance. I explained to him that I was married to someone who had no interest in me sexually. I explained that we had been married for over 13 years. I further explained that I no longer knew what to do and felt that continuing in the marriage was causing me depression and mental stress and that I felt I needed to get a divorce for my well-being. I never mentioned my sexuality except that I was no longer sexually interested in Dan. My pastor's response floored me. He explained that our relationship wasn't following God's design for marriage, so we were essentially living a lie. He explained that he didn't believe living a lie was healthy or desirable. He encouraged me to do everything I could to rekindle the marriage to make it compatible with God's design for marriage. Still, he explained that continuing in the relationship would not be desirable if it was impossible to work with Dan to build the type of marriage and relationship God described in the Bible. He explained that he believed Dan had long ago left the marriage by ignoring God's design for marriage and that he didn't think God would want me to stay in a destructive situation.

The conversation was enlightening. My pastor's perspective was less legalistic and more relational, portraying a God who wanted his children to be happy and not expecting them to remain in the bondage of a bad marriage when the marriage didn't reflect anything like the type of marriage God described in His Word. I knew I had reached the end of my patience and desire to keep working at something I believed couldn't work. I knew I could no longer live in a marriage where companionship and intimacy didn't and likely would no longer exist, no matter the reason. By realizing God didn't want me to live in a situation like the one I was living in and knowing that I could change the problem, I began to feel strong again. I knew I wanted to live an honest, open life. I left the closet, hopefully for good.

As the summer passed, Kathy and I speculated why Dan encouraged me to visit my parents every weekend. She wondered what he did all the time by himself. I wondered if he was by himself or had other people to spend time with. His behavior was very different this summer, and both Kathy and I didn't believe it was because he had to be available every weekend to sign warrants. I confided in Kathy that I planned on looking for teaching jobs at other colleges beginning in the fall. She was very supportive.

In the fall of 1996 and early months of 1997, I began acting on my decision to leave. It was no longer if but when. I started actively looking for college teaching positions. I applied to a couple but felt unlikely to hear from them because my background wasn't exactly what they sought. Unfortunately, I had to put my job search on hold when my mom was diagnosed with another cancer, this time in her jaw area. She had previously fought breast cancer several years ago, so when she passed the five-year post-breast cancer treatment mark, my dad and I thought she was past the worst. However, recently, she had a toothache that didn't go away. She scheduled a dentist appointment to see what might be causing the pain. The dentist couldn't find anything and recommended a CAT scan. She scheduled the CAT scan, and when the results came back, the doctor found a small mass under the tooth, which he labeled abnormal. Because she had breast cancer before, he recommended removing the mass and sending it for tests. The surgery was successful. The mass was sent off for tests and tested positive for cancer.

The positive test resulted in my mom needing radiation treatments for several weeks to kill off any remaining cancer in her jaw area. My mom was relieved that she didn't need chemotherapy like others in her family had endured. She faced the radiation treatments in good spirits, joking that she expected a better tan in the summer than I would have. She was happy that the treatments would be completed in May, allowing her and my dad to spend the summer at their lake house in northern Michigan on weekends. Also, the treatments would occur early in the morning, allowing her to continue to work for Dan at the law office. The radiation had few side effects beyond dry skin and a constant thirst. Consequently, my mom began carrying a water bottle everywhere she went. She also included non-alcohol-based lotion in her purse, applying it to her face several times per day.

The early months of 1997 passed quickly as our family was focused on her cancer treatments. In May 1997, my mom announced her retirement from Dan's law office. In her last working week, she was diagnosed with another cancer, this time in her lungs. Her oncologist believed that the tumor he saw in her lungs was the same type of cancer that had appeared in her breast. Consequently, he decided to treat her with the same drug he had used as a follow-up to her breast cancer. Her prognosis was good. I spent most of the summer of 1997 at my parent's house. I knew my time with my mom might be short. My mom responded very well to the treatment, and the cancerous legions on her lungs disappeared. As a result, the oncology doctor wrote up my mom's case for the American Medical Journal. He explained that researchers studying breast cancer were beginning to believe that breast cancer could spread to other parts of the body rather than remain in the breast, as was the conventional thinking. He wanted our permission to share the case because he believed her situation would help inform the research.

The fall of 1997 began, and I started applying for jobs at other colleges in and out of state. I knew the Christian College would fire me if I were to get a divorce. I had several promising leads. I had shared with Kathy that I would file for a divorce once I had a new job. The plan was in place, and I was confident of finally taking care of myself, which seemed to keep the depression at bay that I had so profoundly experienced in the summer. I hoped to find a teaching job in the state because I feared my time with my mom was short because of another bout with cancer. I shared my prospects with Kathy, and we prayed fervently for each application I submitted. In the meantime, I continued to live with Dan and tried to be patient.

The only thing Dan and I spent time doing together was attending church on Sunday mornings. Kathy often attended church with Dan and me, so it wasn't like we were spending time together.

Then, that Sunday came. It was in November and was no different. We picked Kathy up on our way to church. All three of us sat together during the service. On the way home, Kathy and I sang and enjoyed a conversation. Dan commented on my singing. His comments were less than flattering. Of course, I didn't expect anyone to say anything positive about my singing because I certainly did not have that gift. However, he not only picked on my singing, but he started picking on several things. It felt like he was trying to create a fight. This was certainly not his usual behavior. I felt like he was being mean. I hadn't known him to be mean, just distant and absent. I decided it may be time for a heart-to-heart talk because I knew I wouldn't stand for being treated disrespectfully or being bullied. I believed people could be angry and still be respectful.

We dropped Kathy off and went home. Once home, I confronted him.

"What is your problem this morning?" I asked. He went off before I could finish what I was trying to say. I was surprised. After listening to his rant, I looked at him and responded.

"Well, if you are so unhappy, you should just leave," I baited.

"We should get divorced," he responded.

Dan explained that he wanted a divorce without missing a beat or taking a breath. He justified his comments by telling me he was unhappy and would be better off without me. We were stunned that the divorce word was finally out in the open. Yet, at that moment, we were more authentic and honest with each other than at any time since the early days of our marriage.

After the rather tense exchange, I got in my car and left. I told Dan I wanted time to think about what had happened. I went to Kathy's house and explained what had happened. She and I both knew at that moment that the marriage just ended, and all that was left was the formality of filing the paperwork and making it official. We prayed together. I shared my fears about losing my current job before finding another job and, as a result, becoming homeless and unable to meet my financial responsibilities. Kathy reassured me that if this was God's plan, everything would fall into place. She shared with me several passages in the Bible that led her to believe that God would provide. It was hard to imagine that something like divorce could be in God's plan. Still, getting a divorce felt like the right thing for me. I just had to trust God to find a job, do my part by looking, and let the details work out one moment at a time. Despite the heaviness of the reality that set in, I finally felt free.

Chapter Twenty-Nine: The Beginning or the End?

> *"I know what it is to be in need, and I know what it is to have plenty. I have learned the secret of being content in and every situation, whether well fed or hungry, whether living in plenty or in want"*
>
> -Philippians 4:12 NIV.

It is one thing to have a tense exchange and say you want a divorce; it is quite another thing to act and file for divorce. The next morning, Dan left for work just like every day since we were married a little over fourteen years ago. I spent the day teaching and continuing my job search. I couldn't help but wonder throughout the day what to expect that evening. Before I knew it, I was driving home. I arrived home around five, like every day of the week. I went for a run. Upon returning home, I wondered if I should start supper. I decided against it. I showered, grabbed a sandwich, and began grading papers.

The telephone rang. It was my mom. She frequently called during the week to see how things were going. When I answered the phone, I had to decide whether to tell her about the weekend exchange or wait until I knew more. My mom and I had a close relationship, and I would typically tell her about many things. She was battling cancer, and we never let a moment pass us by when we didn't share openly and honestly about our lives and what was happening in our days. We figured our time together might be short, so we embraced every opportunity to be authentic and present with each other. I appreciated being close, but now I was facing the dilemma of communicating with her what would undoubtedly be a difficult conversation about divorce and sexuality. I decided to go where the conversation went.

As usual, we talked about our day. Then, we began to talk about Thanksgiving. Usually, I had the family over to our house for Thanksgiving. This year would be no different. What was different was that I didn't know whether Dan would be there or if he would be moving out by then. I decided it was necessary to let her know about the weekend. I began by telling her I agreed to have Thanksgiving at our house again; then, I began to explain why I wasn't sure Dan and his mother would be attending. As I carefully recounted the weekend, I was aware of the silence on the other end of the telephone. When I completed my recollection of the exchange, my mom carefully chose her words. She understood our struggles and stressed the importance of our happiness. She said that no matter what might happen about the marriage, she was there for me, and perhaps a divorce was necessary. She encouraged me to think about it carefully and not do anything reactionary.

As I hung up the telephone, I couldn't help but wonder if she saw this coming. She had worked for Dan for ten years. She saw the numerous times I had visited her and Dad without Dan accompanying me. I also wondered where things stood between Dan and me after we agreed to divorce the previous day. By ten that night, Dan was still not home. I decided to move my things into the guest bedroom and stay there tonight and every subsequent night until I filed for a divorce and we could determine how to proceed.

It wasn't until Thursday that I finally had any communication from Dan. While I hadn't seen him come home any night since our Sunday exchange, he must have come home Thursday while I was running and left a note on the table. The letter indicated that we should talk on Saturday. He said he would pick me up for breakfast on Saturday at 7:00 am. The note also indicated he wouldn't be home anytime soon. I resented that he told me what I would do on Saturday morning. He could have asked me if Saturday morning would work for me. That lack of respect reinforced my commitment to a divorce. Saturday morning came, and Dan pulled up at 7:00 am. We headed for breakfast at a local, family-owned restaurant close to the house. We rode in silence. After we ordered, Dan began the conversation.

"We should talk about the divorce," he said. "I want to get moving so we both aren't left hanging."

"Sure," I replied. "I can appreciate you wanting to file now, but I would like to ask if you would be willing to hold off filing until I can secure a job elsewhere. You know the college will not let me teach there if I'm divorced, right?"

"Oh. That's right. Ok. When do you think you will know about another job?" Dan asked.

"Generally, colleges like to have decisions made by May. They want to fill any open faculty lines before faculty leave for the summer so that the fall schedule is set," I replied. I continued, "I have several applications out there and believe I will have a job by May."

"Ok, I will wait to file until April less you tell me you have another job sooner. Will that work?" he asked.

"Sure. I will let you know who my attorney is as soon as I have decided."

"You don't need an attorney unless you want one," Dan continued. "We can agree on how to proceed and divide up our assets without involving another attorney. We can draft the divorce papers ourselves. I can file the paperwork and do the work and save us the headache and money by doing it for us."

"Ok, I'll try it, and if it seems fair, I'll do it your way. If I think you are trying to take advantage of me, I'll get an attorney, understand?" I replied with a hint of anger.

After a prolonged silence, Dan shared his thoughts regarding dividing the assets with me. We spent the rest of breakfast finalizing our divorce plans. He also talked about how he thought we should handle the upcoming holidays. Dan agreed that we should proceed with Thanksgiving as planned and that he wanted to wait to tell our parents about the divorce until after Thanksgiving. I didn't tell him that I had already told my parents. Dan explained that he was looking for an apartment. We agreed to cohabitate until Dan found a place. It was clear from this conversation that Dan had been thinking about this for some time. I couldn't help but wonder when he decided to exit the marriage officially.

Thanksgiving Day came. We hosted the dinner as usual at our house. The day was surprisingly comfortable, which led me to believe that Dan hadn't told his mother about the decision to divorce. I found myself wondering how Christmas would be spent. We had decided to wait to determine how to spend Christmas until after Thanksgiving. As the snow began to fall and the day turned to night, our guests began to leave. Dan helped me clean up after dinner. We talked comfortably, almost like we knew the end was near, and we were trying to figure out how to be friends. As I fell into bed that evening, I prayed that God would help me find a job, and I thanked him for all that had happened.

Dan and I spent little time at home between Thanksgiving and Christmas. We avoided each other and ran out the clock until he found an apartment. He kept me updated on his progress. He informed me one evening that he had found an apartment but couldn't move there until January. That conversation led us to discuss how we would handle Christmas. We agreed that we would spend Christmas with our own families. He informed me that he had told his mother and sister that we were divorcing. I shared with him that my parents also knew.

I spent Christmas with my parents at their house up north. Kathy came with me to visit them over Christmas vacation. The college was closed, and Kathy and I had the week off, so getting out of Grand Rapids was like putting the past behind us for now. Dan was still at the house and beginning to pack up his things so he could move into his apparent on January 1st. It was a very snowy week in northern Michigan. I loved being away from the house and the awkwardness of living with Dan. The snow allowed me to enjoy the opportunity to ski with Kathy and spend time away from the stress of my situation.

On New Year's Day, Dan and I talked about the logistics of his moving to an apartment. I explained to Dan that several of his friends and family had approached me about hosting a birthday party for him on the weekend of the 11th. I told him I had agreed to throw him a fiftieth birthday party. By this time, my anger at Dan had subsided because I knew it was a foregone conclusion that I would soon be legally out of the marriage despite already being emotionally out of it. Generally, I liked Dan as a person, but I was not in love with him. I also couldn't just pretend that 14 years meant nothing. We had some good times. We had enjoyed each other's company for many years. The past several years, the relationship dissolved into a distant cohabitation that was now ending, but that wasn't cause to be mean. Dan agreed to attend the birthday party and move out the next day.

The day of his birthday party came. His friends and family began to arrive. Kathy helped me with food preparation and getting ready for the day. She stayed through the party; after all, she had been his friend while we were married. We enjoyed the day with family and friends. At one point during the day, his aunt shared that they were so glad when Dan started dating me and decided to get married. She continued her story by explaining that the family was worried and wondering if Dan was gay. Kathy and I shot each other a surprised look. We both noticed Dan switched the subject, recounting how he was too busy going to law school to date.

After Dan's friends and family left, he and Kathy helped me clean up. Once everything was put away, Kathy left for her house. Dan then said goodbye and reminded me that he planned to be at the house around 9:00 am the next day. He said he had lined up some friends to help him move to his apartment. He explained that he had a truck but was hoping I would help, too, and asked if I would be willing to use my vehicle. He said his goal was to have everything out of the house by the end of the day so we could go on with our lives. I agreed to help. I wanted this transition over as much as Dan did.

The next day, I helped Dan move into an apartment he had rented closer to his law office. We all finished before 5:00 pm that Sunday. After dropping off the last load at his apartment, I said goodbye and wished him good luck. I got in my truck and headed home. I drove through a drive-through to get supper. I arrived home, changed, sat at the table, and ate. I contemplated the day and the future. I could feel relief wash over me. I was living alone for the first time. Despite my depression and loneliness living with Dan in an empty marriage, I was not feeling lonely then. That was such a strange paradox. I was glad to be out of the marriage. It was over for me. I didn't feel anger. I didn't feel fear. I just felt relief. I also felt the peace of God. Granted, the divorce wasn't filed yet, but I knew it would be filed in April. Indeed, there were many unknowns, specifically whether I would have a job next fall. Still, there was peace in this situation. There was also the presence of God. Somehow, I felt He was there with me. Ironically, I was alone but not lonely.

As the days moved toward April, I devoted more time to securing a job. I widened the area where I would relocate to secure a job, so I began applying for additional opportunities. In February, I was afforded several initial interviews at colleges in-state and out-of-state. I began praying earnestly, asking God to strengthen my faith and trust that He would provide a job for me. I couldn't believe that God would bring me to this point to leave me unemployed. I continued to hope and pray that one of the three institutions I had an initial interview with over the telephone would afford me an on-campus interview. Two colleges invited me to campus within a week of my telephone interview.

One day in late February, the vice president and provost at the Christian College where I taught asked me to stop by his office before leaving. After class, I went to meet with him. He said he had heard that my husband and I had separated. I confirmed that we had. I asked about my job status. He reminded me that the present policy forbids someone from teaching at the college if they are divorced. He said that as long as there was a chance of reconciliation, separation wasn't a problem. He said he planned to recommend a change to the divorce policy to the board of trustees at the April meeting. The previous academic year, two other instructors faced situations where their spouses filed for a divorce despite their objections. The college released both instructors after the semester. The provost said he was committed to challenging the policy because people were not always in control of situations, and just because one spouse wanted out of the marriage didn't mean that college should further punish those individuals who have no way to stop a divorce. He continued that because of Michigan's no-fault divorce law, people were powerless and had no say when spouses wanted to divorce, even if the other party didn't want one and was willing to try to make something work.

He told me he would do everything he could to change the policy. He promised me his support and agreed to be my reference while I continued looking for a job. As I left his office, I felt he understood what I was going through and wanted to support me. While I thought he was committed to changing the policy on divorce, I couldn't count on the policy changing, no matter how dedicated he may be. However, I was happy to know someone else realized that the policy was unfair and punished individuals who may have no control over their circumstances. I continued my job search earnestly while doing my best every day in the classroom. I also knew in my heart that even if the policy changed and I wanted to stay, I still needed to be true to myself, and expressing my sexuality would be something the college wouldn't ever tolerate. One way or another, I knew my time working at that college was short.

In March, I interviewed on campus at two different colleges. One was close to home, and the other was in Illinois. I was hoping for an offer from a college close to home because my mother continued to battle cancer, and I wanted to be close to her during this time. However, I would be happy to receive an offer from either school. I was also hearing from other schools, letting me know they had filled the open position and wanted to set up initial interviews. I knew I would accept the first offer if it were reasonably competitive. I liked the security of knowing I had a job in the fall. I continued to pray and remained confident that it was only a matter of time before I would secure a teaching position. As April arrived, I had yet to secure a job. I was close to receiving an offer. I knew that April was the deadline Dan gave me, and he would be filing for divorce any day now.

On Friday of the first week of April, Dan called to tell me he had filed our divorce papers just as he said. He explained that it would only take a couple of weeks, and I would receive documents confirming the court had granted the divorce. As I hung up the phone, I felt a sense of joy. I hadn't received a job offer yet, but I knew each college was getting closer to deciding. I also knew the provost at the college had submitted a resolution to remove the divorce stipulations from the policy. If the resolution passed and I could stay despite the divorce being final, I knew that would give me additional time to find the perfect teaching job if nothing materialized this spring. I felt I had options and was beginning to believe everything would be just fine.

Finally, after a few days, I received calls an hour apart from both colleges, extending me an offer of employment. I told both that I would let them know the next day. I called Kathy and told her about the job offers. We agreed to go to dinner and talk about the options. Both offers were similar concerning pay, benefits, and tenure provisions. Each job was a bit different. The job in Illinois was a teaching job. The position in the state involved supervising student-teachers in the Grand Rapids area. I liked teaching. I hadn't managed student-teachers full-time before, so I was unsure how well I would like that job. Kathy and I talked through all the pros and cons over dinner. By the time dinner was over, I had come to a decision. I called the in-state university the next day and accepted their job offer. I called the other institution, thanked them for the offer, and told them I had taken another offer elsewhere. That night, I prayed and thanked God for showing me the way and answering my prayers for a new job. The road hadn't been easy, but my faith and relationship with God gave me the strength and confidence to move forward into a life I believed would be more fulfilling, genuine, and enjoyable.

The next day, I arrived home from college and picked up the mail as usual. After changing and going for a run, I showered and began to make dinner. As dinner was cooking, I picked up the stack of mail and ruffled through it. I noticed a letter from the county court in the pile of mail. I carefully tore open the letter, wondering if I had been caught speeding by the intersection cameras recently installed all over the city. I pulled out the document, unfolded it, and slowly read it. It was official. Our divorce had been approved and signed by the judge. I could now be myself and figure out my journey from here. I felt a great weight lift. I called Kathy, and we went out and celebrated. I stepped out of the closet, and there was no turning back.

I knew I had to let the provost at the Christian College know that I had accepted another job and that my divorce was final. When I arrived at work on Monday, the provost requested a meeting. When I walked in, I could tell he was glad to see me. He explained to me that over the weekend, the board of trustees had changed the policy at the college about being divorced and teaching. He said the trustees altered the policy to allow divorced individuals to teach at the college if they were not teaching within the Religion Department or the Seminary. I listened politely and smiled. I was proud of him for taking this on. The policy was wrong and needed to be changed. I congratulated him on his accomplishment.

Next, he informed me that I had been nominated and selected to win the Provost Award for Teaching Excellence. This was the highest honor a faculty member could receive at the college. I was thoroughly honored and thanked him for the recognition. He explained that he and the awards committee strongly believed I deserved the award, and they had voted unanimously in my favor. After thanking him again, I explained that I had accepted a position at a nearby university. I handed him my letter of resignation. He asked me a bit about the job I took. He asked if I would reconsider and stay. I explained that despite the trustees having changed their policy and I enjoyed teaching there, I needed to accept this job that included better pay and benefits because I needed to take care of myself now that I was alone. I explained that I was also concerned that the Christian community would treat me differently now because of the divorce and that I didn't want to impact my effectiveness or the college's reputation. I welcomed the change separating my career from the Christian community in case I experienced their judgment like I had seen others experience. We talked for a while. He congratulated me again, and I left. As I returned to my office, I knew that while this chapter of my life ended, another chapter was beginning. There was one thing I had yet to do, and that was to tell my parents that I was gay.

The following week, I decided to tell my parents about my sexuality. I felt the need to begin living a more authentic life, and the people I wanted to know before I told anyone else were my parents. One day after work, I stopped by my parents' house. It was not unusual for me to drop by and visit on my way home. However, today, I knew I was going to share with them about my sexuality. It was ironic because Ellen DeGeneres had just come out on her television show earlier in the week.

Consequently, my mom and I discussed Ellen's show the day. Ellen's coming out had been the topic of many news shows, social interactions, and my president's chapel sermon. My previous conversations with my mom did not indicate that she was homophobic. I remember when my mom called one of the collectors at the collection agency where we both had worked a "gay boy." At the time, I wasn't sure how to interpret her remarks. I believed my dad's brother, Uncle Doc, was gay, but I never remember my dad or his family discussing it. I couldn't even recollect why I had concluded that I thought Uncle Doc was gay. But somehow, I was aware that Dad's entire family believed that. Given these few interactions with my parents concerning homosexuality, I had no idea what they would say or how they might react.

As I sat in their living room, about to tell them, a car pulled up in my parent's driveway. My mom's sister, Sally, and her husband, Jack, had just arrived. Now what, I thought. After a moment of panic, I figured I might as well tell all of them. I got their attention after Sally and Jack entered the house. I explained to them that I wanted to share something important, and I wanted them to listen with an open mind and heart. I explained how I thought Dan might be gay and how that burdened our marriage, but that was not the ultimate reason we had divorced. I also explained that his sexuality wasn't the only challenge leading to the divorce. I continued by explaining that I had determined I, too, was gay. As soon as the words left my mouth, I started to cry. Fear rushed over me. I was trembling inside and out. This was the hardest thing I had ever done. I was so worried about being rejected, judged, or disowned.

My mom's immediate remarks to my dad revealed her gut reaction. While elbowing my dad, she said, "Doug, I told you she was gay. I knew it all along".

My dad said nothing. I could tell he was processing what I just said. My Aunt Sally asked several questions, and the five of us talked for a while about how I had come to figure this out and how I felt about this revelation. I cried now from both relief and fear. I finally felt honest. I was no longer living a lie. I felt like the last barrier between my parents and me had come down. I felt my parents better understood why I was so unhappy and perhaps why the marriage ended after over 14 years. My family had always liked Dan, even though they didn't always like how he put me second to his work. Sally and Jack both reacted supportively as well. I didn't stay long after coming out because I had a date that night. I didn't want to tell them that I was already dating. I certainly didn't want to drop too much on them all at once. I figured telling them I was gay was plenty for anyone to hear. I was out of the closet for good.

As I drove away, I knew my parents loved and supported me. I finally felt free. A heavy burden had lifted from my life. I knew the road ahead would have its challenges. I claimed the truth in Psalm 139:14 (NIV), which states, *"I praise you because I am fearfully and wonderfully made; your works are wonderful; I know that full well."* I also believed God had always known. I embraced the truth in Jeremiah 1:5, *"Before I formed you in the womb, I knew you; before you were born, I sanctified you; and I ordained you a prophet to the nations."*. While this was spoken to Jeremiah the prophet, it had to be equally as valid for me.

God had been faithful to me and remained through it all. Throughout the journey, I realized that what mattered most was getting to know the God of the Bible. By coming to know God more and more through reading His Word, it became clear that my focus was wrongly placed on getting to know the church's doctrines. While knowing doctrine and theology is important, what must be preeminent is getting to know the God of the Bible and His Son, Jesus Christ, and the Holy Spirit. To do that, we must first accept that our sinful nature separates us from God (Romans 3:9-12). By accepting that Jesus died on the cross as atonement for that sin and believing in our hearts that we are saved, the sin that separates us from God has been paid for, allowing us to get to know the God of the Bible (Romans 5:1-2).

Instead of unthinkingly accepting pastors' and self-proclaimed Christians' interpretations of scripture, I began to test those proclamations against the Word of God. As I did, I realized that people's interpretations may not always stand up to what I think the Bible says. I also realized that I was not infallible either. However, I have concluded that, just like in Jesus' day, there are Pharisees and Sadducees, and we each need to take responsibility to test what we were told and not unthinkingly accept what others say.

Epilog

I recalled, as a kid, my parents talking about how they remembered where they were when they heard about the assassination of President John F. Kennedy. I couldn't relate to those conversations until March 30, 1981, when I vividly remember driving down Ottawa Avenue in Grand Rapids on my way to visit Julie when I heard on my radio that President Ronald Regan had been shot. Whether or not we know about those events, national and world events shape our daily experiences.

Another one of those life-shaping national events occurred on Friday, June 26, 2015. I remember that event as vividly as I remember the assassination attempt on Ronald Regan. I was walking from my hotel to an office building when I heard a CNN report that the Supreme Court, in a 5 to 4 landmark ruling, determined that gay couples could marry throughout the United States. Joy overtook me while I texted several friends with my most immediate reaction. So much has changed for the LGBTQ+ community since my divorce in 1998. At that moment, I hoped that the Supreme Court ruling might mark another opportunity for young people who, like me, might struggle to understand and accept their sexuality.

Since 1998, society has become more aware that some people identify as queer. I think attitudes have changed, and more individuals within society are accepting individuals who are questioning their sexuality or identify along the LGBTQ+ spectrum. While I believe attitudes have changed, and some for the better, individuals in our society still exhibit hate and judgment. Churches and religions continue to wrestle with how to minister to individuals who question their sexuality, accept gay marriage, or identify as queer. I have not found acceptance in organized religion. However, I have found favor by many who proclaim they are Christians and rely on the Bible to share their faith and relationship with God.

As I sat down to write about the most vivid memories of my journey, it soon became apparent that these moments have shaped the person I am today. These memories represent not daily events but the most significant moments of wrestling with my sexuality and faith and the eventual understanding and acceptance. This exercise showed me how many people influenced me positively and negatively. I have also realized just how powerful the context of events can be in shaping individuals' attitudes and behaviors and how those attitudes and behaviors impacted me. I have also learned that many ideas about God, faith, and religion impacted my decisions and journey positively and negatively.

My journey has strengthened my resolve, self-awareness, and faith. I am one of the lucky ones. Since this formational journey, I have often spoken with other gay, lesbian, bisexual, transgender, and questioning people. Everyone has been at different points in their journey of understanding and acceptance of themselves. Through those conversations, I have heard about their spiritual journey. Some have rejected faith, religion, and God. Many have shared with me how they have found their religious institution to be the place of the most hateful interactions they experienced. Many have walked away from their church or theology. I can still recall the varied responses of my Christian "friends" to whom I came out. Many of those people knew me intimately as a "straight, Christian woman." When I told them I was gay or dating women, our relationship immediately changed. Their responses ran the entire gamut from accepting to hate. What was astounding to me was my belief that I was the same person before I told them I was gay. It was evident that I hadn't changed but that they had changed simply because they knew something more about me now than in the moment before. These reactions helped me realize that their response was entirely about them and not about me. I became more authentic by taking a step closer to them and sharing more about myself. In that moment of authenticity, they were confronted by facts that challenged them in ways I would not understand unless they chose to open their hearts to me. Most just walked away from our friendship. In many ways, they became more authentic also.

A friend once told me that her father often said, "People come into our lives for a reason, a season, and a lifetime." I thought that insight was very profound. This memoir reinforced that insight. I also realized that while many people in my life were there for a reason or a season, their influence shaped me for the remainder of my lifetime. Indeed, no man or woman is an island. It may not surprise you that one of those friends who have remained in my life was Faith, who was the most authentic friend when I needed her most.

My spiritual journey is much more complicated than this work can explore. My relationship with God through faith in Jesus Christ is still strong. While my faith in God is unwavering, my skepticism of organized religion grew and remains. I am skeptical of "easy believe-ism" and "legalism." Rather than walking away from God because I have become wary of religion, I have chosen to focus on understanding the God of the Bible and deepening my relationship with God rather than deepening my connection to an institution. For those who may remind me of Hebrews 10:24-25 (KJV), *"...let us consider one another to provoke unto love and to good works; not forsaking the assembling of ourselves together, as the manner of some is; but exhorting one another; and so much the more as ye see the day approaching."* Let me say I believe I am practicing that verse as I congregate with those who have accepted Christ but have rejected religious institutions that are antithetical to the truths in the Bible. Further, I would provide examples of how I am living out this verse by gathering with believers in Christ and how we study together and encourage one another. So, while we may be skeptical of organized religion and churches, we are living out our faith like believers in the early church age did by assembling to strengthen our faith.

I am drawn to the Apostle Paul's words in First Corinthian 1:27 (KJV), *"But God hath chosen the foolish things of the world to confound the wise, and God hath chosen the weak things of the world to confound the things which are mighty."* I consider myself one of those who confound the self-proclaimed wise religious leaders who have determined that homosexuality is an unforgivable sin. I proclaim that there is no unpardonable sin other than unbelief and that *"...whosoever believes in him shall not perish but have eternal life"* (John 3:16, KJV). Don't be deceived; God wants all of you, queer or not, to believe in Him and enter a relationship with Him through faith.

Throughout my journey to understand, accept, and embrace myself, God used individuals to lead me to learn more about him despite Satan's attempt to deceive me by using others to tell me that God hated, rejected, and despised me because of my attraction to women. Those relationships have been like "iron sharpening iron" (Proverbs 27:17 KJV). Those relationships drove me to the Bible to read and study about the God of my faith. I chose not to accept these Christian friends' interpretation of scripture but committed myself to seeking the answers within the scriptures and forming my own beliefs. As a result, my faith in God was strengthened. I ask those of you reading this who are tempted to reject God because of what others tell you about God to realize that what others tell you may not be accurate, that you can know God by reading his Word, and that He may not be the person others portray.

I didn't seek out Biblical interpretations that were easy for me to agree with, but I sought all perspectives, reading multiple commentaries, even those that were hard to read or hear. Because of the varied interpretations of scripture, I cling to the knowledge that by *"grace we are saved through faith and that it is a gift of God, not of works…"* (Ephesians 2:8, KJV). I don't pretend to understand or know everything the Bible communicated about sexuality, nor do I think I ever will. In that gap is where faith in God becomes paramount. I'm not saved because I'm somehow perfect, free of sin, or completely understand the Bible. I'm saved because of the grace of God and the death of his son, Jesus Christ, who paid the penalty for my sins. I don't believe my sexuality is an unpardonable sin. I have plenty of other sins I can point to. I know that the blood of Jesus pays for my sins, and I strive each day to reflect my gratitude for Jesus' atonement and extend the grace I experience from Him to others. My faith gives me the freedom to have a relationship with God, and I reject the church's legalism.

The most common question I get from others seeking to reconcile their faith and homosexuality is whether homosexuality is a choice. Based on my lived experience, I would have to say it is not a choice.

The homosexual feelings and attractions to women you read about in this autobiography were not conscious choices for me. They were just there, and they were always there. What I did about those thoughts and feelings was a choice. My actions based on my feelings and attractions were choices. If you are a heterosexual reading this memoir, consider whether your heterosexual feelings were a choice for you or were they always there. The heterosexual feelings that people feel are innate. That was my experience with homosexual feelings. No matter how hard I tried to change those feelings, how many verses I memorized, and how many heterosexual acts I imagined, my homosexual feelings were naturally there. They remained, no matter how hard I tried to eliminate or ignore my attraction toward women.

The second question I get from others seeking to reconcile their faith and homosexuality is whether faith in Jesus Christ is a choice. I believe my faith in Jesus Christ and trust in his death as atonement for my sin is a choice. I have chosen to believe that after hearing a message about the meaning of the Gospel. That choice has been affirmed over and over by reading the Bible. While my faith is a choice, I am saved by the grace of God because His son died to atone for my sins. I am a sinner, not because I have homosexual feelings, but because I was born into a fallen world affected by sin because of the choices of Adam and Eve, whom the serpent deceived. Satan uses people, circumstances, and events to deceive, distract, and destroy. Whether we know it or not, we are all involved in a spiritual battle between God and Satan. *"For we wrestle not against flesh and blood, but against principalities, against powers, against the rulers of darkness of this world, against spiritual wickedness in high places"* (Ephesians 6:12 KJV).

The third question I get from people trying to reconcile their faith and sexuality is whether homosexuality and faith in Jesus Christ coexist. I believe it can. I experience that very co-existence daily. I cringe when I hear the phrase, "Hate the sin and not the sinner." It implies that homosexuality is a sin. Is homosexuality a sin? The Bible speaks frequently about sexual sins. Those include extramarital affairs, sexual exploitation, rape, incest, bestiality, and adultery. The Bible also addresses homosexuality, but far less often than other sexual sins. I do not believe homosexuality is a sin. Many people do think homosexuality is a sin. I believe exploiting anyone for sex is a sin, whether using same-sex or opposite-sex partners to satisfy the lusts of the flesh. I think someone can commit to a lifelong relationship with someone of the same sex in a way that is faithful and honors God. I accept that by faith. I challenge you to read the Bible for yourself, study what the Bible says about homosexuality, and come to your conclusion.

The mysteries of scripture are not fully understood, nor do I claim to understand them all. It is in the absence of absolute certainty that my faith begins. My faith was deepened when the easy "believe-ism" of Christianity failed to provide me the easy answers I searched for when trying to figure out why I felt one way when I wanted to feel another way.

Perhaps my homosexuality is a "thorn in the flesh." The Apostle Paul in Second Corinthians explained, *"For though I would desire to glory, I shall not be a fool; for I will say the truth. But now I forbear, lest any man should think of me above that which he seeth me to be, or that he heareth of me. And lest I should be exalted above measure through the abundance of the revolution there was given to me a thorn in the flesh, the messenger of Satan to buffet me, lest I should be exalted above measure"* (2 Corinthian 12:6-7, KJV). The Apostle Paul seems to indicate that his "thorn in the flesh" keeps him humble and close to God. I have thought of the "thorn in the flesh" as a trial. The Bible is clear that we all will face trials and tribulations. The test isn't from God, but because we live in a fallen world impacted by sin. Additionally, we are in a spiritual battle between good and evil. As we stand in the middle of this battle, we each face things in our lives that could be used by God for good or by Satan for evil.

My simplistic thoughts of God punishing me while I struggled to come to terms with my homosexuality were not accurate and more rooted in the interpretation of the Bible by others. As I added to my faith, wisdom, knowledge, and self-control, I began to see more clearly the God of the Bible. Our choices have consequences, but God doesn't set out to punish us directly. *"The Lord is not slack concerning his promise, as some men count slackness; but is longsuffering to us-ward, not willing that any should perish, but that all should come to repentance"* (2 Peter 3:9 KJV). God is trying to get our attention and wants us to seek Him, believe in Him, and enter a relationship with Him. He gives us as many chances as possible to choose Him. The only unforgivable sin is unbelief in God, not homosexuality.

Because I have embraced my faith and sexuality, I look forward to spending eternity with God in heaven. Once there, I will ask Him about the truth regarding homosexuality. In the meantime, I will continue my journey of faith and freedom, telling others about my story. After all, how can they hear without a preacher?

About the Author

Dr. Scott has spent over 35 years as a faculty and administrator in higher education. She has authored articles and book chapters and presented on topics such as American history, instructional design, and leadership. She has spoken to various groups about her coming out journey and LGBTQ+ issues throughout her lifetime. She maintains her faith in Christ. She currently lives in the Southwest with her partner, where she enjoys an active life through golfing, bicycling, hiking, and various outdoor activities.

www.ingramcontent.com/pod-product-compliance
Lightning Source LLC
Chambersburg PA
CBHW041315110526
44591CB00021B/2794